FORMOSA

A Study in Chinese History

Formosa

FORMOSA

A Study in Chinese History

W. G. GODDARD

Order of the Brilliant Star (China)

Michigan State University Press

1966

© W. G. Goddard 1966

First American edition 1966

DS
895
F72
G6

MACMILLAN AND COMPANY LIMITED
Little Essex Street London WC 2
also Bombay Calcutta Madras Melbourne

THE MACMILLAN COMPANY OF CANADA LIMITED
70 Bond Street Toronto 2

Library of Congress catalog card no. 66-14852

PRINTED AND BOUND IN THE UNITED KINGDOM

TO JESSIE

my companion in Formosa

Contents

List of Illustrations		*page* viii
Introduction		ix

CHAPTER

1. The Beginnings — 1
2. Captain China and his Corsairs — 35
3. The Dutch Interlude — 49
4. The House of Cheng — 63
5. The Age of Unrest — 92
6. The Literati at Panch'iao — 111
7. Liu Ming-ch'uan the Master Builder — 124
8. The First Asian Republic — 140
9. The Japanese Occupation — 158
10. Sun Yat-sen and Formosa — 168
11. Formosa since 1945 — 177

Postscript — 202

Books Consulted by the Author — 222

Index — 225

List of Illustrations

Reconstruction by Hata Sada-nori in 1803 of a
primitive sea-going Taitung raft as used on the
eastern coast of Formosa   *page* 4

Chief Mao of the Tsou tribe with the author
in 1959   *facing page* 63

Cheng Cheng-kung (Koxinga)   78

Shen Pao-chen, the architect of modern Formosa   111

Liu Ming-ch'uan, first Chinese Governor of
Formosa   126

Lien Heng, anthologist of the Japanese occupation
period   159

Ch'iu Feng-chia, founder of the Republic of
Formosa in 1895   159

Chen Cheng, pioneer of land reform in Formosa   174

Chang Chi-yun, former Minister of Education
and now Director of the Institute of Advanced
Chinese Studies   191

Chiang Kai-shek and the author in 1956   206

MAPS

Formosa   *Frontispiece*

Mountains of Formosa   9

Distribution of aboriginal tribes in Formosa   18

Regional distribution of migrants and aborigines 27

Formosa, as it was known to the House of Cheng   79

Introduction

WHAT is Formosa?

An island, just under 14,000 square miles in area, or slightly larger than Holland, shaped like a huge tobacco leaf, and with a range of high mountains running like a spine through the centre from north to south, somewhere in the western Pacific?

A place of refuge for Chiang Kai-shek and his followers, from which they hope, forlornly or otherwise, to return one day to the Chinese mainland?

Or is there a deeper meaning? Islands have played a decisive role in past history. There was Salamis. In our own time there was Britain. Both saved civilization. Can it be that Formosa has a significance, far beyond the fate of any individual or group, some connection with the future of the hundreds of millions on the mainland of China? Has it any relation to the Asia of tomorrow and indeed to the lands beyond, such as Australia for instance?

If so, what is this meaning?

It was in search of some answer to this question that the author of the following pages went to Formosa in 1953 and since then has made six visits to the island, each of protracted length. During these visits the whole island has been traversed, from Keelung in the north to Hengchun in the south. There have been many talks with Chiang Kai-shek and high officials, past and present, in both the National and Provincial Governments. Long hours have been spent with scholars of the Academia Sinica at Nankang, outside Taipei. As for the ordinary people — the wharf-labourers at Keelung and Kaohsiung, cigarette-sellers on the streets of the main cities, farmers, factory-workers — their views have been sought. Every section of the population has been interviewed, with the aim of presenting as complete a picture of Formosa as possible.

The picture emerging gradually over the past ten years will be seen by the reader as he turns the following pages.

However, this can only be understood and appreciated when set against the background of the past. Formosa today is not just an accident. It has not come about by chance. Whatever meaning it has is the result of centuries, and the Formosa of the present cannot be divorced from the Formosa of the past. Its significance did not erupt into history with the coming of the Nationalists in 1945 in the same way as the island itself suddenly appeared above the waters of the Pacific in prehistory. The historical significance of Formosa has been a cumulative process, each century adding its own dynamic urge.

No attempt is made in the following pages to write a history of Formosa as that term is generally understood, with dates, with the story of battles lost and won, and with the clash of personalities and the struggles of rival groups. Formosa, too, has had all these. Our search has been not for details of these dramas, but rather for the vital mainstream, which, Arethusa-like, flowed on through the centuries, at times underground, then in the full glare of the sun, at times slowly between broad banks, then strong and turgid through the narrows, ever gaining strength, till at last it spread over the vast plain with its life-giving water.

This is not a history of Formosa, but an interpretation of Formosa.

To trace the course of this stream, we must know something of its source and the nature of the land through which it flowed, for Formosa has it own peculiar geographical setting, geological structure, and subjection to the typhoons that have done so much in shaping both the physical nature of the island and the course of this vital national stream.

Geologists tell us that Formosa was not always as it is today. It was born out of violence, and turbulence brought it into the world. At some remote period in the Tertiary Era an extensive subsidence had taken place along the eastern seaboard of the Asiatic continent. The waters now known as the Okhotsk, Japan, Yellow, and China Seas, together with the Strait of Formosa, cover the submerged lands. It is a fact that the maximum depth of water between Formosa and the Chinese mainland is 100 fathoms, whereas the soundings on the eastern side of Formosa fall suddenly to 1,000 fathoms, then to 2,000, till farther out the unsounded depths of the Pacific Ocean are reached. There is a vast difference between the depth of the ocean bed on the eastern side and that of the continental shelf at the bottom of the Strait of Formosa.

Later, in geological time, terrific volcanic action flung up huge igneous rock-masses as high as 1,500 feet above the ocean, carrying with them vast amounts of coral. This was the birth of Formosa, shaped then not as the island is today, but as ranges of high mountains above the level of the ocean, isolated in the vast expanse of water.

Then came the typhoons. Through the centuries torrential rains carried out to sea, especially on the western side, the debris, the wear and tear of the mountain-sides, and the coral, gradually forming the rich and fertile plains, one of which now extends the length of 100 miles along the western side of Formosa. In the great cosmic drama Nature's anger was to prove a blessing to man.

Through subsequent centuries, in the historic period, man was to claim what in prehistoric times Nature had disclaimed and then sought to rectify — that Formosa is an integral part of China.

But it did not end there. Great physical changes have been transforming the face of Formosa since the first wanderers landed on its shores. They saw in the north of the island, between what is now Taipei and Keelung, a vast lake in the mountains, around which they built their rude dwellings and formed their villages. They lived mainly on fish from the lake. But Nature did not take kindly to this intrusion. The succession of typhoons brought the detritus down from the mountains and deposited it in the lake till the bottom began to rise higher and higher. Today what was once that lake is a plateau. During this process of transformation, Nature, in another of her whimsical moods, rent a spur in the surrounding mountains, with the result that the remaining water rushed towards the sea in wild abandon, cutting what is now the channel of the Tamsui River.

Still the increasing ravages continue. What the earthquake begins the typhoon carries on. Mountain slopes are cut into precipitous valleys, destroying what man has cultivated. And the field of activity is vast, for 68 per cent of the area of Formosa is mountainous or hilly country. Born in the mountains, the rivers, swollen with typhonic rains, rush into the plains, threatening to hold everybody and everything to ransom.

But the skill and ingenuity of man have now combined to meet this challenge. The Shihmen Reservoir, the largest and highest in Asia, a triumph of modern engineering, is the symbol of man's answer to the typhoon. Much of the sting has now been taken out of that seasonal destroyer. Similar projects in other parts of Formosa promise victory over those forces that in the past have wrought untold havoc and destruction.

The earthquake and typhoon have played an important part in the formation of the Formosan character. The fierce spirit of independence, so marked throughout the history of the island, was born of the perpetual struggle with the elements of Nature, the trembling earth and the wind that snapped giant trees into matchwood. The Formosan had to match his spirit to survive with these forces that knew no mercy and favoured no weakness. The island was no place for weaklings. It afforded no sanctuary for the indolent. Only the strong could survive. The men and women who crossed the water from Fukien and Kwangtung were the sturdiest of spirit, the most determined of will, of the original stock. Otherwise they would not have dared the crossing of the sea, and otherwise they would never have survived the rigours of pioneering in the face of these hostile forces of Nature.

Out of this struggle with the elements, with earthquake and typhoon, was born that passion for freedom which has been one of the cardinal characteristics of the Formosan throughout the centuries.

There was a striking similarity between the making of this Formosan character and that of the Australian. In each case the early migrants had to face the inclemencies of Nature and dare the dangers of an inhospitable land. In Formosa there was

the earthquake and the typhoon ; in Australia drought, burning
sun, and destroying bush-fire. In both cases the toll of life and
labour's enterprise was terrific. The climate showed no mercy,
and only the resolute of will had any hope of survival. The
weak fell by the wayside.

In both cases another element, this time human, entered into
the struggle to intensify it and add to the casualties. In Formosa
the first known Chinese migrants, the *penti*, so called because
they claimed to be the original settlers, spread out over the
unmapped, unclaimed, and unsurveyed coastal lands. When
later migrants arrived, they were resisted and treated as intruders.
They were permitted to hold only small areas. Gradually there
developed those feuds which stained the history of the island
with much blood. A similar clash left its mark on the early
history of Australia. The first free migrants ' sat down ' where-
ever they chose and on land as extensive as they wished. Hence
the name given them, ' squatters '. Masters of vast areas, they
made their own laws, appointed magistrates from among themselves, and, like the Chinese in Formosa, reigned as feudal lords.
Some of their clan names still persist as holders of large estates.
When, later, land-hungry migrants arrived in the colonies, they
had to be content with smaller areas. These were known as
' selectors '. Much of the early history of New South Wales
and Victoria was shaped by the conflict between these two
groups.

Historians have recorded the lawlessness that resulted, but
out of the struggle with the elements of nature and the clash of
squatter and selector developed that spirit of independence and
that love of freedom, so characteristic of the Australian. And
also, perhaps, that resentment against authority.

The early histories of Formosa and the Australian settlers run
in parallel lines.

Another factor favoured the growth of the spirit of independence and passion for freedom in Formosa. The migrants
from the mainland of China went there of their own choice.
They left their homeland and ventured across the sea to escape
discrimination and oppression. Of the population in 1945

before the coming of the Nationalists, and with the exception of the 140,000 tribesmen in the mountains, 40 per cent were of Hakka stock, the untouchables of south China, and the remaining 60 per cent descendants of migrants from the depressed areas of Fukien province. In both cases, their ancestors had migrated in search of freedom and independence.

Later centuries took the scholars in their thousands to Formosa in the same quest, the search for freedom from official censorship. These literati were to become the dominant force in the history of the island. Coming from south China, there were no eunuchs among them, a most fortunate circumstance, as in Peking there were eunuchs among the scholars who used their position to clamp down on the activities of the more progressive and liberal-minded among the literati. There was the case of Li Lien-ying. As Chief Eunuch, he was the real power behind the throne, appointing and dismissing officials, especially such as were reformers. He decided which memorials should reach the throne, and many of these must have gone into the waste-paper basket.

An entirely different position existed in Formosa. There the literati were free from such censorship and tyranny. When the so-called Reform Movement did eventually get launched in Peking in 1898, all its main provisions had been operating in Formosa for the past eighteen years. What Viceroy Chang Chih-tung advocated in his *Ch'uan-hsueh p'ien*, published in 1898, the Governor of Formosa, Liu Ming-ch'uan, had put into operation as far back as 1880. At the very time when Peking was reading Chang's book, urging the modernization of China whilst retaining Confucian standards, Taipei in Formosa was electrified, the railway from Taipei to Keelung was in use, industries on the Western model were functioning, and cable communication between Tainan and the Pescadores was established and was being continued beyond to the mainland itself.

In the great task of modernization, Formosa was a generation ahead of the Chinese mainland.

Liu Ming-ch'uan had had experience of the intransigence of the clique behind the throne in Peking. He had good reason to remember how his recommendation on strategy, in the clash with Russia over the mountain passes on the frontier, had been ridiculed and rejected. He could never erase from his memory the bitter sarcasm of Liu Hsi-hung when he had urged the construction of a modern railway for the rapid movement of troops. In Formosa his plans for the modernization of the province had met with some resistance, but this had soon been overcome. Peking had opposed many of his proposals, but he had the people behind him in Formosa, especially the literati. As a result he had been able to set the foundation that was to make possible the later spectacular progress of the island.

As the reader turns the following pages and follows the course of this mainstream of life and thought in Formosa through the centuries, the meaning of Formosa will become clear. Fashioned by earthquake and typhoons in the heart of the mountains, guided by the unremitting toil of a people determined to be free, this stream has worked out a pattern of life that might well prove to be the prophecy of what all China will be in the future. It may take many years, even a century. But then China is a timeless land and its people have an infinite patience. They have lived very long and survived all the ideologies imposed upon them. They have known most of what human ambition and cupidity have foisted on mankind.

If, then, Formosa is the pattern of the China of the future, just how and when this will be adopted on the Chinese mainland must remain matters of conjecture.

There are problems, not the least of these in Formosa itself. And it will be fatal to ignore these and disastrous to delay the search for their solution. Formosa is moving, slowly perhaps, but nevertheless surely, to a crisis, not from without but from within. This may not be apparent on the surface, and not spectacular, but there are some on that island who see the danger ahead and are very concerned ; not for the security of Formosa, but for what they believe to be the meaning of the island.

These problems are dealt with in the postscript to this book. For the comments on these, the author alone is responsible.

One thing is certain. The solution of these problems will not come through the United Nations, membership of which exercises the official mind of Formosa unduly to the detriment of more important issues. The meaning of Formosa has been the work of centuries, and its continuance will not be determined by what happens in a debating society across the seas, especially by such a disunited one as the United Nations Organization. Whether Formosa is or is not a member of that organization, the meaning of Formosa can only be determined by Formosa itself. For an answer to these problems, which will assume ever-increasing proportions with the years, Formosa must look into its own past history. There, and there only, will the solution be found, for the most serious of these problems is strikingly similar to what Formosa had to face in the past, especially during the Governorship of Liu Ming-ch'uan.

For convenience' sake the name Formosa has been used throughout, as it is the recognized title in the West. To have used the period names would have confused those readers not acquainted with the history of the island. The first name, still preserved in tribal tradition, was ' Pekan ', a Malayan word originally applied to a resting-place after a long journey. This was the name given to south Formosa by the early Malayan migrants. In the third century A.D. the island was referred to in Chinese geographical records as 'I Chou', signifying ' a barbarous region in the east '. Then, from the year 607, in the Sui Dynasty, until 1570, in the Ming Dynasty, it was known to the Chinese as ' Little Liu Ch'iu '. Why it was called Taiwan, the name by which it has been known among Chinese since then, is not clear. It appears to have been employed first by the Dutch to designate the small area around the present Tainan, where they were first established. Chang Chi-yun holds the view that Taiwan was the name of an aboriginal tribe in the vicinity. Certain it is that quite a number of place-names in Formosa are derived from tribal names. Yosaburo Takekoshi, the Japanese historian and an authority on Formosa in his time, suggested that Taiwan might be a corruption of *tung-huan*, a Chinese equivalent of ' eastern savages '. To the Japanese, the island was

'Takasago'. Later the Chinese name 'Taiwan' was adopted. In 1590, Linschotten, a Dutch navigator on a Portuguese vessel, sailing along the west coast of the island, was so impressed with the lush beauty of the coastal plain that he located the island on the chart as 'Ilha Formosa', the Beautiful Island. This Portuguese name has been adopted by the West ever since.

Thanks are due to the many Chinese scholars who have readily responded to inquiries for information by the author. Special mention must be made of Chang Chi-yun, former Minister of Education in Formosa and now Director of the Institute of Advanced Chinese Studies, who supplied source-material not otherwise obtainable, elucidated obscure points in Formosan history, and made available the photographs of Shen Pao-chen and Liu Ming-ch'uan ; Ling Shung-sheng, of the Academia Sinica, for permission to use the drawing of the Taitung raft ; and the Cartographic Department of the National War College, Taipei, for preparing the maps dealing with the distribution of population. Hsu Shen-mo, of the Chinese Geographical Society, prepared for this book the map of Formosa as it was known to the House of Cheng. Angus & Robertson Ltd., of Sydney, Australia, kindly permitted the author to quote from Bernard O'Dowd's poem 'The Poet'.

While this manuscript was in preparation, the Commission in Taipei entrusted with the compiling of the historical documents relating to Formosa published these under the title *T'aiwan Shih Hua*. This could well be an appendix to the present book, as document after document adds support to the interpretation of Formosa outlined in the following pages.

A list of the books consulted by the author appears at the end of this volume.

The Wade spelling of Chinese names has been followed throughout, but, as in most modern Chinese works, the diacritical marks have been omitted. These are valuable to those students interested in the correct pronunciation of Chinese words, but to the ordinary reader for whom this book is intended, such marks only prove confusing.

B

CHAPTER ONE

The Beginnings

THE first rays of the morning sun stabbed the summit of Mount Tawu in south-east Formosa. The day of the great festival had dawned.

Along the coast from Taitung to Taniao, spread over the coastal plain from Lachia in the north to Hsinhua in the south, and in the western mountains, the villages were soon throbbing with excitement. In some places the trek to the coast had already begun, thin streams of villagers trickling through the paddy fields and across the groundnut farms. Long before the sun had flooded the plain, these would swell into human torrents as the mountain people, led by their *popuroasis*, regional chiefs, came down, those from the Peinan region in the north with orchids in their hair and those from Tawu in the south to the accompaniment of innumerable nose-flutes and mouth-harps. The priestesses could be picked out by the large square of white on their chests, symbol of their tribal status.

All were moving towards Chinlun on the coast, but their eyes were turned to the south, across the sea, in eagerness to catch the first sight of the incoming canoes.

Out there, somewhere between Chinlun and the island of Lanyu, the five canoes had been waiting since midnight, large stones anchoring them to their moorings. Enveloped in darkness and with no other sounds to break the silence than the murmur of the water lapping against the canoes, the paddlers peered across the sea, waiting for the first glimmer of light on Mount Tawu. The moment it appeared the stones would be raised and the canoes turned towards the shore.

Arriving off Chinlun, where hundreds of tribesmen would dash into the sea to escort them to the shore, the fifteen paddlers would be greeted by shouts of welcome from the crowds lining the water's edge. As the canoes grated on the sands, the paddlers would be ceremoniously received by the *sakaka'ai*, the premier chief, and, amid the cheering crowds, led to the feasting-house. There, in the presence of the chiefs and priestesses, the *mivtek*, the age-long ritual wine ceremony, would be performed, to invite the ancestral spirits to attend the celebration. Meanwhile, outside the feasting-house, the *rimbas*, jungle rattles made from the hooves of deer such as the ancestors had used, would rend the air, as excited men, women, and children welcomed the coming of the ancestral spirits back to their ancient haunts. Then for three days the festival would continue with feasting and dancing, the places of honour being accorded the fifteen who had come from the south in their canoes.

Food-gathering would be the central theme of the festivities. One of the fifteen would be chosen to impersonate Riru and plant the millet, as the ancestors had done when they had landed on the same spot many centuries earlier. Then all would gather in the outer part of the village where the temporary bachelor-houses had been erected, to witness and applaud the deer-slaying by the young unmarried tribesmen. These would vie with each other in displaying their prowess, as a highly coveted prize would go to the young man who gave the deer the death-blow. A sign would be tattooed on his forehead, the greatest honour that any young tribesman could receive. More than that, he would be noted by *tsune*, the chief priestess of his tribe, who would later be arranging the marriages of the year.

The festivities ended, the movement back home would begin, to the coastal villages, to those spread over the plain, and to those in the foothills and the mountains. The tribesmen would not meet again for a year.

With the mountain people, most indolent of all the tribe, it would be a leisurely return. Loitering by streams that flowed down from their mountains, they would seek amid the cascades to catch sight of the minivet, the bird of good omen. Had not the ancestors told how a flock of those grey-throated choristers, brilliant in their red and yellow plumage, welcomed Riru and his companions when first they had wandered into those foothills ? Had they not flown just above the tree-tops and shown the way through the dense jungle ? Meanwhile, the priestesses, with the younger women, would scour the valleys in search of medicinal plants, *Amaranthus*, *Dendrobium*, and the many *Limaciae*.

This commemoration, enacted each year through the centuries, although in recent times reduced to the simple canoe ceremony, was designed to keep alive the oldest tradition in Formosa, the coming of Riru and his companions to Pekan, as they called that coastal plain, from their ancestral homeland away in the south. Pekan, a Malayan word, originally signified a haven gained after a long wandering. Later it was applied to any settlement. The Canadian missionary, George Leslie Mackay, recorded in 1895 his conversation with an eighty-year-old Formosan tribesman, who told how his grandfather, with others, disliking the typhoons that swept over the island, decided to seek out the land of their ancestors. They felled some trees, lashed the trunks together, and on that simple raft put out to sea — southwards.

However much time and fancy may have garnished this tradition of a migration across the sea from the south, anthropologists have been disposed to lend credence to it. One of the early workers in this field, the French scientist Hamay, suggested in 1896 that these tribesmen of south Formosa were of Proto-Malayan stock, and others have since taken the same view. In the early years of this investigation, attention was drawn to the striking affinity between many words in the dialects of these tribes and those in the Malayan language. It was noted, for instance, that at least one-third of the basic terms in those dialects were similar to those in Malayan, a striking fact when we recall that over the centuries there have been no contacts between Formosa and South-East Asia. It would be reasonable to conclude, then, that the languages of the tribesmen of south Formosa and the Proto-Malayans derived from a common source. However, it has long been recognized that language, in itself, can never be taken as an infallible guide in the study

Reconstruction by Hata Sada-nori in 1803 of a primitive sea-going Taitung raft as used on the eastern coast of Formosa

of racial origins. But when, as in the case of the south Formosan tribesmen and the Proto-Malayans, language similarities are accompanied with likeness of physical characteristics, social organization, and primitive crafts, it must be admitted as a probability that some ethnological relationship exists.

Our knowledge of the early history of South-East Asia, limited as it is at present, indicates the possibility of such a migration from that region to Formosa at a very early date. The primitive inhabitants of that region, extending from south-east China through Indo-China and the Malayan peninsula to the islands of the East Indies, were the peoples referred to by anthropologists as Proto-Malayans. Unfortunately we do not have such accurate knowledge of the earliest Proto-Malayan movements of population as we have of migrations elsewhere, as for instance of those from Rome to Byzantium and from the steppes of central Asia into China. In the early centuries of the Christian era, when the politico-cultural centre of gravity moved from Rome to Byzantium, many who could afford to make the migration did so, including ' opulent senators of Rome '. Constantine encouraged this movement of population with offers of land and many other privileges. The new capital was a powerful magnet, attracting merchants with an eye to financial gain, and who were followed by ' hosts of artisans and innumerable servants, who hoped to gain a better living by supplying the wants or catering to the luxury of their superiors '. At the same time, across the world, waves of migrants from central Asia were moving into China, where they hoped to find abundant food. Climatic changes in central Asia were forcing these hordes from a land rendered destitute to one where they hoped to find subsistence.

Although we have not such detailed information of the mass movements of the human herd into South-East Asia at that time, we do know that from the end of the first century of the Christian era onwards, Indian culture and colonization had been spreading throughout South-East Asia, with the result that during the fourth century Indianized kingdoms had been established as far east as Java. At the time when large numbers of scholars

were leaving Rome for Constantine's new capital, Buddhist
monks, scholars, architects, builders, and hosts of officials from
India were flooding the lands of South-East Asia. Chinese
monks, in their search for Buddhist literature, made pilgrimages
across central Asia to India and returned to China by way of the
Indianized kingdoms of South-East Asia. One of these, Fa
Hsien, after fifteen years in India, proceeded to Java. He was
there in the year A.D. 413 when the aggressive kingdom of Sri
Vijaya, from its capital at Palembang, was subduing the minor
states of Malaya and extending its dominion over most of
Indonesia. In his record Fa Hsien noted ' the large number of
merchants and traders' passing between India and this kingdom. On one occasion he nearly suffered the fate of Jonah, when,
during a storm, the merchants were about to fling ' this religious
mendicant' overboard, and would have done so had he not
been saved by the protests of one merchant who happened to be
' a Buddhist believer '.

This domination of the Proto-Malayans in South-East Asia by
the powerful newcomers was strongly resisted from the outset.
Their ancestors had migrated from south China at a remote
period, and prior to the Christian era had spread throughout
South-East Asia, reaching as far north as the Philippines, where
they became known as Tagalogs and Igorotes. They resented
the intrusion into their peaceful life, the usurpation of their lands,
the imposition of a foreign religion, and the domination by those
who imposed their will by force. To what extent this resistance
to the Indianized culture and martial strength of the Sri Vijaya
aggression went we do not know, but the sea presented an escape.
As pressure of population increased, with the advent of more and
more foreigners, the sea must have proved more and more
inviting. For such reasons peoples had taken to the sea in earlier
times and migrated over long distances, as to the Marianas as
far back as the fifteenth century B.C. and to the Marquesas in
150 B.C., if we are to accept the findings of such authorities as
Libby and Shapiro.

In the case of those Proto-Malayans who turned to the sea as a
way of escape, favourable currents would have taken them to the

Philippines and further north to the east and west coasts of Formosa. One of these, sweeping through the Java Sea, would have carried their rafts between Borneo and Malaya, and thence into the China Sea and on to the western coast of Formosa. Another current, coursing between Borneo and Celebes, then through the Celebes Sea, and passing the eastern shore of the Philippines, where it becomes part of the North Equatorial Current, would have borne their rafts along the east coast of Formosa where the current is known as the *heh ch'ao* or 'black stream'. Swept along these currents and guided by such sea-marks as the direction of waves, land-smell, the flight of birds, and floating seaweed, the rafts of the migrants, with their sails of pandanus leaves and their raised platforms for the storage of food, seeds, and plants, would have little difficulty in making land on the east and west coasts of Formosa.

Most ethnologists are agreed that the ancestors of the present inhabitants of Lanyu, the island to the south-east of Formosa, arrived by way of the Philippines. They too have their annual ceremony in celebration of the coming of their ancestors from across the sea. This takes the form of casting into the sea offerings of fruits and flowers in honour of the 'Sea God', the tutelary deity of these Yami tribesmen.

These Proto-Malayan migrants soon reacted to their new environment in south Formosa. The Central Range shut off those on the coastal plains of the east from those on the west coast. Lateral spurs of this mountain range created in turn pockets of habitation, with the result that the geographical conditions resulted in the rise of tribal separatism. Much the same position had prevailed on the Chinese mainland through the centuries. Gradually, each settlement in south Formosa developed its own characteristics, so that, with the passage of time, different cultures developed, changes in language appeared, and varied religious concepts emerged. So it is that anthropologists write of different tribes in south Formosa, the Paiwan in the remote south, the Puyuma in the south-east, the Ami in the eastern-central area, and inland the Bunum and the Tsou, with the Yami on Lanyu. As long as the coastal plains and the

lake region provided food without effort, there was no necessity
to wander far afield, with the result that no contacts were made
between these settlers. But such isolation could not continue.
Sooner or later, the hunters, seeking flesh for food and skins for
clothing, were destined to meet in the mountains, and thus
began the tribal warfare that was to persist through the centuries.
But it must be noted that originally all were of the same Proto-
Malayan racial stock.

One sees a parallel in the Hebrew tribesmen, who migrated
from the south to Canaan. Though a common kindred, they
remained for some centuries independent tribes, governing
themselves after the patriarchal manner. The *shophet*, or ' judge ',
was at one and the same time warrior, priest, and arbiter of
disputes. ' In those days, there was no king in Israel, but every
man did that which was right in his own eyes.' The geography
of Canaan was an important factor in bringing out the separatism
of the twelve tribes, and caused the interminable feuds that
existed among them. No sooner had the migrants crossed the
Jordan and entered Canaan than the tribe of Judah separated
itself from the rest and went south. Even when external pressure,
in the form of Philistine aggression, created a certain tribal unity,
which cried out for an overlord as king, it was not a unanimous
decision. Samson was the chief dissentient. Then, when the
monarchy was established, it was short-lived and soon there were
two overlords, one in the south, the other in the north.

From traditions still current among the south Formosan
tribesmen, it is possible to reconstruct the manner of life among
those early migrant-settlers. They lived in houses made of
reeds. Nature was kind. Probably nowhere else, save in the
jungles of the Amazon, had she provided such an abundance of
building material, ready for use and easily worked. Little
exertion was needed, for the rattan stems, as thick as a man's
leg, were to hand. These could be bent to any angle, and as
they often measured up to 500 feet in length, one stem would
provide the entire framework for an entire dwelling. Thinner
stems covered the floor, with reeds and grasses providing the
thatching for the roof. No housing problems existed among

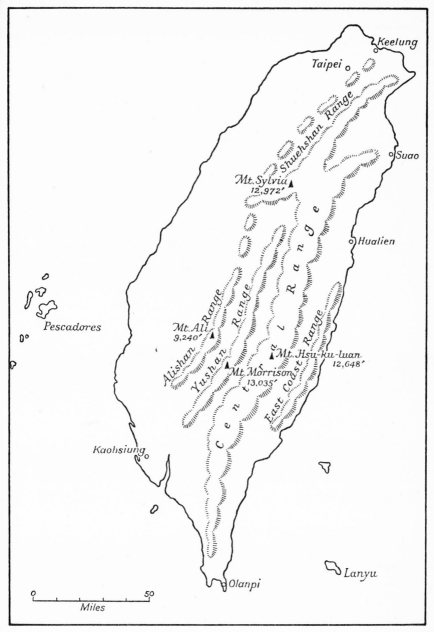

Mountains of Formosa

those Proto-Malayan settlers in south Formosa.

The main food-plantings were sweet potato, millet, taro, and a type of pomelo resembling a grapefruit. Rice was unknown. When, later, contact was made with the rice-eating Chinese, they were regarded as unclean. This prejudice was, in time, overcome, but some tribesmen maintained the tabu even up to very recent times. The only instrument available was the pointed bamboo hoe, sufficient however for working the coastal plains. But when pressure of population forced a movement into the foothills, the jungle had to be dealt with. Here, what is known as the *kaingin* method of agriculture was adopted. A small area was slashed, the larger trees left standing. A fire then went through it and the seeds were sown. When the crop was harvested, no attempt was made to feed the soil for future replanting. It was simply abandoned and another area slashed and fired.

This form of agriculture took the tribesmen further and further from the coastal plains into the high country, and with them went their families. The result was that gradually the foothills and then the mountain slopes were settled with villages. With this settlement of the hills the regular hunt developed, as it was soon discovered that the high country abounded in both deer and wild pigs, the former providing both food and clothing. As long as the minivet, the bird of Riru, sang in the mountains, there would be good hunting. So said those early settlers in the mountains of south Formosa in their traditional songs.

Domestic vessels were first made of interwoven rattan stems. Later, the water-jars and cooking-vessels were of pottery, an art which became highly developed, especially among the Ami tribe on the east coast. This ' moulding of vessels from earth ' began with a framework of bamboo, coated inside and out with clay. The wheel was unknown. Then the bamboo was discarded and its place taken by a stone, shaped by rubbing with other stones under water till the required shape was obtained. This stone was inserted into a mass of wet clay and the exterior shaped with paddle-shaped bamboo sticks. The stone was then removed and the vessel left to harden in the sun. The workmanship of some of those early pots exceeded anything of later centuries, and such as have survived the wanderings of the tribes are today regarded with such veneration that it is *parisha*, forbidden, for other hands than those of the priestesses to touch them.

Time was reckoned by knots tied on tall grass stems.

The system of control was matriarchal. Each village was part of a community directed by a *popuroasis*, a regional chief, who himself was subject to the orders of the priestess in all major matters. These chiefs were themselves descended through the female line. They were the leaders of the hunt and the fight, but it was the prerogative of the priestess to determine the time of seed-sowing, the time of hunting, and the time of the attack on the enemy. In all disputes her word was final.

The priestess was the guardian of the ancient customs and the custodian of all tribal ceremonies. She alone could give consent for marriage. Each male member of the tribe left the home of his parents on his sixteenth birthday to enter the tribal ' bachelor-house ', and from that time he was not permitted any association with females. In the bachelor-house he received instruction in the arts of war and the technique of the hunt. It was from the bachelor-house that he later went to his marriage, his bride having been selected by the priestess in seeming consultation with the families concerned.

Under the influence of the sacred *samshu*, a spirit distilled from the sweet potato, the priestess held communion with the ancestral spirits and interpreted their will to the chiefs. She was the mediator between earth and heaven. With the aid of this potent *samshu* she danced till she swooned her way out of this world to take up temporary residence in the realm of spirits. On her return, she brought with her the divine directives.

The house of the priestess was always on the highest ground in the village, preferably on a hillside, for the mountains spoke, but in a language that she alone could understand. The echo was the voice of the ancestral spirit. But the priestesses of south Formosa were not above tricking the tribesmen over the echo in the hills. There was the famous case of Wu Feng, who, in later years, lived among the Tsou tribe, and fought for the abolition of head-hunting. All the regional chiefs favoured his campaign, but with the priestess it was a different matter. She would seek the mind of the ancestral spirits on the issue. So, with her hierarchy of maidens, she resorted to Mount Ali, the mountain of echoes. Taking her place in a ravine, she stationed members of her court in various parts of the mountain. Soon the mountain was resounding with voices, with the result that she reported to the chiefs that the holy mount simply reverberated with the anger of the spirits of the ancestors at the very suggestion that head-hunting should cease.

The chiefs believed their priestess. It would have been most perilous to offend the dwellers on Olympus, for, at death, they would have to cross the narrow bridge over the mighty chasm and they would need the assistance of those spirits if they were to pass safely to the abode of the blessed.

Tribal separatism resultant on geographical conditions, together with Chinese and other contacts, were in later centuries to modify much of this primitive community life, so that each tribe gradually developed its own form of society, its corpus of beliefs and habits, to such an extent that they appeared to have lost all signs of their original ethnic unity.

These early Proto-Malayans thought themselves to be the only inhabitants of Formosa. Whatever the pressures that had driven them from their homeland in the remote south, they had now attained an idyllic state of existence, with food-gathering easy as a bounteous Nature provided all that life asked for or they could dream of. Much like the Maoris, who, centuries later, were to traverse the vast expanses of the Pacific, and, reaching the shores of New Zealand, believed themselves to be the first to discover a land where food was to be had for the taking, these migrants to south Formosa, as they roamed at will and revelled in their freedom, which they imagined nobody could contest, thought that the only other dwellers on the island were the deer and wild pig in the mountains, the rock monkeys in the foothills, the snakes and hedgehogs that abounded everywhere, and the innumerable highly-coloured twittering and at times screeching birds.

They had reached Karuruvan, the earthly paradise.

But, as with the Maoris, this state of bliss was soon to be shaken. Disillusionment was on the way. With the increase in population, the urge to push further north became imperative. Then came the shock. They found their way barred by others. As the Maoris were to find the Moriori well established in New Zealand, so the Proto-Malayans in Formosa were amazed to see villages in the north of the island, and their leaders ready to resist the newcomers from the south. These northerners were the ancestors of the tribes known today as Taiyal and Vonum and are generally regarded as the original inhabitants of Formosa.

Who were these people?

Various theories as to their racial origin have been put forward. All agree, however, that they were not of Proto-Malayan stock. They differ physically, being decidedly prognathous, and both their social organization and crafts were dissimilar to those of the Proto-Malayans. Ludwig Riess, one of the first to note this, suggested in his *Geschichte der Insel Formosa* in 1897 that these northern tribes had reached north Formosa at least a thousand years before the Christian era by way of the Ryukyus and were a branch of the people known as Lonkius, who had retreated from the cold north and spread over the Kuriles and Japan, being represented today by the Ainus of Hokkaido. Some Japanese anthropologists regard the Taruko, a subdivision of the Taiyals in north-east Formosa, as descendants of the vanguard of this migration. The story of the ' Cutting of the Sun ', still told by Taruko tribesmen, may preserve some ancient tradition of such a trek from the Arctic region to warmer lands in the south. In this legend the long cold night of the north is mentioned together with the exploit of cutting off half of the sun so that the northern days might be longer and warmer.

Chinese anthropologists and ethnologists, on the other hand, have maintained that the earliest migrants to north Formosa were from the Chinese mainland, who crossed the sea at a very remote period. North Formosa is seen as the first stage in the movement from continental China to Micronesia and beyond into the far reaches of the central Pacific. The beginning of this migration

has been set down at about 1600 B.C., that is, during the Shang
Dynasty. In 1896 a Japanese teacher, Dennojo Awano, discovered near the present Taipei the now famous Yuan-shan
shell-mound, which some believe could have been a settlement
of these early migrants. The bearers of this culture were fishermen and gatherers of molluscs, who buried their dead in
kitchen-middens and practised the custom of extracting four
upper teeth. They were head-hunters.

From what part of China could such migrants have ventured
over the sea to north Formosa? Were there in China, at that
early period, any tribes with customs and traits similar to those
which we know were peculiar to the tribes of north Formosa and
which differentiated them from the Proto-Malayans of south
Formosa?

The aborigines of the forests of Kweichow in central China
have long been the subject of speculation by scientists, all of
whom agree that the primitive Kweichow culture was distinct
from what we understand as the Chinese civilization of the Shang
Dynasty. It has even been suggested that the region from
Kweichow to Upper Siam might have been the 'womb of
humanity', and that traces may yet be found there of the
connecting-link between *Pithecanthropus* and *Sinanthropus*.

However, we do know that at a much later date the agricultural
programme inaugurated by Emperor Yu, founder of the Hsia
Dynasty, in the twenty-second century B.C. did result in a
massive dispersion of the early inhabitants of Kweichow. He
constructed many thousands of water-channels to curb the
flooding of the rivers, and, in so doing, gave China its first
effective irrigation system. This, in turn, intensified the zeal
for agriculture. Soon there was a land shortage, as the area
under Yu's control was comparatively small. All available
land was soon covered with paddy plantations. The hunger for
land then turned the eyes of the landless to the south, where the
primitive tribesmen of Kweichow hunted in their forests with
no care for agricultural pursuits. Their food was at hand and
could be secured with little effort.

Emperor Yu made several futile attempts to secure control of those forest-clad lands of the south. But the men of Kweichow loved their lakes and forests too dearly to suffer such intrusions without vigorous protests. The men of the northern plains were no match for the sturdy hunters of those southern forests, and again and again Emperor Yu had to retreat and lick his wounds.

But Ch'eng Tang, founder of the succeeding dynasty, the Shang, was a man of different mettle. He was confident that he could succeed where Yu had failed. In the year 1740 B.C. he announced a national crusade to conquer and possess Nan T'u, as he called the south country, and subdue the ' barbarians ', whom he compared with *ch'un*, ' creeping insects '. This clarion call brought to his banners many thousands of the landless, who, though they could have been conscripted, offered their services willingly. They were prepared to offer their lives as the price of land for their families. After a bloody struggle in the forests, Nan T'u was conquered, but not the tribesmen. Ch'eng Tang of China was to learn what many since his day were to discover : it is one thing to possess territory by force, but quite another to conquer its people. Rather than submit to the Shang, the tribesmen of Kweichow decided to migrate. And so the great diaspora began. The proud and independent tribesmen moved to the east, to Kiangsi and the coastal districts of Chekiang ; to the west, to Yunnan and Szechwan ; and to the south, to Kwangsi and Kwangtung, and thence into Annam.

This great dispersion began about the year 1700 B.C.

Some Chinese historians believe that these migrants to the east and south were the ancestors of the people subsequently known as the Yueh, who in the seventh century B.C. had established their own kingdom, reaching from Chekiang in the north to Annam in the south. From Chinese records we learn that these Yueh were skilled navigators, who were not content to hug the coast, but ventured out into the open sea. One of their kings, Kou Chien, in the fifth century B.C., was very maritime-minded. He built a port at Lang Yah, which became one of the most important in east China, and constructed a fleet of rafts, manned by 3,000 sailors. This fleet carried on regular trade

C

with villages along the coast of China and Annam, the southern
part of the Yueh kingdom, then known as Nan Yueh, ' South
Yueh '. These sailors brought home tales of the *chiu chou*, the
nine regions, ' encircled by sea ', and it was on these stories that
Tsou Yen later built up his geographical theories of the nine
continents in a vast encircling sea.

In correspondence with Chang Chi-yun on this subject, this
most eminent of living Chinese historians assured the author
that there are clear indications that there was migration from the
Chinese mainland to Formosa as far back as the period of the
Ch'un Ch'iu (Spring and Autumn Annals), that is 770–469 B.C.
He also asserted that ' the aborigines of the mountainous sections
of Taiwan [Formosa] still observe many of the customs of the
ancient Yueh tribe '.

Such a migration of Kweichow tribesmen to the China coast
and thence across the sea to Formosa would have been spread
over a long period. Shen Ying, writing in the third century A.D.,
made various references to Formosa. In his best-known work,
Lin Hai Sui T'u Chih (Geographical Records of Lin Hai), he
mentioned the island ' I Chou ', which Ling Shun-sheng of the
Academia Sinica has identified as Formosa. Shen Ying dwelt at
some length on Sun Ch'uan's expedition to the island in A.D. 230.

If, then, Kweichow tribesmen or their descendants crossed the
sea to Formosa, we should expect to find there some footprints
of their wanderings, some practices in north Formosa that were
peculiar to the forest-dwellers in primitive Kweichow.

One such discernible trace of such a migration is the practice
of *couvade*. Among the aborigines of Kweichow, when a wife
was lying in, it was obligatory for the husband to take to his bed
and feign illness. This custom was also observed among the
Yueh in coastal China and is still observed among the descendants of the Yueh people in Vietnam, Laos, and Cambodia.
There is no record of this custom elsewhere in China, and it
seems to have been a characteristic of the primitive tribes of
Kweichow which they took with them to the different regions
of their dispersion. Among both the Taiyals and Vonums of
north Formosa, even to this day, a husband may not engage in

hunting or any other activity until ten days after the birth of the child. During that period he never leaves his house, but may receive visitors, who come to inquire about his health, as he must pretend illness. The early missionaries in north Formosa were so impressed with the rigidity with which the *couvade* was observed that one of them, George Mackay, noted: 'at the time of childbirth, the mother seems to receive much less attention than the father, who becomes the centre of all inquiry, and indeed the mother returns to her tasks much earlier than the father himself'.

Then there was the close connection between head-hunting and tattooing. Neither of these customs was common among the early Chinese, but each was practised in various parts of South-East Asia. However, only among the tribesmen in Kweichow and the Yueh people and in north Formosa were these two customs associated in a unique way. Among the artifacts discovered during the excavations at Yin Hsu in the south Shang region of China was a tattooed statue, concerning which Chang Chi-yun has commented, 'such a practice had certain connections with the Yueh tribe'. The area where this statue was found verged on the Kweichow country. Liu Hou-tze, in one of his poems, described the river traveller with 'the pigment of war [head-hunting] grained into his chest' and Ch'u Yuan, greatest of the poets of the Chou twilight, in his anthology of the region between south Hupeh and Kweichow, has one lament for those whose 'heads were cut from their bodies' and the survivors 'with the tattooed bodies'. Among the Taiyals and Vonums of north Formosa, heroes of the head-hunt bore the tattooed chevrons of their valour on their bodies. The young warrior, on production of his first head, was decorated with two parallel lines on his forehead. Later, as more heads were gathered, other chevrons were tattooed on his body in such a way that he came to look like the braves of central China described by Liu Hou-tze. Status in the tribe was immediately clear by these tattooed lines on the body, showing at a glance the number of heads taken.

Samuel Clarke, a missionary working in Kweichow in 1904, wrote of one tribe in a remote part of the province as worshipping

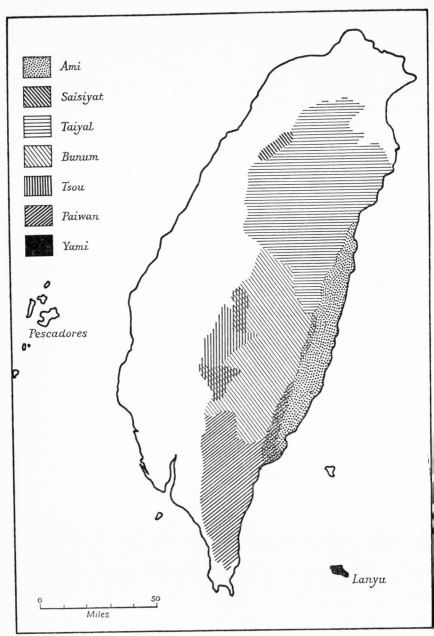

Ami

Saisiyat

Taiyal

Bunum

Tsou

Paiwan

Yami

Pescadores

Lanyu

0   50
Miles

Distribution of aboriginal tribes in Formosa

a *chei*, a dog supposed to embody the spirit of the creator of the tribe. The Taiyals of north Formosa believe that they are the offspring of a marriage between a princess and a dog.

But to return to our story. The northern tribesmen, Taiyals and Vonums, resisted the Proto-Malayans moving up from the south. No details of the struggle have been recorded but we do know its approximate date and result. In the *Sui Shu* (History of the Sui Dynasty), we read that Emperor Yang Ti sent Shu Kuan to investigate a report that ' in spring and autumn, when the weather is fine, and there is no wind, a smoky haze can be seen across the sea, extending for hundreds of miles along the eastern horizon '. Crossing the ' Tung Yang ', the Eastern Sea, Shu Kuan reached a land, the inhabitants of which were peaceful in their approach, but owing to language difficulties no converse with them was possible. Capturing several natives, Shu Kuan returned to China and reported to the Emperor. For four years the matter was forgotten. Then, in A.D. 611, it came up again. The existence of such an extensive land, not far from the coast of China, ribboned with many rivers, could not be ignored. So General Ch'en Ling was ordered to fit out a second expedition and ' explore the new land '. There, to his amazement, he met not peaceful natives but a very bellicose group. Fortunately he had with him one of the natives Shu Kuan had taken back to China and who, during his four years there, had gained sufficient knowledge of Chinese to interpret for Ch'en. From the tribesmen it was learnt that the former inhabitants of the plains, whom Shu had met, had been driven into the foothills. When Ch'en demanded tribute as recognition of the sovereignty of Emperor Yang Ti, not only did he meet with a flat refusal, but also with a challenge to arms. As nothing was to be gained by remaining longer, Ch'en returned to China.

It is clear from the above that the Proto-Malayans, moving up south, must have outfought the northern tribesmen and forced them into the foothills some time between A.D. 607 and 611.

Although the land visited by Shu Kuan in 607 and Ch'en Ling in 611 was called 'Liu Ch'iu' in the Chinese dynastic record, Chinese historians have never doubted that it was Formosa.

In 1296 Admiral Yang Tsiang, on his way to establish a base in the Liu Ch'iu Islands from which Japan could be attacked, made land at a place very similar to that described by both Shu and Ch'en. Realizing that this could not be his objective, he sailed farther north till he reached the island now known as Okinawa. There he met with such opposition that he returned to China, but he had proved that Formosa was an island quite distinct from the Liu Ch'iu group. Some twenty years later the historian Ma Tuan-lin published his *Wen Hsien T'ung K'ao* (General Study of Literary Remains), in which he accepted Yang's conclusion and named Formosa ' Little Liu Ch'iu ' to distinguish it from the northern group. He dealt in detail with the Ch'en expedition, the burning of native buildings by the Chinese, and the caulking of their boats with the blood of the slain, the ' wild men from the south '.

The Japanese, however, did not agree with this. As late as the year 1609, when, under the sponsorship of Iyehisa Shimaszu, the Daimyo of Satsuma, they landed on Okinawa and carried off the king, Sho Nei, to Japan, they maintained that Okinawa and not Formosa was the island visited by Shu Kuan and Ch'en Ling. Generals Kabayama and Hirata, commissioned to prepare an official history of Okinawa, collected all the records of native annalists, gave them a strong pro-Japanese flavour, and produced what is known as the *Munuscript History*, as it exists only in manuscript form.

According to this record, Shu Kuan arrived at Okinawa in the year 607 and again in the following year, to be followed by Ch'en Ling in 611. It contains most of the incidents mentioned in the Chinese official *Sui Shu*, but in one particular goes further. It attributes to Shu Kuan the naming of the island on which he landed :

When Shu Kuan first came to this country, he saw that its shape was like a *kyu*, floating above the waves, so he called it Ryukyu, meaning floating *kyu*.

Kyu is the Japanese equivalent of the Chinese *liu*, ' a precious stone ', and *ryu* that of *ch'iu*, ' round ' or ' spherical '. Hence

Liu Ch'iu, the name Shu gave to the island, according to the Japanese account, became the Japanese Ryukyu, the original Japanese name for Okinawa.

But to return to Emperor Yang Ti. In spite of his intense interest in the world outside China, he made no further attempt to follow up the discovery of the new land in the Eastern Sea. The reasons for this were obvious. The court at Chang'an had received news of the rebuff of Ch'en Ling by the ' barbarians ' at the time when the remnants of the imperial armies were struggling back to the capital after their third futile attempt to subjugate Korea. This was a crushing blow to the ambitions of Yang Ti. He fumed at what he regarded as an insult to his majesty and then vented his anger on both the commanders of the Korean campaigns and Ch'en Ling. All were summarily demoted.

Yang Ti had a vile temper. Irascible like most men of consuming ambition, he would stop at nothing when his schemes were thwarted. His closest friends were always the first to feel the blow. Like the fabled Sardanapalus, he would not hesitate to strike down, in anger, ' the very men who held him on his throne '.

But the storm had to abate, and then wiser counsels prevailed. Yang Ti decided to concentrate, for the time being at any rate, on consolidating the plans of his father, Yang Chien, and to forget Korea and the ' barbarians ' of the Eastern Sea. He would strengthen the forces in the north-west so as to drive back the Turco tribesmen who were nibbling away at China's frontier.

No time was lost in carrying out this purpose. He travelled along the frontier of Kansu, inspecting the troops, and receiving the homage of the western oases, and being acclaimed as far afield as Turfan. These submissions helped to heal his wounded pride. When he found time to relax from these excursions, he set about building his second palace at Loyang in Honan, with its artificial lake bordered with luxuriant villas for his favourites. Far better to sail on the lake on moonlit nights with his bevy of beauties as they improvised verses and sang songs, than torment his mind with the thoughts of the insults hurled by the

' uncivilized ' Koreans and the ' barbarian ' natives across the sea. Here there was nothing to oppose his imperial will. His favourites could, for his pleasure, defeat even the seasons, for if the maple leaves of autumn strewed the banks of the lake with their faded glory, artificial blooms glistened in their place. All through the year, despite the changes of the seasons, lotus blossoms bedecked the surface of the lake, even though, at times, they were made by delicate hands.

Emperor Yang Ti succeeded in forgetting the island across the sea, as did his successors on the Dragon Throne for a thousand years.

But not so the people of south China, especially such as lived at Chaochow, the port which from Ch'en Ling had set out on his expedition and to which he and his sailors had returned with their strange tales of that fabulous land across the water. Popular imagination had been fired with the stories of its extensive coastal plains, through which numberless streams raced from the mountains to the sea. There, indeed, was something to allure the minds and inflame the hopes of the depressed multitudes of south China. The Emperor and his court could give their undivided attention to the west, but the people of Kwangtung and Fukien looked more and more to the east, to the sea. Who could say what other lands than that discovered by Shu Kuan and Ch'en Ling were out there beyond the horizon? It only needed some venturesome rafts to give the answer. After all, Shu and Ch'en had only confirmed the story, told hundreds of years earlier by fishermen to the soldiers of Emperor Wu of the Han Dynasty and retold through the centuries, of mystic islands, far, far out beyond the rim of the sea.

By the end of the seventh century south China, in the face of official opposition, was becoming maritime-minded. Then, as always and everywhere, private enterprise was showing that courage and vision that officialdom has always lacked. An ever-increasing fleet was crossing the sea to the Penghu Islands, the Pescadores. Doubtless some of the more daring junks crossed the narrow strait to Formosa. Merchants in Chuanchow and Canton had begun to establish relations with traders in the Ryukyus, believed at that time to be the most northern part of the Liu Ch'iu group of islands.

This maritime-mindedness of the merchants of south China was not limited by narrow horizons. Not only the Eastern Sea but also the Southern Ocean invited their attention. Soon Chinese rafts were on their way to Tupo, as Java was then called. By the end of the eighth century the Chinese were controlling the sea routes to South-East Asia and as far as India. In the middle of the eleventh century this commerce had reached such proportions that the merchants were forced to make special arrangements to control operations. Records of the year 1280 show that Chinese merchants were doing business in countries as far from their home ports as East Africa, and with their own ships.

It was only to be expected that the discovery of lands beyond the sea would inspire migration, especially of the depressed people. Within fifty years of the death of Yang Ti in A.D. 618, so many of these were migrating from south China that the T'ang Emperor T'ai Tsung issued a decree prohibiting Chinese from leaving China to live abroad. But this proved ineffective in face of internal forces such as drought, famine, and the political chaos that was beginning to cloud the closing years of that dynasty. During the century that followed the passing of the T'angs the economic crisis reached its peak, and, as one writer of the time recorded, ' people died like flies ', adding, ' as for the landlords, they regard the life and death of their tenants as of no more importance than a blade of grass '. It was estimated that, in the fifty years (A.D. 910–60) between the T'ang and Sung Dynasties, at least a million families migrated from the western provinces to central China and 700,000 families moved into south China, only to swell the numbers of the destitute already there.

The records of the time paint a sorry picture of these migrating processions, ragged, hungry, many dying on the roadside, their ' parched tongues having not known the taste of food or water for days '. From his cottage-door Wang Yu-ch'eng watched one of these families limping along the road :

There is a famine.
Everywhere food is lacking.
No smoke rises from the chimneys.
A group of beggars is passing on the road :
They are a family,
Three children, following, weeping,
They have but a quart of grain for the journey.

These migrations were overland. But now a new escape was
offering, with the opening-up of the sea lanes. These had a
special attraction for the landless, who had suffered so much
under landlordism that their one dream was to own their own
plot of land, however small. Perhaps, beyond the sea, in one of
the lands of which men were talking, the dream could be realized.
This dream begat a hope, a hope on which many lived in the
absence of food. The urge to migrate was becoming, to many,
the one authentic imperative. Then life would gain some
meaning and a sense of security wipe away the tears of the
past.

The first to respond to this urge to cross the sea in quest of
a new life, based on the ownership of land, were the Hakkas, the
untouchables of China. For centuries these unwanted had been
on the move from their ancestral homes in Honan province.
Their wanderings had begun as far back as the Ch'in Dynasty,
when a bloody persecution had driven them on to the roads.
They had sought a home in Anhwei and Kiangsi. Then, in
A.D. 419, a pogrom, which developed into a general stampede,
forced many of them into the mountainous regions of Fukien.
Such as remained behind were subsequently uprooted in the
days of the T'angs (618–907), to take refuge in the caves and
mountains of Kwangsi and Kwangtung. When they did emerge
they were hounded by the *penti*, the big landowners, who
treated them as outcasts. They were branded as ' strangers ' in
their own country, hence the name Hakkas. They could not
own land ; their sons, however efficient, were excluded from the
public examinations, and thus from official positions. This
latter prohibition was to remain in force until the enlightened
Emperor K'ang Hsi removed it in the seventeenth century.

A kindly fate had led these Hakkas over the mountains and the centuries nearer and nearer the sea, which was to prove their great salvation. As long as they remained on the Chinese mainland, there was no hope for them. Now they began to look across the sea to the Penghu Islands as their El Dorado. There they would have land of their own and enjoy the fruits of their toil.

But it was not to be — at least, not on those islands. The vanguard of the Hakka migration soon realized that the land, fertile land, which they had set out to find and possess was not there. True, there was good fishing, but they could have remained in China as fishermen. It was land they wanted, land that would respond to their tilling. So they moved on across the narrow strait to Formosa. A few remained, but by the end of the twelfth century the Hakkas on the Penghus numbered less than a thousand. On the southern part of the great western plain of Formosa the migrants found the land they sought. The age-long dream had come true. The long bitter persecution of the centuries had ended. They had their problems, not the least of which was the enmity of the natives, descendants of the Proto-Malayans, whom they had dispossessed of their land and driven into the foothills. No Hakka would think of penetrating far into that region without adequate support, for a Hakka head was the greatest prize for a native head-hunter.

Those migrants possessed the drive and optimism of true pioneers. They were the first to demonstrate just what the Formosan soil, when tilled, could produce. Soon the western fringe of that coastal plain was green with sugar-cane, and rice production was so extensive that Formosa was forecast as the ' future granary of Fukien '. Tea culture was proceeding rapidly. Such was the progress that, during the year 1000, arrangements were completed for the export to south China of sugar, rice, tea, and dyes. Peikang was the port from which the junks sailed with their cargoes, initiating the first trading concern across the Strait of Formosa. Encouraging as it was, much more could have been accomplished had there been draft animals on the island. As it was, all labour was manual, and centuries were to pass before the first water-buffaloes appeared in 1520, introduced by the Dutch.

News of what was happening across the sea in Formosa gradually percolated into the Hakka villages in Fukien and Kwangtung. As the junks unloaded their cargoes of food at Chaochow and Chuanchow, it became clear that what the villagers were hearing were no idle tales. Each loaded junk from Formosa added a further stimulus to the urge to migrate. During the closing years of the Sung Dynasty, with the dread of Mongol domination becoming more and more a reality, this urge gained momentum, and during the period 1250–79 one-third of the Hakkas of Kwangtung crossed the sea to settle in Formosa.

This flooding of south Formosa with settlers from China aroused the natives on the coastal plains of the north, the descendants of the Malayans. Panic-stricken, they feared that they would suffer the same fate as their kinsmen in the south. But they knew that their rude weapons of bamboo pikes would be no match for the Chinese with their pikes and swords of iron. Their only hope was to have similar arms. But where was the iron to be found ? There was only one way out : raids on the land from which the invaders had come. So, in their rafts of bamboo poles, they set out, pillaging and plundering village after village, in search of armour and any bit of iron available. In the *Sung Shih* (History of the Sung Dynasty), Tuo Tuo recorded that during 1174–89 :

> Hundreds of natives of Liu Ch'iu [Formosa], led by their chiefs, suddenly appeared at Shui-ao, Wei-t'ao, and other villages on the coast of Fukien, robbing them of all the iron and armour.

Hardly had they returned to north Formosa than the expected attack eventuated. In their quest for land, Hakka migrants penetrated right up to the northern plains, determined to expel the natives, whose resistance, even with their newly fashioned weapons, proved no match for the newcomers. Driven into the foothills, these descendants of the Malayans had once more to face the original inhabitants, whom their ancestors had centuries

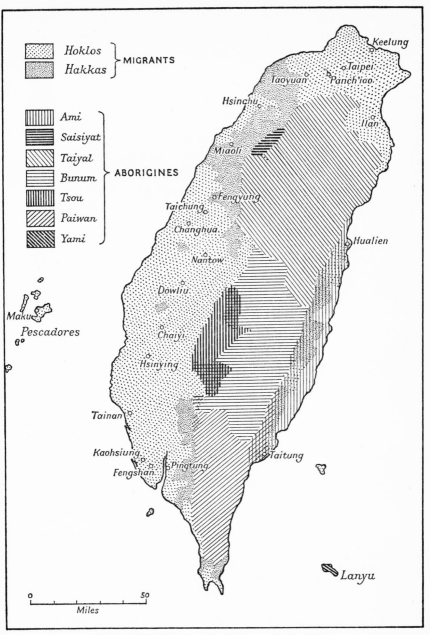

Regional distribution of migrants and aborigines

earlier forced out of the coastal lands. As for the Hakkas, they were in control of the rich coastal plains and Formosa bid fair to become a Hakka kingdom.

But it was not to be. Their tenure of that rich land was not to last, for other Chinese, not Hakkas, had already cast envious eyes on that coast. These were the Hoklos, from Amoy and other parts of Fukien province, who had long felt the lure of the rich island across the sea, where ' sugar-cane grew and covered the land from the mountains to the sea ' and where the thriving port of Peikang was filled with ' junks laden with sugar and rice for transport to Amoy '. Chinese have always been born traders, and the commercial potential of Formosa made a strong appeal to any Fukienese with assets.

In the early years of the thirteenth century this second migration was in full swing, with settlers and traders well prepared for what might lie ahead. After many bitter struggles, these Hoklos drove the Hakkas from their coastal lands into the foothills, where, once again, they had to face the Malayan descendants whom their ancestors had centuries earlier forced out of the plains. Once again the Malayans had to retire, this time into the mountains, and come to terms with the original inhabitants. From that time the integration of these two began, and the so-called ' aborigines ' of Formosa in the mountains today are the amalgam of those two races. With the passage of time the tribes of the different regions developed their own characteristics, and these have given rise to the ethnological classifications we know at present.

The distribution of population resultant on these migrations has remained very much the same through the centuries since. A British shipping agent, W. A. Pickering, who lived in Formosa a century ago, noted the sharp lines of this distribution :

The West coast and all the alluvial plain, from north to south, is inhabited by immigrants from the Chinese province of Fuh-kien, and these speak variations of the language called by Europeans the Amoy dialect. These emigrants are called Hok-los.

In the villages between the lower ranges of the mountains and at the South Cape, indeed everywhere on the borders of the savage territory, we find another and totally distinct race, called Hak-kas, or strangers, in their own language, and termed by the Hok-los, Kheh-lang.

We now come to the Ch'i-hoan, or raw savages, of the high mountains.

The Hoklos from Fukien took to Formosa not only their grim determination to possess the rich coastal lands and control the export trade of the island, but also the Maid of Foochow, the Goddess Ma Tso-po. There are many variations of the story of this maid and her apotheosis, but all agree that she was born on an island off the coast of Foochow, and, as a reward for her virtuous life, was endowed by Heaven with supernatural powers. On one occasion, during a very violent storm, her brothers at sea were about to founder, when she suddenly appeared on their fishing junk and commanded the waves to subside. When her miraculous intervention became known on the island, she was elevated to the guardianship of sailors and became known as the ' Holy Mother '. Temples were soon erected in her honour and her fame crossed to Foochow on the mainland, where a splendid temple was erected, which remained through the years one of the most impressive sights in Fukien province. Temples for her worship were built in all the fishing villages and as far south as the estuary of the Pearl River. Macao was probably a Portuguese corruption of her name. With the coming of the Hoklos to Formosa, Ma Tso-po became the tutelary divinity of the west coast, where she is worshipped today as Matsu.

What, then, was the manner of life in Formosa in the twelfth and thirteenth centuries? On the whole it was a prosperous existence. No attempt was made, from any quarter, to establish a central control. With both the Hoklos and Hakkas, it was the age of the pioneer, unhampered by authority and free to expand. That zest which had inspired the primitive community on the Chinese mainland at the time of Emperor Yu had been recaptured in Formosa as men went forth to conquer the new land with their ' drains and ditches '. No limited acreage warped the vision, for, as far as the eye could see, the rich earth invited the husbandry of the tiller.

Among the Hoklos on the western plains, control was in the hands of the clan elders. Each clan settlement was a state in itself — very much the situation that existed in ancient China in the time of the Chou, except that there was no overlordship from the centre. A kind of gentlemen's agreement existed, which, however, was broken at times when members of one clan trespassed on the domain of its neighbour. This was inevitable in an unmapped and unsurveyed island where boundaries were uncertain. We read of feuds between the Tsengs and Changs, which tended to become hereditary, much as was the case among the Highlanders in Scotland, and for much the same reason.

The Hoklos fished along the coast and the inland streams. They cultivated rice, millet, sugar-cane, and such vegetables as melons, cucumbers, and pumpkins. On the extreme east, verging on the Hakka lands, the women cared for silkworms and the plantations of *shulang* and tree-indigo, from both of which dyes were extracted. The ports on the west coast were entirely in the hands of the Hoklos, who reaped rich rewards from this highly lucrative business. During the middle of the thirteenth century there was such a boom in prosperity that several of the more powerful clans acquired land near these ports and soon a keen rivalry developed in the acquisition of trading junks for the conveyance of rice to Fukien, then in the grip of a severe famine. The dye trade was increasing, and Amoy merchants set up their own receiving stations at Peikang, the most important of the ports. On the return journey to Formosa, the junks acted as migrant vessels, bringing more Hoklos to the island.

The Hoklos lived in timber houses, the frames being of the hard *kosan* wood, to which planks of *chengpi*, a kind of pine, were attached. The Amoy style of clothing was retained, the more prosperous wearing a loose jacket and wide breeches, reaching a little below the knees, with light turbans twisted about their heads. The poorer class had just the waist- and loin-cloth as covering. The women dressed much like the men, with the addition of a few bracelets. White cords bound the braided tails of their hair, and ornaments of silver were added according to the finances of the individual.

The Hakkas in the foothills lived a more precarious life. Proximity to the mountain tribesmen made existence much more hazardous, and they had to be on the constant alert for marauding head-hunters, ever determined to seek revenge for the loss of their former lands. The density of the jungle favoured these hunters, as they could lie, unseen and unheard, ready to pounce on the unwary Hakka who chanced to stray too far from his own territory. This uncertainty was reflected in the type of houses in which they lived. These were not of timber but of earth, pounded into solidity, each a miniature fortress which could not easily be burnt. A framework of bamboo in parallel walls was erected, the space between filled with earth, and when this had been pounded and hardened, the bamboo was removed; similar to the dwellings in primitive China associated with the name of Fu Yueh. A number of these houses were surrounded by an earth wall, thus forming a stockade.

As hunting was the chief source of food while the forests were being cleared, the Hakkas could not avoid some contact with the men of the mountains. At times they were able to come to terms, thus enabling the Hakkas to instruct the natives in efficient methods of agriculture. Such as responded to these overtures of friendship and showed a willingness to adopt the Hakka way of life, especially in tilling the land, became known as *sek-huan* or 'ripe barbarian', i.e. semi-civilized; such as resisted all approaches were *chin-huan* or 'green barbarian', entirely uncivilized. These were not tribal or ethnological terms, but purely indications of adoption or rejection of Chinese standards and customs.

The ever-present fear of attack created among the Hakkas a much greater degree of unity than was the case with the Hoklos. They were compelled by circumstances to form a common front, and this took the form of villages in which many families lived. This emergence of village life as distinct from clan life was the first step towards Formosan nationhood. It was born in the hills, in marked contrast to the feuds and rivalries which were already dividing the Hoklos in the west and which were to have a marked influence in the future of Formosa. History was to record, and

D

at no distant date, the debilitating effect of those clan divisions, and at a time when unity was urgently needed.

The dress of the Hakkas, like their houses, was a reflection of their uncertain life. The wild fibre known as *dolichos* had to provide the cloth, coarse as it was, for their garments, as well as for such footwear as the women needed.

Meanwhile the mountain people carried on their primitive way of life, hunting, feasting, and worshipping their tribal deities. When failure in the hunt or paucity of crops, such as they were, occurred, the divine displeasure had to be appeased, and this was done by offering a Hakka head as a propitiatory sacrifice to the offended god. When not gathering food or hunting for heads, the days were passed in a carefree manner. The men told and re-told the heroics of the past, and the women, with their *sapteads*, wooden beaters, prepared the bark of the *roran*, the mulberry tree, for the making of cloth. According to one Chinese record, some of this cloth was decorated and known as *pan-wen-pu*. The *Sui Shu* tells how Shu Kuan took with him from Formosa in A.D. 607 ' fine cloth made from white bark, also mottled cloth '. Among some tribesmen in the central mountains, carving in wood and stone had reached a high degree of efficiency. One family, the Tarusagiu, was setting the foundation of a reputation which was to persist through centuries even to the present day. Carvings by members of this family centuries ago, which today stand as frontal posts of *khuva*, meeting-houses, have been compared most favourably with the best work of the Maoris on their *whare whakairo*, carved meeting-house. It is doubtful whether such a long tradition in decorative art existed at any time, in East or West, comparable with that of the Tarusagiu family. On the eastern slopes of the central mountains a high standard in pottery-making was attained, but the art was subsequently lost, and only a few worth-while specimens remain to indicate the degree of excellence attained in the past, especially among the Ami and Paiwan tribesmen.

In all the mountain villages, the so-called Jew's harp, made of thin bamboo slits, and similar to the primitive Chinese *sheng*, was the favourite musical instrument. In the twilight, its soft tones, carrying a far distance, seemed to be the expression of a soul that was leaving its body to enter the spirit-world of the ancestors, or perchance calling its absent mate. Nancy Chang Ing, in one of her choicest nocturnes, has caught the mood of the mountain musician :

> Stars hang low,
> Half-moon, yellow, vibrant glows,
> Distant hills, dark cloaked
> In mystic, silent splendour.
> Ginger blossoms, dew-soaked
> Fragrance, heavy laden.
>
> Quiet, my heart, beat light —
>   Listen to night.

One has to spend nights on the Formosan mountains to feel the deeper meaning of this bewitching mysticism.

Somewhere, in a secluded spot, back in the twelfth and thirteenth centuries, eligible maidens vied with one another in making tubes of bamboo, into the ends of which brightly coloured yarn or blooms of gentian blue were thrust to form rosettes. One of these tiny tubes would be inserted through a hole cut in the lobe of the right ear, so as to attract the attention and win the approval of the priestess, as the time of marriages is drawing near. Then, later, when the priestess had made the selections, had we stood on a headland overlooking that dream-water high up in the mountains of central Formosa, now known as Jih Yueh T'an, ' Sun Moon Lake ', forest, mist, and water would have reproduced for our delight one of Wang Wei's masterpieces. Then, as night closed on, we would have heard, coming across the water, the Tsou epithalamium, that bridal song now almost forgotten :

> For nights I have not slept,
> In the light of the bright moon
> I have wandered, seeking you.
> Now, at last, I have found your door,
> And a great joy fills my heart.

The moral standard of all the Formosan tribes was high.

Their code was enforced with Mosaic firmness. Indeed, as that code is set down side by side with the Decalogue, the similarity is remarkable, for at that time no white man had set foot on the island.

Although, with the passage of the centuries, the tribes became more and more separate entities, each developing its own customs and language, and at times engaging in bloody struggles among themselves, there was, in the earlier period, a common meeting-place. There are reasons for concluding that the festival known as *Mavayaiya*, and still celebrated by the two neighbouring Paiwan and Piyuma tribes, was, in the twelfth and thirteenth centuries, a kind of Panathenaic gathering. It was held once every five years, when the expert huntsmen of Formosa gathered together to prove their skill. There were races to a spot where a Hakka head was tossed into the air, the competitors jostling each other to be the first to impale it on a bamboo pike thrown from a specified distance. Later a bundle of bark was substituted for the human head, into which the competing archers shot their arrows.

The prize awarded at this *Mavayaiya* was the most highly coveted honour in Formosa. It took the form of a crown, surrounded with tiger's teeth, from the centre of which a single white feather denoted that the wearer was alone in skill, and in valour ' nonpareil '. The festival today is but a shadow of a former splendour.

We are reminded here of the Australian aborigines, among whom time and locality developed differences in language even when the same thing is referred to. The dreamtime, when their ancestors had food in abundance and met in friendly competition, is *ngerewat* to the north Australian aborigines, the Wargaitj tribe, but to the Aranda tribesmen of central Australia it is *alcheringa*. And that great carnival of the dreamtime has now become just a tribal corroboree.

Such, then, was the Formosan scene, amorphous perhaps, but prosperous, when, according to Chinese historians, the ' authentic ' history of the island began, with the landing of Wan San-ho on its southern shore in the year 1430.

CHAPTER TWO

Captain China and his Corsairs

WAN SAN-HO, better known as Admiral Cheng Ho, an honorific borrowed from the days of Chou, was the most travelled of the seafaring Chinese of the time. He had led no less than seven expeditions to the South Seas, and had voyaged as far as the Somali coast of East Africa and Ormuz on the Persian Gulf. Returning from an official visit to Siam, a typhoon had driven his junks out of their course as far east as south Formosa. There he was taken ill and 'all the remedies known to his physician failed to give relief'. Thereupon the local physicians were called in, with immediate beneficial result. So impressed was Wan with his speedy recovery that he directed his physician to make a collection of as many Formosan herbs as possible.

In his report to Emperor Ming Hsuan Tsung on his return to Peking, Wan stated that ' the natives of the magnificent island, though barbarous in character, are of a kind disposition, even providing me with the means of returning to my own land '. The Emperor was so impressed with the account of Wan's rapid recovery, due to the efficacy of Formosan herbs, that he called in the Court physicians and ordered them to make an examination of the plants Wan had brought back with him. There might be, among these, some unknown in China. One such was found, the *Hydnocarpus*. Instructions were issued that this plant be cultivated and incorporated in the pharmacopoeia, under the title *Ta Feng-tʒu*. It was the drug made from this plant that enabled the Western physician, Hobson, to achieve startling results during an epidemic in Canton in 1855.

But perhaps Wan had got his plants mixed. The *Hydnocarpus* was not known in Formosa, but was widely used as a medicinal plant in Siam, where its lucraban seeds were believed to be effective in dealing with skin complaints.

However, Formosa got the credit, and Wan's story of the island created quite a sensation at the Ming Court. For months it was the one topic of conversation and speculation. Every official had something to say about the island in the Eastern Sea. The literati delved into the ancient records to find any reference that might be applied to the mysterious island. From south China detailed reports were received of the remarkable prosperity of the island and the trade that had been carried on with its merchants for years. That Peking could have been hitherto ignorant of this was incredible.

Then, suddenly, interest flagged and died. Formosa was no longer mentioned in Peking. Wan died in 1435, and with him all concern about the island that, for a brief period, he had made the chief topic of talk in Peking. The subject was to remain dead for more than two centuries until it was revived in 1684, when an inspector-general, under the jurisdiction of the Fukien authorities, was to be sent to Formosa.

Historians may well seek some explanation of this apparent disregard of Formosa over such a prolonged period in official circles in Peking. The records had preserved the accounts of the expeditions of Shu Kuan and Ch'en Ling, and Peking could not have been unaware of the large-scale migrations from south China to Formosa over the centuries. In 1367 Yang Tsiang had proved that Formosa was not one of the islands of the Liu Ch'iu group. In the following year the Penghu Islands had been attached to the T'ungan prefecture of Fukien province, thus incorporating those islands in China itself. Officials stationed in the islands must have known what was happening just twenty-five miles across the water in Formosa. The increasing activity of the trading junks laden with Formosan products destined for Fukien, which called in at the Penghu Islands, must have arrested their attention. Then sixty years later, Wan's story of ' the magnificent island ' had, for a brief period, focused attention on Formosa. Yet in spite of all these, no attempt had been made to claim the island. One might have thought that the expanding south China–Formosa trade, in itself, would have excited the interest of Peking. But it was not so. In fact, the first claimant to Formosa was to come from the West.

There was an explanation of this official attitude over the centuries. During the Sui Dynasty (589–618) the constant threat of invasion from the north-west diverted attention from discoveries in the Eastern Sea; the T'angs (618–905), in spite of their great achievements at home, were strongly opposed to migration from China, and even when famine and political chaos rent the country in the closing years of the dynasty, prohibition of migration was enforced with Draconic severity; the Sungs in north China (960–1126) could not afford to take their attention from the menace in the north as the shadow of the Mongol became more and more ominous, and later, in south China (1127–1278), they had to fight for their very existence; then, as for the Mongols, who controlled all China (1279–1368), their time and energy were fully occupied in futile attempts to impose their rule on a resisting people, who remained throughout loyal to Sung ideals. It was not until the restoration of domestic peace with the advent of the Mings in 1368 that the strategic moment in opportunity arrived.

This was the age of decision. A Government was in control which had popular support. The fear of invasion had vanished. A new inspiration, such as China had not known for a thousand years, surged through the land. The Court of Peking was now to determine China's place among the countries of the world. Chinese ships were soon to be seen on all the seas of the western Pacific, and sailing the Indian Ocean to the African coast. At the same time, ships from the other side of the world, from Europe, were crossing the Indian Ocean on their way to the China Sea, and some had already been seen in the South Seas. Peking had now to make up its mind and formulate its policy.

The literati, many of them eunuchs, made the decision. They were opposed to foreign conquests, which they considered ' useless and costly '. China, as the unrivalled civilization of the world, the *Chung Kuo*, the Middle Kingdom, whose political administration was the ideal for all men to follow, had no need to embark on such ventures. China was the one and only land favoured by Heaven. She was *T'ien Hsia*, 'Under Heaven'. All that China required from others was that they should recognize this unique position she held and adopt her civilization. Physical possession was out of the question. That was the way of the barbarian, the uncivilized.

This attitude of the literati was not just a negative approach. The physical conquest of newly-discovered lands was ruled out, not only for economic reasons as 'costly' and philosophical reasons as 'useless', but because another policy, of a positive character, was preferable. They sought for and discovered this in China's past. This was the doctrine of *tsung chu ch'uan*, which had bound together the different states in the time of Chou. Then, the states (*tsung*), each self-governing, had acknowledged the overlordship (*chu ch'uan*) of Chou, with the result that China had enjoyed its golden age. Had not the Confucian *Ta Hsueh* (Great Learning), set forth a model for all mankind, in showing how 'the moral sense of the world could be enlightened' by following the way of the Chou? If such a doctrine could operate with such success in the past in China, why should it not succeed in the China of the Mings and, through it, in all the world?

So it was that the literati at the Ming Court developed the characteristically Chinese concept of suzerainty. Contact with other lands and peoples there must be, and especially those newly discovered, but nothing in the form of colonization There must be no interference with the way in which others governed themselves. Such ideas as 'spheres of influence' and 'protectorates' found no place in such a philosophy. Chinese civilization rather than Chinese swords must conquer. All that China demanded was that her civilization, as represented by the Emperor, be recognized as superior to all others and tribute paid as a sign of such recognition. In all things else, others could do as they pleased.

The literati, in spite of some opposition, won the day and, to the undoing of China, their doctrine of *tsung chu ch'uan* became the official policy of China.

A false picture of China, however, has too often been presented by Western historians. These have seen her as a sleeper in splendid isolation, awakening at times to the din of thunderous legions passing by, only to retire to her couch again when the noise and tumult have subsided. Some have pictured her, rudely aroused, only to grant concessions to the armed intruder, then retire again to her deep slumber. Unfortunately, these have looked at China through Western eyes, so long accustomed to viewing colonization by the sword. The Greeks, in spite of their boasted culture, sought to hellenize the world with the sword. The Romans followed in the same way. The Western nations inherited the technique, improved on it, and then went out to compel the peoples of new lands to bow and submit. The long record of their colonization was a bloody story as they gained their colonies and won their spheres of influence at the point of the bayonet.

Who will say that the Chinese doctrine of *tsung chu ch'uan* was not superior ? Who will deny that conquest by culture is the mark of higher civilization ? However, we can only speculate on what might have been the fate of Asia, if, when Europeans first penetrated into the Far East, they had found the sea-lanes controlled by Chinese war-fleets and the islands manned by Chinese battalions.

This policy, formulated by the literati of Peking in the days of the Mings, had an important bearing on the history of Formosa. No plans for the colonization of the island were drawn up and no attempt was made to take over possession, although Wan San-ho and others after him had urged such action. The literati pointed out that Chinese culture, then well established in the Liu Ch'iu group, would gradually percolate to Formosa, where it would find a kinship among the thousands of Chinese settled there ; meanwhile, from the Penghu Islands, where Chinese officials were stationed, a similar cultural stream would move in the direction of Formosa. As a result, the entire region, from the Penghu Islands to the Liu Ch'iu group, would become a suzerainty of China, and Chinese civilization would spread throughout. There were sufficient Chinese in Formosa, the centre of this region, to give momentum to this cultural occupation. Those Chinese literati, five hundred years ago, seemed to have grasped a fundamental truth that the British Commonwealth leaders are only now beginning to grasp.

Chinese history, especially the views of the literati of the period under review, needs to be rewritten for the edification of the West at the present time. Huang Tsung-hsi wrote a treatise on the thesis that ' The world is too big for one man to govern by force of arms ' ; Wang Fu-chih followed this with a tractate, setting forth the position that ' Chinese culture must be the instrument of the extension of China's influence in the world ' and that ' the adoption of Chinese civilization by others will solve most of their problems '. Mei Wen-ting later summed up the situation and the attitude of the literati by affirming that ' what was valid in the civilization of the West was not new but had earlier been emphasized by China '. It is highly significant that among these literati, special attention was given, in their search for a policy, to the most ancient of Chinese guide-books, the *Yih Ching* (Book of Changes). This classic, dubbed by Western scholars as ' rubbish ' and ' gibberish ' in the past, is, in our scientific age, being re-examined, and is being treated by Sinologues with much greater respect than in the time of Legge and Giles.

However, the plan for the peaceful conquest of Formosa might have succeeded, had it not been for the Dutch and the crafty Hsiung Wen-ts'an, then Governor-General of Fukien and Chekiang. It is sufficient to note here that when Martinus Sonck arrived in Formosa in 1623 to inspect a suitable site for a trading station, he was met by Li Han, a Chinese from Japan, who was to act as his interpreter. As ' Captain China ', Li was to become one of the most colourful and dynamic characters in Formosan history.

Born in Fukien, Li had gone to Manila as a young man to try his fortune as a trader. To further his interests there, he had become a Christian ; at least he had attached himself to the Christians. For some offence, evidently not trivial, he was sent to the galleys. But this slavery did not last long, as he succeeded in stowing away on a ship bound for Japan. Settling at Hirado, he set himself up as a merchant, and in 1616 received a Red Seal Licence from the Shogun to engage in overseas trade.

Prosperity was rapid and in a short time Li Han was the head of the Chinese community at Hirado, hence the title ' Captain China ' which was to remain with him during the rest of his life. His influence and standing were recognized far beyond Hirado, as Iwao in his *An Inquiry into the Life of Li Han* refers to him as ' Chief of Chinese residents in Japan '. Japanese records of the time mention his commercial activities at Nagasaki, where he had established a trading-house, from which he carried on business with both south China and Formosa. It would appear that Nagasaki was the centre from which his overseas business was conducted, with Hirado the place where he acted as business agent for the English and Dutch. There is reason to believe that, at the same time, and with the connivance of and possibly support of the Daimyo Matsuura, he engaged in certain piratical ventures. Withal, his varied activities paid handsomely, as we find him mentioned in the records as ' a very wealthy merchant, with considerable property in Hirado and Nagasaki '.

He seems to have had it all his own way as far as his dealings with the English were concerned. At the time, the chief factor of the English East India Company in Japan was the elderly and, it would appear, very gullible Richard Cocks. The wily Li managed to ingratiate himself into the goodwill of Cocks so successfully that the Englishman acted as godfather to Li's daughter Ignacia, and indeed chose her additional name, Elizabeth.

As we read Murakami's *Diary and Correspondence of Richard Cocks*, it is not difficult to see the game that each was playing. Cocks was trying to use Li for his own ends, and Li was pitting his skill and subtlety against the Englishman. Believing that Li, in spite of the Chinese prohibition of trade with Japan, could work things for his company, as he seemed to have friends at various south China ports, Cocks paid over large numbers of silver bars. The Company would soon gain its objective, Li assured him, but

' we must be patient '. In a letter to his company in 1621 Cocks
wrote :

I am now informed that the ould Emperour hath resigned the government into one of his sonnes ; and that the new Emperour hath granted
our nation trade with China for two shipps a yeare, and the place
appointed near to Fuchchew.

But the official permission did not reach Cocks. So, to
expedite matters, more silver bars were paid over. Still nothing
eventuated, and on 31 December 1622 Cocks had to inform his
company :

Our friend, the Captain China, still mentayneth that our nation
may have trade into China if they will, but not the Hollanders ; which
God grant may once take effect.

By this time London was awake to Li's ' fraudulent practises '.
Cocks was reprimanded for his ' simplicitie ', directed to procure
' all satisfaccon from him [Li Han] for all that he owes to the
Company ', and return to England. But it was too late. Li had
left for Formosa, under engagement to the Dutch. Cocks
himself died at sea.

Li Han was now to embark on the most exciting period of his
career. He was quick to see the possibilities of the new situation.
Vast fortunes were to be made in Formosa, and his earlier
experiences in piracy would stand him in good stead. Neither
Chinese nor Japanese authorities could hamper his operations,
as neither made claim to the island. The field was thus free from
all restrictions and only the Dutch had to be dealt with. He
suggested to Martinus Sonck that in the north of the island ' the
inhabitants are a very murderous people, with whom they [the
Dutch] would find it difficult even to speak ', so it would be
better to confine activities to the south of the island. Already
the crafty Li had his own plans for the north, especially the coast
around Keelung.

From the outset the Dutch suspected Li. ' Had we been able
to use anybody else,' wrote Sonck to Batavia in 1624, ' we
would not have trusted Captain China as much as we are now
forced to do for lack of an alternative.'

Li did not remain in Dutch employ long. The call of the seas and the rich harvest to be reaped there was too strong for him to resist. His one ambition was to become master of the Strait of Formosa as well as of the China Sea. And this, not as a legitimate trader, but as the doyen of pirates. Never was there such a golden opportunity, as the seas, easily reached from a haven on the west coast of Formosa, were becoming alive with trading ships — English, Dutch, Spanish, Portuguese, and Chinese. Pirated goods, taken to depots in north Formosa, could easily be sold in both Chinese and Japanese ports, and he had friends in all of these.

Such a vision was irresistible, especially to such as Li Han. The possibilities were unlimited. But there was one snag. Others had seen what he saw and, indeed, were already operating. There were the Japanese, who, having lost all their belongings during the civil war at the close of the Ashikaga regime, had taken to the sea as pirates, and from their base in the Liu Ch'iu Islands were ravaging the China coast from Shantung to Fukien. Flying the flag of Hachiman Daibosatsu, the Japanese patron deity of warriors, they were terrorizing village after village. *Ming Shih*, in its history of the time, recorded that their exploits in Fukien villages resulted in a pitched battle with Chinese forces, in which, after a running fight, they were driven back to their base. Then, in south Formosa, Chinese pirates had bases from which they scoured the sea, seizing goods from vessels on their way from Nagasaki to Formosa. Back in 1592 the Shogun had issued permits to merchants at Kyoto, Nagasaki, and Sakai to engage in this trade. These Chinese were building up a lucrative business with the stolen cargoes, in Macao, Annam, the Philippines, and as far off as Java and Siam. The seas abounded with fish and these Chinese fishermen were reaping an abundant harvest from the waters.

Li Han studied the position and formulated his plans. He would build up his own vast pirate confederacy, with the Japanese operating from north Formosa and the Chinese from south Formosa. His corsairs, owning no allegiance to either China or Japan, would regard him as their director and final

arbiter in all things. He himself would be the law. From
Keelung to Tamsui in the north, along the west coast south of
Lukang, and in the remote south, from Fengshan to Henchun,
villages for the families of his pirates would be established around
the depots, where the pirated cargoes would be stored, and from
which, in turn, these would be sent to ports, from Japan to south
China and as far away as Siam, where his agents would handle them.

It was a daring conception, the like of which had never been
known previously in the history of piracy. And it worked.

Li invited the chiefs of the Japanese and Chinese pirates to
meet him at a small cove south of Anping, known as Kansan. He
set before these his plan and won their approval. This in itself
was a remarkable testimony to Li's standing, as at that time
China and Japan were estranged to such a degree that war
between them was a possibility at any time. Yet Li was able to
bring about harmony between the Chinese and Japanese outlaws,
who recognized him as their leader and whose instructions they
swore to obey at all times and in all circumstances. He was their
' pirate-chief'. In recognition of this it was agreed that their
flag would bear the emblem of a tortoise-shell, which signified
Li's supremacy.

No time was lost in carrying out the decisions of the conference.
From his base in Formosa, Li Han directed the far-flung activities
of his pirate empire. The whole situation was nothing short of
fantastic, and the closer our investigation of it, the more incredible
it appears. From Japan to Java and beyond, the orders of Li
carried more weight than the injunctions of Governments. His
ships, flying the tortoise-shell flag, were masters of the seas and
the dread of all engaged in legitimate trade. His connections
reached from Hirado and Nagasaki in Japan, down the China
coast, where members of his family in Fukien were co-partners
in the gigantic scheme, right down to Batavia. Records of the
period suggest that the Daimyo Matsuura in Japan and So Bing
Kong, head of the Chinese community at Batavia, were more
intimately involved in Li's piracy than purely as agents for the
disposal of his stolen goods.

For a brief period Formosa was the most important spot in the

Far East. For twelve months in 1624–5, Li Han — ' Captain China ' — was the uncrowned king of the western Pacific, ruling his maritime kingdom from the island of Formosa.

Li Han was the pioneer of trade in the Far East. His corsairs roamed the seas seizing the goods which his ships later transported to Japan, south China, Annam, the Philippines, Borneo, Malacca, Java, Siam, and according to some records to distant Acapulco in Mexico. It was business on the grand scale. The lanes of commerce opened up by this piratical business were to become the acknowledged channels of legitimate world trade.

Such an empire as Li had established could only survive as long as harmony prevailed among his corsairs. However ruthless they were on the high seas, all the available material suggests that, when on shore, there was no strife among them. This is most remarkable when we recall how considerable the settlements must have been, with the families of the pirates and the large number of employees required to handle the receiving and dispatching of goods at the depots. Leaders were chosen by ballot to administer the affairs of these communities. Laws were enacted and honoured and there is no record of rebellion. Li spent much of his time in inspecting these depots and directing the operations of the various fleets. It speaks much for his strength of personality that the settlements carried on in such a harmonious manner.

This was the first semblance of government in Formosa.

Li seems to have had a working agreement with the Hoklos in Formosa, especially the traders at the port of Peikang. He never interfered with their ships on their way to and from Fukien. His brother, a merchant at Chuanchow in Fukien, seems to have acted as agent both for Li and the Hoklos traders. There is no record of any clash between the pirate settlements in Formosa and the Chinese populations there.

As for the Dutch, they acted as realists in their dealings with Li Han. They had never trusted him and had only retained his services earlier out of sheer necessity. Martinus Sonck, the Dutch commander in Formosa, in a letter to Batavia, had expressed the hope that ' the services of Bencon ' might be secured, but, of course he did not know that this 'Bencon', as he called So Bing Kong, was closely associated with Li Han. However, the Dutch did not object to Li's ships transporting silk and other goods for them to south China and there disposing of them. Li suggested that he should fly the Dutch flag on some of his ships, for which he would pay compensation, but the Dutch refused to take the risks. Still, in rejecting the suggestion, they did not want to alienate Li, so they made him considerable gifts, as 'he has been so helpful to us in everything and in order to increase his partiality for us'.

Were the Dutch shutting their eyes to Li's piracy in the hope that his 'partiality' might spare Dutch ships on the high seas? In any case, Martinus Sonck probably never stopped to think that posterity would one day read his correspondence.

Li Han was not just a buccaneer. The pirate settlements he set up on the Formosan coast were not designed to be Utopias, where wild roamers of the sea, weary of their wanderings and their wounds, might rest in peace. He was no Misson, urging his fellow pirates to build their 'Libertatia' settlement in a secluded Madagascan bay, 'a place of our own and a haven, when age or wounds have rendered us incapable of hardship and where we might enjoy the fruits of our labour and go to our graves in peace'; no John Phillips, swearing loyalty with his fellows on a hatchet to a code of rules, as they planned their sanctuary in Newfoundland, where they would retire, shut off from the world; no Mansvelt, urging his company of corsairs to one last 'grand deed' of piracy before they settled on their dream island off the Colombian coast, 'enjoying peace and dying unhunted'. Li was not of this order. His settlements were busy with the noise and bustle of commerce, the arrival and departure of trading ships, the filling and emptying of warehouses. He and his confederates were not seeking a place of rest but were building a new world, a Chinese world. On the foundations they were laying were later to rise the prosperous ports and coastal cities of Formosa.

Then suddenly, in 1625, Li Han disappeared. Captain China was no longer to be seen moving from settlement to settlement, giving his directions, and supervising the enlargement of the empire he had built up. The next and last notice of him was at the end of that year at Hirado in Japan, when his death was reported.

Had Li Han just faded out of the history of Formosa? If so, who had taken his place? Or could it be that only the name of Captain China had vanished?

In Chinese records the name of Yen Ssu-ch'i appeared as leader of the pirate band from the time that the name of Li Han disappeared in Formosa. However, it is significant that although British and Dutch ships were active in both Chinese and Formosan waters, no mention was made, in their reports, of Yen Ssu-ch'i. One might have expected the Dutch especially to have known something of his activities. And to aggravate the problem, the Japanese, who were aware of Li Han's movements right up to the time of his death, make no mention of this Yen Ssu-ch'i.

Who, then, was he?

There is little doubt that the Li Han and Yen Ssu-ch'i of Chinese and later Western historians were one and the same. Why he changed his name we do not know. That he did so should occasion no surprise. In Fukien, where he was born, he was known as Li Han; in Manila, the scene of his first trading venture, he was Andrea Dittis, the meaning of this surname not being clear; in Japan, he was Captain China, the name by which the Dutch knew him. It would not be surprising if Yen Ssu-ch'i was a sobriquet coined by somebody, who observed his countenance (*yen*) as thoughtful (*ssu*) as he planned the extension (*ch'i*) of his empire. Did not the Earl of Rochester, observing the habits of King Charles II of England, give him the name by which every schoolboy knows him, the ' Merry Monarch '?

The Chinese records, which alone mention Yen Ssu-ch'i, can be interpreted as confirming this identification. In these, the birthplace of Li and Yen is set down as Fukien, the occupation of both is ' pirate-chief ', the base of operations is the same, Formosa, and Cheng Chih-lung is the chief-of staff to both. In fact, the sole difference is that these records mention Japan as the place where Li Han died, whereas Yen Ssu-ch'i is said to have

E

died in Formosa. Such coincidences are strong pointers to a common identity.

What, then, was Li Han's place in the history of Formosa, indeed of the Far East? Chinese and Japanese historians have taken more than a passing notice of him, but, strangely, Western Sinologues have ignored his very presence. Li Han was a master among buccaneers, but he was much more. He was of the mould that later produced Cecil Rhodes in Africa. He was the first man to grasp the strategic position of Formosa. What Douglas MacArthur said of Formosa in 1945 had been visualized by Li Han more than three centuries earlier. More than that, long before Buckle, Montesquieu, and Chang Chi-yun, Li Han understood how history is determined very considerably by geographical factors. He saw Formosa lying athwart the sea routes from the Indies to China and Japan, as holding the key to the passage from south China to Japan, and as controlling the lanes to the lands beyond the Pacific.

Li Han believed that whoever held Formosa held the trade of the western Pacific, and history proved him right. A Japanese shogun, a Chinese emperor, and a Dutch governor sought his help and alliance, as they knew that their own security depended, to a great extent, on the friendliness of whoever held Formosa.

CHAPTER THREE

The Dutch Interlude

WHILE Li Han had concentrated on the economic build-up of the scattered settlements he had established, the Dutch embarked on their ill-fated colonization of Formosa. It was a brief adventure, and when, in 1661, they were forced out, no lasting impression of their experiment remained. Never, in the history of East–West relations, has a European power been presented with a greater and more promising opportunity; never has there been such a disastrous failure.

For years the Dutch had wanted to enter the China trade, then monopolized by the Portuguese. In 1595 Cornelius Houtman had been successful in opening up trade with Java, and this had led to the formation of the Dutch East India Company seven years later and the annexation of the Indies. Encouraged by its success there, the Company then decided to challenge the Spaniards, who had established a trading-base in 1571, and the Portuguese, who from their base at Macao had controlled the China trade since 1557.

This Dutch ambition was not lacking in religious zeal. Neither the English East India Company nor the Dutch East India Company was happy with the prospect of the lucrative trade of the Orient falling entirely into the hands of their Catholic opponents.

From 1607 to 1622 the Dutch had made several requests to the Chinese for permission to establish a trading-post, but had always met with polite refusals, characteristically Chinese. The Portuguese were *kuei k'e*, honoured guests, of China, and it would not be courteous to permit opposition to those who were treated as such. The authorities regretted that the observance of good manners towards honoured guests made it impossible to grant the Dutch requests. But the Dutch were not interested in protocol and etiquette. They made a display of force, but when Hsiung Wen-ts'an, under orders from Peking, prepared to meet force with force, the Dutch abandoned the project for the time being. In the Pescadores they began the construction of a naval base, from which an all-out assault on Macao could be launched. If the Chinese would not permit the feelings of their honoured guests to be offended by competing traders, then the only course was to drive those guests out of China. Perhaps then the Dutch could become the honoured guests themselves.

News of the construction of the naval base in the Pescadores put Governor Hsiung into a flurry. He feared that, in reply to the refusal to allow the Dutch to set up a station in south China, they might take over the Pescadores. Knowing that China was in no position to face Dutch naval power if it came to a show-down, Hsiung worked out a subtle plan to outwit the Dutch without fighting. Why not a Dutch trading-base on Formosa? Of course China had no authority to suggest such a thing, as she had no jurisdiction over the island. The Dutch might not be aware of this. At any rate, it was worth the venture. The ruse worked, and the Dutch imagined that they were to become *kuei k'e* on Formosa, much like the Portuguese at Macao. This was to preclude any other country from entering into competition with them. After all, the Chinese were being generous. Early in 1623 Commander Sonck arrived from Batavia to complete arrangements with China. He was fêted at Foochow in the grand manner. As a mark of goodwill, the Chinese would not only allow the Dutch to set up their base on Formosa, but would provide considerable merchandise to assist in the establishment. But that was not all. A Chinese official would proceed to Batavia to cement good relations between China and the Dutch East India Company. Delay on the part of Batavia in implementing the agreement annoyed the Chinese, who considered that the Dutch were showing very bad faith. So Governor Hsiung staged yet another ruse. He put up a sham fight off the Pescadores, which decided Sonck that the best thing to do was to ratify the agreement at once and thus retain the goodwill of

China. Otherwise the Chinese might become embittered and that would close the doors to the possibilities of trade.

Hsiung's cunning had won the struggle with the Dutch.

When Commander Sonck arrived in south Formosa in 1623 he got a shock. There was no official with whom he could confer as to the location of the trading-base; indeed, nothing to suggest Chinese authority on the island — no official buildings, no signs whatever that Peking was interested. Li Han, who had been engaged by the Dutch station at Hirado to act as Sonck's interpreter, may or may not have made him wise to the situation. We do not know. There were Chinese, many of them, to be seen. Some lived in pretentious red-brick houses and appeared to be very opulent. These were the Hoklos. In marked contrast with these, and a few miles inland, were others, not Chinese in appearance, who lived in grass houses, and were referred to by the Chinese as *pepo-huan*, ' savages of the plains '.

In spite of this shock, Commander Sonck was deeply impressed with what he saw — the apparent richness of the land, especially on the plain, and the abundance of water. It was a most inviting prospect, the more so as it seemed to be an unclaimed land and without any central authority. Why so much concern about driving the Portuguese from Macao or the Chinese from the Pescadores, when Formosa was just waiting for a claimant? Of course, much would have to be done to develop the island, especially in the construction of harbours. Then there were the pirates, of whose exploits he was hearing much already, but the Dutch fleet, if strengthened from Batavia, could easily clean the sea of these. Batavia and the Company at Amsterdam would be thrilled when his report reached them.

But the vision of Commander Sonck was not to be realized. Plans drawn up in far-away Amsterdam were to be only drawings on paper. Then, as so often in the years to come, the West was to fail completely to understand the mind of the Orient.

From the outset the Dutch were destined for disaster in Formosa. On receiving the report that the island was unclaimed, even by China, the Governors of the Dutch East India Company decided, as in the previous case of the Indies, to annex the island.

With Formosa a Dutch colony, they would be in the position of controlling all trade, in and out of the island, and from the reports this was already considerable, especially with south China. The Governors knew that once their success in Formosa became known, there would be a scramble among the European powers for a footing there, with a serious challenge from a Spanish–Portuguese Catholic coalition. And both China and Japan had to be reckoned with.

In making this decision, which must have conjured up visions of quick, fabulous fortunes for the merchants of Amsterdam, the Governors were sowing the seeds of the destruction of all Dutch opportunities in Formosa. Had they been less avaricious and content with trading-posts on the island, their future would have been much brighter. As it was, their policy of greed, based on colonization, was to clash from the outset with the Chinese doctrine of *tsung chu ch'uan*, and, in the not distant future, lead to war. The policy of annexation, based as always on oppression of the domestic population, was to antagonize the Chinese in Formosa, and to arouse China herself to take up the sword and demonstrate that the Dutch could be beaten at their own game. The weapon that the merchants of Amsterdam selected for use in Formosa was to boomerang back and make them bite the dust in the most abject humiliation, and at the hands of an Oriental country.

How painfully slow has the West been in learning the lesson that China was to teach the Dutch in Formosa !

Once committed to the task of making Formosa a Dutch colony, the sword became the symbol of occupation, both to the inhabitants of the island and to all beyond its shores. Casteel Zeelandia, the fort erected at Anping, at the entrance to the harbour that serves the present city of Tainan, was a warning to Spaniards, Portuguese, and others that the Dutch were in control. The very bricks of the fort, all brought from Batavia, were a stern reminder that behind it was the full power of the Dutch fleet. Two smaller posts, Utrecht and Provintia, each a ' pistol shot distance ' from the main fort, and nearer the mainland, were designed as intelligence centres as well as symbols of Dutch power before the eyes of the population. Three thousand Dutch troops manned these forts and a Dutch governor, under the jurisdiction of the Governor-General at Batavia, was responsible for carrying out the complete colonization of the island.

Formosa was incorporated within the Dutch East Indies.

The inevitable scramble for a place in Formosa was not long delayed. The Spaniards, fearing that the Dutch, from their base in south Formosa, would interfere with their trading ships bound for Japan, decided to establish their own base in north Formosa. In 1626 they built their fort, Santissima Trinidad, at the entrance to Keelung harbour, and the flag of Castille was soon flying above it. Friars were brought from Manila to convert the tribesmen, and in the new city that was laid out, San Salvador, a Christian church was erected under the guidance of Friar Francisco Mola. In 1629 a second settlement was established on the north-west coast at the mouth of the Tamsui River and a fort erected. In this city of San Domingo a church was built and more friars arrived from Manila.

From the outset the Spanish purpose seemed to be the safe-guarding of their trade and the conversion of the natives. There is no record of a seizure of land or attempts to enforce native labour in productive enterprises. They had no colonizing plans, nor did they dispute the Dutch position in the south of the island. They followed very much the Chinese philosophy of *tsung chu ch'uan*, with the difference that the Christian way of life, as Spain understood it, and not Chinese civilization, was to be the norm of life among the people. This Spanish policy was much closer to that of China than to the Dutch. Had the Spaniards prevailed in Formosa the history of the island might have been entirely different and much bloodshed and disorder prevented.

But this was not to be. The Dutch viewed the advent of the Spaniards as a direct threat to their colonization programme. Pieter Nuyts, Dutch Governor of Formosa, reported to Batavia :

If they [the Spaniards] are once established, it is to be feared that they might incite the natives and Chinese to revolt against us.

But Batavia did not take this warning seriously, and for the next twelve years the position remained as it was, with Spanish trade prospering.

Governor Nuyts must have known that sooner or later the Chinese population of the island would revolt against the rule of the Dutch, which was becoming more and more oppressive. In this case it would be most convenient to have the Spaniards as scapegoats on whom the blame for any uprising could be placed. Such a rebellion did occur in 1640, and the Spaniards were blamed. Conveniently for the Dutch, the warning of Governor Nuyts was remembered, and they were given the word to expel the Spaniards. On 26 August 1641, Paulus Tradenius, commander of the Dutch forces in south Formosa, sent a dispatch to Gonsalo Portilio, commander of the Santissima Trinidad fortress at Keelung, demanding his capitulation. On his blunt refusal, the war was on. The Spaniards were no match for the Dutch. Manila could not send reinforcements, as the rebellion in Mindanao was taxing the resources of the Spaniards in the Philippines. On 24 August 1642 the flag of Castille was hauled down from Santissima Trinidad and San Domingo.

The Spaniards had been in north Formosa for just sixteen years.

Now in undisputed mastery of Formosa, both the Chinese revolt of 1640 and the brief struggle with the Spaniards in 1642 having ended in their favour, the Dutch embarked on subduing the entire island. Prior to the coming of the Spaniards, all attention had been given to south Formosa, but recent happenings had emphasized the necessity of bringing north Formosa under Dutch control as well. A series of forts was built on the central western and northern coasts, and by the end of 1650 twenty-five military centres had been established throughout the island. The Chinese population, comprising some fifty clans, were brought under rigid control from seven administrative centres, with jurisdiction over 300 towns and villages. Colonization was reaching its peak, and the Dutch were determined that the 1640 uprising was not to be repeated.

As colonizers, the Dutch in Formosa were most inept. In their complete ignorance of the Chinese, they imagined that they could change the centuries-old Chinese way of life, even to attempting to impose on them the Dutch language. They did succeed, in large measure, in maintaining control by sheer force, often brutal, but they failed completely to win over the people. Their determination to make the Chinese population of 100,000 pay for the elaborate defences of the island only exacerbated the position and stiffened popular resistance. As the capitation taxes increased, so did the bitterness of the population. Had the Government in Holland been in charge of affairs, many of the impositions might have been reduced, or possibly have never even existed, but the entire control was in the hands of the Dutch East India Company, a private undertaking, concerned only in squeezing out of Formosa the last guilder, without the slightest regard for the condition of those whose labour produced such wealth.

Rarely, if ever, had the people of an Asian country been so ruthlessly exploited by conquerors from the West. Never had the escutcheon of Western honour been so shamefully besmirched with disgrace. It was colonization at its worst — sweated labour in Dutch factories and on the rice and sugar-cane fields owned by the Dutch East India Company ; Chinese families, seeking to eke out a precarious livelihood in remote places, reduced to beggary by impositions of every kind ; a licence fee, payable to the Dutch, for permission to hunt a deer in the mountains, fish in the rivers, with each member, however young, in every Chinese family, forced to pay a capitation tax. The very food the farmer produced to feed his ill-fed family meant so much more for the pockets of the merchants of Amsterdam. From their former peace and plenty, Dutch colonization was reducing the Chinese in Formosa to want, and want was daily begetting unrest and the spirit of rebellion.

The rapacity of the Dutch East India Company was silently digging Dutch graves.

The Japanese on the island were less patient than the Chinese in their resentment of this oppressive rule. They refused to pay taxes on the ground that they had been in Formosa long before the coming of the Dutch. When threatened with severe

penalties for this refusal, they retaliated with threats of interference with Dutch commerce at Nagasaki, Hirado, and other
trading stations in Japan. Not anxious to force the issue, the
Dutch refrained from putting their proposed measures into
operation. This, in turn, aggravated the Chinese population
still further, as they found themselves compelled to bear the
entire burden of taxation. Having won the day, the Japanese
extended their sympathy to the Chinese, and formed with them
a common front against the Dutch. An island of comparative
peace and plenty had been transformed into a place of seething
discontent as the long arm of Western cupidity reached out into
the remotest corners to seize financial gain for foreign merchants
who had not the slightest interest in or concern for the people
of Formosa.

As for the Japanese, matters came to a head with the Yahei
incident of 1628. A merchant-pirate, Yamada Yahei, living at
Nagasaki, had clashed with the Dutch some years earlier, when,
on his way to China, he had suffered from ' Dutch interference '
in the Pescadores. Hearing of the treatment meted out to his
fellow Japanese in Formosa, he decided on revenge. With the
assistance of the Daimyo and possibly of the Shogun, he mustered
five hundred men, some of them Chinese, and sailed for Formosa.
When the expedition arrived off the island, Governor Nuyts
insisted that all arms be handed over into custody during Yahei's
visit. This was reasonable, as Dutch ships entering Japanese
ports had to observe a similar custom. When Yahei refused to
comply, the Governor had him confined to his official residence
while Dutch officials boarded the ships and seized the arms and
munitions. Infuriated, Yahei decided to leave Formosa, on the
pretext that he proposed to visit China to recover goods stored
there. His arms returned to him, he sailed from Formosa. But
he was soon back. His trick had worked. Making his way to
the Governor's residence, he set upon him ' like a wild cat '
and had his men bind Nuyts hand and foot. The alarm was
raised, and a general mêlée followed. In the midst of the
uproar, the Governor called for ' some peaceful discussion ',
as he feared for his own life. A Dutch official involved

in the struggle noted later in his diary :

The Governor told me to stop the firing at once, otherwise his life
would be in danger. The Japanese also informed me that if I did not
stop the firing, they would present me with our chief's head. I at
once ordered our soldiers to cease firing. . . .
There is a report that the Japanese, with the aid of native Formosans
and Chinese, intend to attack our fort tomorrow night.

This last entry indicated how unpopular the Dutch were and
how Japanese, Chinese, and natives had formed a common
front against them.

However, the ' peaceful discussion ' did not yield any positive
result. Many of the Japanese settlers decided to leave Formosa
and return to Japan, taking with them a deep-seated hatred of
both the Dutch and their religion. This was to flare up into open
hostility in the near future, with the savage persecution of the
Christians, especially at Nagasaki, where Yamada Yahei lived.
The policy of the Dutch East India Company in Formosa was
closely linked with the Japanese crusade against Christianity at
the time.

There were some among the Dutch who could see the
inevitable outcome of the repressive official policy. But they
were few, and themselves employees, without authority. These
were the missionaries, enlisted in Holland to serve the Company
in Formosa. At that time there did not exist any Protestant
missionary societies in Europe. The urge to convert Asia to
Christianity had not yet been born. There were Catholic
societies, which had operated in China since 1583 and earlier in
India, but the first Protestant missionary to arrive in China was
Robert Morrison in 1807. Although the Jesuits were in favour
at Peking at the time the Dutch were in control of Formosa, no
attempt was made to establish the order on that island, probably
because it was known that the Dutch East India Company,
being a Protestant institution, would never have permitted it.
Believing that missionaries could assist the Company in its
acquisition of wealth, a number of these were engaged for work
in Formosa as servants of the Company on its payroll. It was a

strange venture, this enlistment of Christian missionaries in such an enterprise. There were excellent men among them, and had they been free to carry out their activities as they wished, the record of the Dutch in Formosa, instead of being a sordid chapter in the history of East-West relations, might have been one of its brightest, the avarice of the Dutch East India Company notwithstanding. But the Company had engaged them, paid their salaries, drew up the rules restricting their activities, and thus regimented them completely. Thus it was that these missionaries became just one of the instruments of colonialism.

The missionary-employees of the Dutch East India Company were dyed-in-the-wool Calvinists of the Reformed Church. The first to be recruited for work in Formosa were Georgius Candidius and Robertus Junius. Both were worthy men themselves, but were destined to fight, from the day they landed on the island, against their employers. They taught the natives the rudiments of Christianity, practised what medical knowledge they possessed, and introduced an elementary system of education. But beyond that they could not go, as their employers had made it clear that their task was to transform the natives into profitable servants of the Company.

This was surely one of the strangest experiments in the history of missionary enterprise !

These natives from the mountains were permitted to choose their village headmen, and each year a grand ceremonial feast, a *land-dag*, was held, to which the headmen were invited. This took place at the village of Sakkam, near Casteel Zeelandia, so that the military might of the Dutch could impress all present and serve as a warning to any who should be so foolish as to foster the spirit of rebellion. Each headman received a silver-headed staff, bearing the coat of arms of the Company, as the insignia of his office and authority. Psychologically impressed by this attention, the headmen returned to their villages, where the missionaries carried on the good work on behalf of their employers.

However, this devotion to the interests of the Company did not quench their Calvinistic fervour. They declared the worship of the tribal gods a criminal offence ' punishable with public whipping and banishment'. Once a month, it was obligatory for all villagers to assemble at a given place, to hear read aloud a proclamation setting forth the manner of this punishment. When news of this proclamation reached Amsterdam, there was a flutter at the headquarters of the Company, and fears were expressed that the Government might regard it as ' so contrary to the spirit and character of the Dutch nation'. Thereupon Batavia was instructed to inform the Governor in Formosa that ' the ordinance may not be publicly retracted but not put into operation'.

A splendid piece of hypocrisy !

But the Company had a more weighty consideration in mind than ' the spirit and character of the Dutch nation'. It was concerned more with the temper of Japan, engaged at the time in crucifying Christians at Nagasaki and other centres. It would be unfortunate if the Japanese should get the impression that its employees, the missionaries, were over-zealous in Christianizing the natives of Formosa. They might close the Company's posts at Nagasaki, Hirado, and other cities throughout Japan. After all, were not these trading-posts of more importance than the souls of the natives of Formosa ?

When the directive from Batavia reached Formosa, the Calvinist conscience of the missionaries, up and down the island, was stunned. Ever uncompromising, it could not reconcile the prescription of idolatry with the toleration of it. The consistory met to consider the position. Just what transpired on that occasion we do not know, but thereafter a silent struggle between the missionaries and the Company officials went on, and from that time the missionaries did their most creditable work. Possibly they were in the position where they could support themselves and defy the Company. The statistics indicate that a spate of church-building began, the hitherto alfresco worship giving place to orderly indoor services. The small school that Robertus Junius had established with fifty pupils soon expanded into a chain of schools, with more than 500 pupils, using a romanized form of their own languages, which the missionary had devised. Natives were attending the newly erected churches in increasing numbers, and in 1650 the number of baptized members of the native Church was set down at over 7,000.

Encouraged by this success, the consistory made a bold move which was a direct challenge to the policy of the Company. At Mattau, a seminary for the training of a native clergy would be established. It must have taken great courage to do this. At one stage it seemed that the missionaries, inspired by one of their number, Petrus Mus, were on the point of breaking with the Company, but pressure from some source prevented this. When this plan to set up a seminary had been first mooted, Robertus Junius had informed the Governor-General at Batavia, Antonius van Diemen, of the project, and his letter showed clear signs that the Calvinistic passion of the missionaries had in no way been dulled by official interference :

The village of Mattau is situated in the midst of rivers, like Mesopotamia itself, so that many a deserter or runaway will, as it were, be caught in his wicked purpose to escape . . . if the seminary were erected at Mattau, the rapid current and the great depth of the rivers, particularly in the time of the monsoon, would effectually prevent them from doing so.

But the missionaries were fighting a losing battle with the Company. The odds were against them. As profits increased, the missionaries were brought more and more under control. It is a sad reflection that in a few years all that was to remind history of the labours of the thirty-two missionaries, from Georgius Candidius, who arrived in Formosa in 1627, until 1662, when Jacobus Ampzingius left, were a few romanized scripts on the walls of a cave near Keelung. Years later, Wells Williams, in his classic *Middle Kingdom*, was to inscribe their sad epitaph :

The work was progressing favourably, churches and schools were multiplying . . . many thousands of the islanders had been baptized when the Dutch Governors in India, fearful of offending the Japanese, who were then persecuting the Christians in Japan, restricted these benevolent labors, and discouraged the further conversion of the natives.

Throughout, the Dutch East India Company went on piling up fortunes for the merchants of Amsterdam. Their policy was to take out of Formosa the maximum and put back into the island the minimum. In one year alone the capitation tax yielded 300,000 guilders, the raw-silk trade with Japan 980,000 guilders, and the China trade 4 million guilders, to mention just a few of the sources of commerce. As against these, the total amount put back into Formosa in the form of public services, developmental enterprises, and administrative costs amounted to only 215,000 guilders. Officials of the Company were so poorly paid that they had to resort to all forms of the squeeze to augment their low salaries. Once again the people of Formosa, especially the Chinese, paid.

But this state of affairs was not to continue. Slowly the Company was digging its own grave with a golden spade.

Not content with the existing high rate of profit, especially from the China trade, the rise of the Ch'ing Dynasty in 1644 prompted the Company to make yet another bid to set up trading stations in China. But without success. The Goyer–Keyzer mission to Peking in 1655 was, as stated in the official Nieuwhof report, ' as a mercantile speculation, a total loss '. The Ch'ing, like the Ming, suspected Dutch intentions. The fact that they had turned their trading-post in Formosa into a colonial office, from which the whole island had been brought under Dutch rule, deepened the suspicions of Peking, which all the kowtowing by members of the mission could not remove. The Portuguese at Macao had never exceeded their rights or abused their privileges as ' honoured guests '.

The writing was now on the wall. Still the Dutch could not see it. The sight of quick profits blinded their vision. They were dazzled and then bewitched by their own cupidity. They became so profit-drunk that they did not attend to their own defences. Totally unconscious of the movement of history, they gathered in their guilders. Each new migrant to the island meant another capitation tax, another cheap labourer on a Company sugar plantation or paddy field or in one of the factories being erected throughout Formosa. They failed, however, to see in that migrant a potential subversive and a future rebel. As more and more money left Formosa for Batavia on its way to the Company in Holland, more and more Chinese entered the island to strengthen the resistance that was building up.

Time was running out. The Dutch interlude was coming to an end. The curtains were beginning to open on the next act in the drama of Formosa.

From then on, the walls of Casteel Zeelandia started to crumble. In crevices between the bricks, which the Dutch had brought from Batavia, trees began to sprout and their roots to challenge the entire structure. Today a tall banyan rises above the ruins and on its spreading branches the winds of the Eastern Sea play their requiem for the loss of a great opportunity of harmonizing East and West. At times it sounds like a dirge, memorializing the West at its worst.

Chief Mao of the Tsou tribe with the author in 1959

CHAPTER FOUR

The House of Cheng

THE mantle of Li Han, alias Captain China, had fallen on a young Chinese, Cheng Chih-lung, then twenty-three years old.

Born in Fukien province in 1602, Cheng had spent some time in both Macao and Manila and gained a working knowledge of Portuguese and Spanish. Eventually he made his way to Japan, where he married a wife of the Tagawa family, samurai of humble origin, known as *ashigaru*. Settling at Hirado as a trader-cum-tailor, he attracted the attention of both Li Han, then head of the Chinese community, and the Dutch traders by his proficiency in Portuguese, then the lingua franca in the Far East. When Li Han was approached by the Dutch to act as their Chinese interpreter in Formosa, he urged them to secure the services of Cheng also, as he could interpret in relations with Macao.

Cheng arrived in Formosa, under engagement to the Dutch, in 1624.

He was introduced to the West by Bishop Palafox in 1671 as ' Icoan or Jasper ' :

In Macao, he [Cheng] was instructed in the teachings of the Christian religion, was baptised, and given the name Jasper, for what reason I cannot say, unless he thought it more profitable. But as Icoan or Jasper did not succeed in gaining attention, he returned to his own country.

In the following year, 1672, the Belgian Jesuit Rougement added that Cheng's baptismal name was Nicholas and referred to him as Nicholas Iquan, that being the equivalent of the Portuguese ' Icoan '. As a result of these entries, the person mentioned in Japanese and Dutch records of the time as Nicholas Iquan was Cheng Chih-lung. However, it is noteworthy that

when Bishop Palafox published his *History of the Conquest of
China by the Tartars* in 1671, the historic significance of Cheng
Chih-lung had already been recognized.

From the time of his arrival in Formosa a mutual distrust
existed between Cheng and the Dutch, much the same as in the
case of Li Han and the Dutch. Neither trusted the other. The
Dutch paid him ' good wages ' but were suspicious of him. And
for a good reason. He collaborated too closely with Li Han.
' We have a Chinese interpreter from Japan,' reported Commander Cornelius Reijersen to the Governor-General at Batavia,
' but he is of little use to us.' The Dutch, however, were
compelled to retain his services as they were unable to secure any
other ' trustworthy interpreter '. Reijersen had the same trouble
as his predecessor Sonck had had to face earlier.

Cheng's tenure of office as interpreter was brief. When Li Han
left Formosa in 1625, his fleet of pirate ships was acquired by
Cheng, whether by force or legacy it is not clear. He severed his
connection with the Dutch and moved from Anping in south
Formosa, across the strait, to Amoy in Fukien, taking with him
the entire fleet he now controlled. This he increased, so that
at the close of 1626 he commanded a thousand junks. With
these he roamed the seas, seizing goods which he sold in Chinese
and Japanese markets. He had learnt Li Han's technique to
perfection. In 1627 the Dutch Governor of Formosa informed
Batavia :

Over a year ago, a man named Iquan, formerly interpreter to the
Company, left without notice and became chief of a pirate band. He
amassed much shipping and men, and terrorized the whole China
coast . . . and has rendered navigation along the coast impracticable.

Already Cheng was a man to be taken seriously. His pirate
fleet never interfered with Chinese ships trading between China
and Formosa, nor with Japanese ships trading with the island.
The Dutch, Portuguese, and Spanish were his prey. Peking
was aware of this and planned to co-operate with him. Already
the Manchus in the north were threatening China, and in the
south there was the ever-present fear of Dutch intentions. Jan

Pieterszoon, founder of the Dutch East India Company, had stated years before that the China market must be opened by force, and Reijersen's attack on Macao in 1622 had shown that the Dutch had never abandoned that objective. To Peking, the establishment of a Dutch trading station, as in Java and Formosa, was only the prelude to Dutch conquest and colonization. At all costs, then, the Mings must avoid fighting on two fronts. They could deal with the northern threat, and Cheng with his fleet would attend to the Dutch menace in the south. Peking was convinced that whereas the Portuguese at Macao had no hostile intentions, the Dutch were different, and had definite aggressive designs against China.

A mission must be sent to Amoy to confer with Cheng. But the right man must be selected to make the deal. Everything would depend on him and how he handled the negotiations. Ts'ai Shan-chi was the choice, and the selection could not have been better. He had been prefect at Chuanchow and had known the Cheng family. Cheng Chih-lung was only a youth at the time, but the prefect had been most favourably impressed with him. He had discussed with Cheng Shao-tsu, the youth's father and himself an official, the question of Cheng Chih-lung's entering government service. So keen had his interest been in the young man that he had given him instruction, preparing him for his *hsiu ts'ai* examination, the first of the tests for entrance to the public service. But he had been very disappointed when Cheng Chih-lung, then eighteen years old, had decided to go to Macao and enter the business world. Shortly afterwards Ts'ai himself had been transferred from Chuanchow and had lost sight of the Cheng family. Now was the opportunity to renew the friendship of those past years.

At Amoy, Ts'ai and Cheng met again. At once the envoy put all his cards on the table. Peking could deal with the Manchus if Cheng would handle the Dutch. The proposal was favourably received by Cheng, especially as Ts'ai assured him that official opinion in Peking was moving in the direction of forcing the Dutch out of Formosa and setting up an inspectorate there. Nothing could have appealed to Cheng more forcibly, for this had been his secret hope for years. But his brother, with whom he discussed Ts'ai's proposal, urged him to delay any agreement for the present, as there should be some guarantee of their own position when the Dutch were driven out of Formosa.

Treachery on the part of Pieter Nuyts, Dutch Governor of Formosa, decided things. From a document in the Dutch archives dated 1 October 1628, dealing with the terms of an agreement between ' Pieter Nuyts, Councillor of India and Governor of the Island Formosa and Fort Zeelandia, and Iquan, chief Mandarin of the Province of Amoy and Admiral of the China Sea ', we learn that Pieter Nuyts, informed of the meetings between Cheng and Ts'ai, paid a visit to Cheng at Amoy, where he was received with cordiality and suitably feasted. In return he invited Cheng to a function on board the Dutch warship, where he was seized and forced to agree to Dutch freedom of trade in all south Chinese ports. Cheng never forgot that treachery, although he had to wait years for revenge.

But one result was immediate. On his return from the Dutch warship, he contacted Ts'ai and accepted the Peking proposal. He would co-operate to the full with the plan set forth by the envoy. Ts'ai returned to Peking and Cheng was appointed Commander of the Imperial Fleet in south China. Amoy was his official headquarters, but he spent some time at the palatial residence he had built near the site of his ancestral home at An-hai.

The die was now cast. Cheng formulated his plans, which he was to carry out with subtlety, attention to detail, and amazing determination. He was now the Ming hero in south China, who would one day expel the Dutch not only from Formosa, but from the whole of the Far East. They would be permitted to retain Batavia only. Any Dutch ship seen in the waters north of the Indies would be taken over and its cargo seized. Pieter Nuyts would be made to pay dearly for his treachery in Amoy harbour. Migration from south China to Formosa would be speeded up and that island become a centre of Chinese civilization, not as a colony after the Dutch fashion, but a suzerainty of

China, in the Chinese manner. The Emperor in Peking would be the *chu*, the overlord, as the Chou of ancient times, with the House of Cheng as the ruler of the island.

This was an ambitious programme, and although Cheng himself was not to see its completion, he did set the foundation. Developments in China were to distract his attention, especially the decline and fall of the Mings, but he did succeed in plotting the course that the history of Formosa was to follow under the leadership of his son, the famous Cheng Cheng-kung.

While Cheng was working out the details of this plan, Hans Putmans arrived in Formosa as successor to Pieter Nuyts. He was even more aggressive than Nuyts had been and deeply committed to the Pieterszoon policy of bursting open the gates into China with Dutch cannon. On learning that Cheng had torn up the agreement signed on the Dutch warship at Amoy, he decided to force the issue. So, one morning in 1633, he staged his 'Pearl Harbor'. Taken by surprise, Cheng's fleet, at anchor in Chengchow Bay, was decimated. Confident that he had Cheng at his mercy, Putmans named his terms. If Cheng would agree to the establishment of a Dutch trading-post at Foochow and permit freedom of trade with south China ports, the Dutch would supply him with 'cannon, gunners, and soldiers, to fight the Manchu invaders', who were then menacing north China. But Cheng, now more embittered than ever, rejected the proposal with his characteristic determination. His remaining ships, under cover of night, set fire to the larger Dutch warships that were blockading Amoy harbour. Stunned at the sight of his blazing ships, Putmans hastily retired to Formosa to replenish his fleet. But in a more sober moment the fear of Chinese retaliation, which might close Chinese ports to the Dutch indefinitely, prevailed. He wrote to Cheng suggesting that, as his proposal was not acceptable, perhaps Cheng might offer some alternative.

This played right into Cheng's hands. Yes, he had an alternative. He would agree to the setting up of a Dutch trading station at Foochow, provided Chinese junks transported the goods between Formosa and south China. To Putmans, this was something. It would open China to Dutch trade, even though the goods were carried in Chinese junks. To Cheng, this arrangement would enable his fleet to keep him informed of the state of the Dutch defences and there would be no necessity for the Dutch fleet to be active in the Strait of Formosa.

Cheng had won the day.

Formosa was the key to the realization of his plan, and large-scale migration of Chinese from the depressed areas of Kwangtung and Fukien was number-one priority. In the event of the Manchus gaining control of north China, it would be possible, from a base in Formosa, to hold south China. Cheng Chih-lung was the first to see Formosa as the strategic base from which China could be recovered from any foreign usurpation.

But the first authentic imperative was the creation of that island as a centre of Chinese civilization, and that involved massive migration from south China. Putmans' acceptance of his offer now made this possible. Avoiding the watchful eyes of the Dutch, his fleet began to ferry migrants across the Strait of Formosa to places on the central west coast of the island, chief of which was Choshiu-chi, then but a small Hoklos fishing village. From there the migrants made their way inland and established villages which were later to amalgamate to form the city of Changhua. Soon this shuttle service was conveying not only depressed peasants, anxious to escape from famine and the unending processions of funerals, but also large numbers of the literati, who were growing increasingly fearful of the future. Restrictions on Chinese migration to the Philippines imposed by the Spanish authorities in 1594 and rigorously enforced in later years, when thousands of Chinese were expelled, culminating in 1603, the year after Cheng's birth, with the massacre of 23,000 Chinese, had made migration to Formosa most attractive, as it carried with it no restrictive qualifications.

It is difficult to estimate how many migrants Cheng's fleet ferried across to Formosa. Few data are available. However, we do know that the will to migrate was strong. During 1591–3, when no restriction on the entry of Chinese to the Philippines was in force, no less than 45,000 migrated from south China to

Manila and its environs. With that haven for the depressed of Kwangtung and Fukien now closed, it can be assumed that Cheng's fleet never crossed the Strait of Formosa with empty space that a migrant could fill. Japanese authorities set down the number of Chinese on the island before Cheng's activities at 25,000 spread over Formosa, 8,000 of these in the south, where the Dutch activities were then concentrated. This would hardly have been capable of constituting an efficient land force to attack the Dutch in 1661, when Cheng Cheng-kung's fleet appeared off Casteel Zeelandia, as most of them had only ' bows and arrows ', only a few 'having swords, three feet long', whereas the Dutch garrison numbered 5,000 ' trained, disciplined, and equipped '. One estimate mentions 30,000 migrants as ferried across by Cheng, whilst another, probably to be taken with reserve, gives their number as ' countless '.

Whatever the number, it was no merely humanitarian enterprise to save starving people and offer them a new life. Nor did personal gain allure its promoter. Unlike men such as Walter Raleigh, planning a colony in Virginia for his own advantage, or Humphrey Gilbert visualizing fortunes from his El Dorado in Newfoundland, Cheng Chih-lung had one objective only — the peopling of Formosa with Chinese, whose family roots would strike deep into the soil of the island, so that one day the Dutch foreigner would be driven out, and, from a base on the island, the Manchus, if they overran China, might be forced out.

In the mind of Cheng, Formosa was to be a Chinese bastion of the future.

Cheng was a patriot. He believed passionately in Ming values as the true expression of the spirit of China. At his own expense, and seeking no financial return, he carried out a migration unique in history. There have been movements of populations of greater proportions and over greater distances, but carried out by Governments. The migration from south China to Formosa, on the other hand, was inspired, carried through, and financed by one man, who saw that island as the repository of Chinese culture and civilization at a time when both Asian and European pressures were beginning to bear down on China. Whatever the fate of Ming values on the Chinese mainland, his fleet could guarantee them security on Formosa when the Dutch foreigner was expelled. The Manchus would not be in any position to become a threat as they had no sea power. To Cheng it was not merely a migration of people, but the temporary movement of the centre of civilization.

But the darkening clouds in China's northern sky were to divert his attention from the waters of the Eastern Sea. Already reports were reaching him of the march of the Manchus and the chaos and disorder in their wake. The roll of the thunder itself from the heart of those storm-clouds suggested the death-rattle of the Mings, especially when he received word that Emperor Ming Ch'ung Cheng was banking all his hopes on Cheng holding south China. It was an ominous message.

In desperation, he proclaimed the Prince of T'ang, Chu Yu-chien, heir to the tottering Ming throne, now under his protection. He had Chu set up his throne at Foochow, as Emperor Lung Wu. As long as he remained there on the Fukien coast, even as a shadow ruler, he was safe, as Cheng's fleet controlled the sea lanes. With a Chu enthroned, the Ming cause would not die. Still, he knew that sooner or later, with the Manchus moving south, the great decision would have to be made.

For twelve months Lung Wu sat on his Ming throne at Foochow. Supported by Cheng's son, Cheng Cheng-kung, who had been invested with the imperial surname ' Chu ' and popularly known as ' Kuo-hsing-yeh ', ' Lord of the Imperial Surname ', Europeanized as Koxinga, Lung Wu urged Cheng Chih-lung to make this decision without delay. His plan was to attack the Manchus while Chang's fleet sailed north, landed forces, and attacked the Manchus in the rear. Meanwhile, Cheng Cheng-kung would build up the defences of Foochow and the surrounding area.

Cheng Chih-lung hesitated. Would he comply with this strategy ? Or would he sail to Formosa and there build up a base for future operations against the Manchus ? Had he co-operated in Lung Wu's plan of campaign, the history of

China might have been different. Who can say?

Lung Wu was not prepared to wait on Cheng's decision. Leaving Cheng Cheng-kung to hold Foochow and the southeastern provinces, he marched north to face the Manchus. Captured at Tingchow, where the decisive battle was fought, he committed suicide. The doom of Foochow was now sealed. It soon fell to the conquerors from the north. The last hope of the Mings vanished.

> The town is as old as the human race
> And it grows with the flight of years:
> It is wrapped in the fog of idler's dreams;
> Its streets are paved with discarded schemes,
> And sprinkled with useless tears.

Cheng had sent an urgent plea to Japan for help, but it was too late.

Thereafter, Cheng's movements are uncertain. One record states that, in his despair, he made secret overtures to the Manchus to capitulate. Another has it that he was captured by guile. We do know, however, that he was treated as a princely guest in Peking, while the Manchus tried to persuade him to order his son to hand over the fleet in south China waters. When this failed, chiefly because of Cheng Cheng-kung's blunt refusal, Cheng was executed. In his last hours he returned to the faith he had embraced at Macao in his youth but had neglected during the turbulent years of manhood. The last rites were administered by his two friends, the Portuguese Gabriel de Magalhães and the Italian Luis Buglio, in the small chapel where he attended the daily celebration of Mass during his last days in Peking.

It was the year 1661.

Unlike so many famous Chinese of his time, Cheng Chih-lung did not associate Christianity with the West and its exploitation of the East. Unfortunately, historians, attracted by the more romantic career of his son, the famous Koxinga, have failed to see the true greatness of Cheng Chih-lung, the founder of the House of Cheng.

The Manchus were now firmly established in Peking, and their armed might controlled the greater part of China. But the spirit of the Mings was still very much alive in south China. The prophetic gleam had been quenched in the Manchu take-over of the palace of Lung Wu in Foochow, but it lived on in the hearts and minds of many millions who had faith in the final restoration of the Mings. Champions of this faith sprang up throughout south China, including princes, pretenders to the Ming throne. But the son of Cheng Chih-lung was the man to whom the majority looked for the realization of their hopes. Psychological-ly, Cheng Cheng-kung had much on his side. In those fateful days, when Emperor Ming Ch'ung Cheng had known that his cause in the north was lost, he had commissioned the father of Cheng Cheng-kung to hold south China for the Mings. When Emperor Lung Wu had set up his court at Foochow in 1645, Cheng Cheng-kung had been his chief adviser. The imperial surname had been conferred on him as a special mark of favour, making him a member of the imperial family. In the following year he had been appointed *Chao-t'ao Ta Chiang-chun*, ' Field-Marshal of the Punitive Expedition ', and commissioned to guard the ' Hsieh-hsia kuan ', the strategic pass between Fukien and Chekiang. In that same year, 1646, when Emperor Lung Wu had set out on his fateful march to do battle with the southward-moving Manchus, he had placed the responsibility of holding the southern provinces on Cheng Cheng-kung. Who then was better fitted to arouse the patriotic fervour of the people than this man ? Added to this, he alone had what neither the Manchus nor any other Ming champion possessed — a substantial fleet.

Of the early years of Cheng Cheng-kung little is known for certain. Popular legend, especially in Formosa, has filled up the gap. As with people in all heroic ages, their hero was of divine birth. Aeneas was the son of Aphrodite-Venus and Priam, King of Troy, destined to ' establish a city across the sea, after his many wanderings '. There his descendants would rule as the great House of Julian. And so it was with Cheng Cheng-kung. His mother was none other than the Goddess of the Sea, Ma Tso-po, known to the Japanese as Tenjiosego, with whom

Cheng Chih-lung had consorted. Had not this Great Mother come with them, the Hoklos, across the waters of the Strait of Formosa? Had she not marked out her son from all others by his matchless beauty? So handsome had he been that when Lung Wu, Emperor at Foochow, had first seen him, he had exclaimed, 'What a pity that we have no daughter so that you could become our son-in-law!' And had not the Emperor made up for this by giving him the imperial surname? Even as a small boy he had mastered the *Ping Fa*, the Art of War, by that famous military strategist Sun Tzu, and when not studying that treatise he had spent his time in becoming efficient in archery and horsemanship.

Dismissing these fanciful tales, we know that Cheng Cheng-kung was born at Hirado in Japan in 1623, the year before his father sailed for Formosa. His mother was of the Tagawa family. At seven years of age he was taken to China, and at fifteen was registered as a salaried licentiate. His education was completed at the Imperial Academy in Nanking. Returning to Fukien, he became associated with his father's enterprises there. When Lung Wu established the Ming Court at Foochow he was introduced to the Emperor, and from then on his fortunes rose rapidly. Soon he became commander of the Ming armies in south China. When Foochow fell to the Manchus and his father was taken to Peking, he made his way to Kulang-yu, a small island off Amoy, to collect the scattered Ming forces and take over his father's fleet, and plan his future operations.

Whilst there he heard the encouraging news of the progress of Chu Yu-lang, grandson of the great Ming Emperor Shen Tsung, known to history as Wan Li. The western provinces of Szechwan, Yunnan, and Shensi were rallying to the Ming standard, and many officers, who had earlier deserted to the Manchus, had returned to their former allegiance and taken their stand beside Chu. Along the entire western frontier these were now enlisting recruits for the Ming cause.

Such inspiring tidings strengthened Cheng's conviction that the Ming cause was not just a chapter in the past to be remembered but one that had to be restored and continued. The Manchus were interlopers, who were in China only for a time. With Chu, he could create a pincer movement that would crush these Manchus and break them to powder within its mighty jaws. He could campaign in south China, thus complementing Chu's operations in the west. The rising in Kwangsi, of which information had just reached him, would serve to sharpen the prongs of the pincers when the strategic time for closing these pincers arrived.

With Chu's agreement, Cheng lost no time in putting his part of the plan into operation. The Manchus, believing that they had effectively crushed Ming resistance in south China, had retired, leaving only token garrisons in Fukien and Kwangtung. Cheng soon overcame these, gained control of Amoy, and established seventy-two garrisons along the coast. He had under his control 50,000 cavalry and 70,000 infantry. Once again the fire of Ming zeal was burning furiously, and 'daily there were more enlistments than could be handled'.

Cheng's fleet must have been an impressive spectacle on the waters off Amoy. An Italian Jesuit then in Amoy was amazed at what he saw. He was Vittorio Ricci, who later recorded:

Never before nor since was a more powerful and mighty fleet seen in the waters than that of Koxinga, numbering more than 3,000 junks, which he had ordered to rendezvous in the bays and waters around Amoy. The sight of them inspired one with awe. This squadron did not include the various fleets he had, scattered along the neighbouring coasts.

This fleet was soon to be challenged by the Manchus, who had mustered some 800 war-junks. But these were no match for Cheng's experienced captains. After a bloody battle, as one eyewitness recorded, 'for weeks putrid corpses and tangled wreckage strewed the shores of Amoy and Quemoy'.

Encouraged by this initial success, Cheng, himself a skilful horseman, led his cavalry on a mopping-up expedition, clearing out the Manchu garrisons in south-east China, the infantry following to consolidate the positions gained. This campaign continued over twelve years, and at one time Nanking itself seemed almost within Cheng's grasp. He would probably have entered this city, where Chu Yuan-chang had established the Ming Dynasty in 1368, had it not been for the discontent among his troops.

Meanwhile, in the west, the fortunes of Chu Yu-lang were fading. Overwhelmed by superior Manchu forces, Chu had fled to Burma, then crossed into Siam, where he was captured, taken back to Yunnan and there strangled. The rising in the west suppressed, the Manchus moved east to engage the armies of Cheng. The very strategy that Cheng and Chu had planned was now to be employed against himself. With the Manchus moving east and large forces coming down from the north, he was in grave danger of finding himself within the jaws of giant pincers.

Facing this dilemma, Cheng acted swiftly. He would not risk defeat and the possibility of being cut off from his fleet. He would adopt the plan his father had espoused so vigorously. He would remove his naval base from Amoy to Formosa and there rebuild his armies for a future assault on the Manchus. It is most interesting to note that this decision to use Formosa as a base for the recovery of the Chinese mainland and the restoration of the Mings was made in the same year, 1660, that Charles II landed at Dover to restore the monarchy in England under a Stuart king.

Amoy was the scene of intense activity during the first half of that year. Ho Pin, a former interpreter for the Dutch in Formosa, was enlisted as Cheng's chief intelligence scout. He reported that the Dutch defences had been very much reduced and that the main fleet under Jan van der Laan had sailed for Batavia. This was good news, as Cheng had decided to act before the first monsoon, which began early in the second half of the year.

But the Dutch in Formosa, although they had allowed their defences to weaken, were not asleep. They too had their scouts out, and these had informed Governor Coyett of the unusual activity at Amoy. An urgent request for the return of the fleet was sent to Batavia. Strictest security measures were imposed on Chinese entering such ports as were Dutch-controlled. Defence posts, which had been neglected, were speedily put in order again. In the midst of this feverish preparation the fleet suddenly appeared. Admiral Jan van der Laan had not gone to Batavia, but had been working hard at sea on plans of his own. He hated Governor Coyett and was determined on his demotion ; at the same time he was desperately keen on driving the Portuguese out of Macao. He had worked out a plan by which both objectives could be gained.

Arriving off Casteel Zeelandia, he was struck by the signs of activity. Everything was in a state of preparedness for war. All the posts were fully manned, and the former carefree atmosphere had given place to one of military awareness. Governor Coyett informed him of the reports of the intense activity at Amoy, which could only mean that an invasion was imminent. The Admiral then sent a dispatch to Batavia to the effect that there was no justification for the considerable expense involved in putting the defences in order, information which he knew would be welcome in Batavia, as the Governor-General there had on various occasions informed Governor Coyett that too much money was being spent on the administration of the island. The Dutch East India Company did not relish this eating into its profits. At the same time, the Admiral would sail for Macao to engage the Portuguese.

He arrived off Macao just when Cheng had completed his plans and was about to issue sailing orders. The sight of the Dutch fleet standing off Macao diverted Cheng and delayed his sailing, while the first of the monsoons swept down the Chinese coast, causing havoc among the junks in the Bay of Amoy. The Dutch fleet moved out of the danger area, and Jan van der Laan, confident that the Chinese would not embark on any venture for months, at least until the weather was more favourable, sailed south to Batavia. On his arrival there he learned that his dispatch had been successful. Coyett had been recalled and Hermanus Clenk appointed to Formosa in his stead.

In February of the following year, 1661, the weather being favourable, Cheng Cheng-kung decided to embark on the great venture. Summoning a war council, he addressed the officers :

We are not sailing to Taiwan [Formosa] as exiles. Our homes and the graves of our ancestors are here, on this land. For myself, I have no wish to leave this land permanently. You, yourselves, agree with this. My purpose is to drive the foreigners out of Taiwan, which, by right, is ours, and to make there a base, from which we can continue our struggle against the Manchus, foreigners now in possession of our homeland.

The following month, the fleet of 800 war-junks, carrying 30,000 picked troops, sailed from Amoy for the Pescadores, leaving Cheng Ching, son of Cheng Cheng-kung, to hold Amoy with the rest of the fleet and some 50,000 troops. After weathering violent storms, the fleet arrived off Casteel Zeelandia at the end of April. The Dutch defences comprised two frigates with a few small supporting ships, which were no match for Cheng's fleet. But the larger guns of the fort far outclassed those of the Chinese, which had a small range. Cheng, however, was a keen strategist. While the roar of guns continued, waking Governor Coyett from his bed, some of Cheng's junks entered a river mouth north of Casteel Zeelandia, which was too shallow to allow the entry of such ships as the Dutch had, but was quite suitable for Cheng's junks. These junks landed Chinese troops in a constant stream, while the Dutch were misled into thinking that activity was confined to the sea battle that was going on. In a few days a strong Chinese force had landed and had moved to the rear of the Dutch forts. There they were acclaimed by the Chinese population, which, with their own rude weapons, swelled the invading forces.

The siege lasted six months. By that time only 500 of the Dutch garrison remained alive, and these short of both food and ammunition. There was nothing left but surrender.

Cheng Cheng-kung was magnanimous in his terms. The Dutch were permitted to take with them from Formosa everything they possessed but arms and munitions. On a November day, Governor Coyett and the surviving Dutch, with a long column of carts laden with their goods, marched out of Casteel Zeelandia to embark for Batavia. They were a sorry spectacle, victims of an avaricious company so keen on making quick profits for the merchants of Amsterdam that it was not prepared to devote a small portion of those profits to the defence of the island where it harvested its gold. In his *The Island of Formosa*, Davidson summed up this suicidal policy in these words :

Formosa would perhaps have been theirs [the Dutch] to this day had not the Company with extraordinary short-sightedness been so engrossed in making the maximum of profits for the moment, that they refused to expend the money necessary to make themselves secure against Chinese invasion.

On assuming control, Cheng Cheng-kung dedicated himself to the twofold task of building up Formosa into a prosperous island and from there, as a base, launching an expedition for the recovery of the Chinese mainland from the Manchus.

His first move was to wipe out all traces of the Dutch adminis-tration and introduce Chinese laws, customs, and forms of government. His purpose was to restore the Ming way of life. He was never, as many historians claim, a self-appointed king. Such was not his ambition. On the contrary, he regarded himself as the custodian of the Ming way of life and caretaker of what remained of the Ming empire. His work in Formosa was to be a continuation of all his struggles on the mainland of China. To him Formosa was a suzerainty of China, Ming China.

Having appointed a governor to administer affairs in his absence, Cheng set out on a tour of inspection of the islands. He wanted to see the country for himself and meet the people. He had a special interest in many of these, as his father had trans-ported them from China. Records of the time tell of the welcome accorded him on this journey of inspection and how he noted the areas suitable for further settlement. He went as far north as the present Taipei district, and penetrated into some of the aboriginal country. On his return to his capital, the former Casteel Zeelandia, he summoned a conference of officials to hear the results of his survey of the island :

In order to establish our rule, our first concern must be to provide food for the people. Without sufficient food, a family, in spite of the

Cheng Cheng-kung (Koxinga)

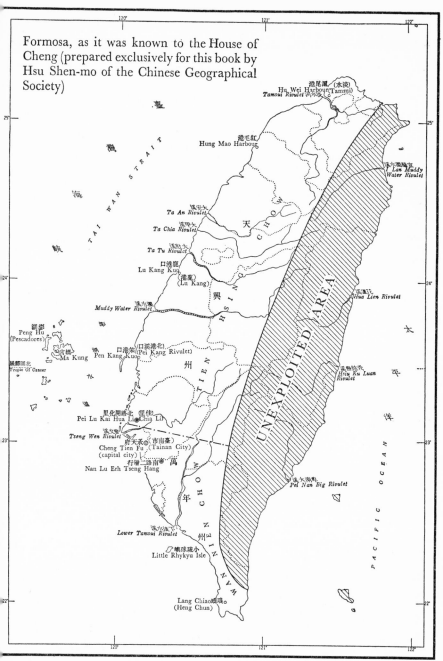

Formosa, as it was known to the House of Cheng (prepared exclusively for this book by Hsu Shen-mo of the Chinese Geographical Society)

臺

鷄

海

峽

TAI WAN STRAIT

港尾溜 (水淡)
Hu Wei Harbour (Tamsui)
Tamsui Rivulet

港毛紅
Hung Mao Harbour

I Lan Muddy
Water Rivulet

大安
Ta An Rivulet

天

興

州

Ta Chia Rivulet

Ta Tu Rivulet

口港鹿
Lu Kang Kuo

(鹿港)
(Lu Kang)

Muddy Water Rivulet

Hua Lien Rivulet

湖澎
Peng Hu
(Pescadores)

Ma Kung

Tropic Of Cancer

口港笨 (口溪港北)
Pen Kang Kuo (Pei Kang Rivulet)

Hsiu Ku Luan
Rivulet

太

平

洋

PACIFIC OCEAN

UNEXPLOITED AREA

里化開路北 (里佳)
Pei Lu Kai Hua Lio Chia Lii

Tseng Wen Rivulet

府天承 (市南臺)
Cheng Tien Fu (Tainan City)
(capital city)

行層二路南萬
Nan Lu Erh Tseng Hang

Pei Nan Big Rivulet

萬

年

州

Lower Tamsui Rivulet

嶼球琉小
Little Rhykyu Isle

Lang Chiao嶼琅 (Heng Chun)

G

ties that bind it together, will become dissatisfied. Our first responsibility, then, is to make it possible for everybody to have plenty of
food.

Our soldiers must be fed. If they are to fight well, they must not
suffer a shortage of food. So, during peace, our soldiers must devote
some of their time to producing food.

Not enough people are engaged in agriculture. The land is
available and is fertile. We must encourage more of the people to
produce food.

The conference then got to work and drafted plans which
became law. Land was to be given, without payment, to those
families which were prepared to settle on it. For an initial
period of three years the family would be exempt from taxation.
Beginning with the fourth year a land tax would be imposed.
Further concessions were offered to groups of settlers who
combined to form themselves into rural villages. But it was
obligatory on all males to undergo a period of military training
so as to be able to defend the island in case of invasion. The
army also was put on the land. On the old T'ang principle that
'having no idle moments they will have little time to cause
trouble', special areas adjacent to the military posts were set
aside for the troops to cultivate.

Formosa now entered one of the most prosperous periods in
its history. Thousands of the depressed peasants in Fukien and
Kwangtung migrated across to the island to find a new life.
During 1662–4 there were six waves of migration — peasants
seeking land they could call their own; whole communities
clamouring for recognition; Hakkas demanding their place in
the national life, free from the restrictions which had been
imposed on them through the centuries.

The literati went also. It has been estimated that close on
a thousand of these scholars from south China made their homes
in Formosa during that period, many of them setting up their
own schools on the island for the promotion of Chinese culture.
On the mainland of China the repressive measures of the Ch'ings
were meeting with stiff resistance, and these literati feared that the
very foundations of Chinese civilization were being threatened.

Houses and libraries were being searched in order to discover the sources of the unrest that was beginning to surge over the country, and monetary rewards were offered those magistrates who could muster the most suspects. The days of the Ch'in had returned, and the shadow of the infamous Li Ssu, who had waged war against the literati in the second century B.C., fell over China. Over the centuries — eighteen of them — the voice of Li Ssu could be heard again in the Court at Peking, denouncing the literati as the mischief-makers, the inspirers of rebellion, and the enemies of the dynasty. The Ch'ing on the Dragon Throne was being urged to cast these literati into prison as the Great Ch'in had done, and burn their books. With such a Damocles sword hanging over their heads, such of the scholars as could fled from south China to Formosa. On that island the flame of Chinese culture could burn brightly and freely.

It is interesting to compare the Dutch map of Formosa with one compiled shortly after the death of Cheng Cheng-kung. The former shows Dutch trading stations, but the latter fills in the gap and locates the many settlements that sprang up as a result of the beneficial planning of Cheng Cheng-kung. What were vacant patches on the Dutch map show the names of Lantao in the remote south, Fengshan where Kaohsiung now stands, Benkong on the coast a few miles from the present Changhua, Chucha, Tamsui, and Keelung in the north, whilst between the mountains and the coast we see Hsinying (the present Chiayi), Penhsi (the present Taichung) and many villages dotting the whole area.

As one travels up and down Formosa today, especially through the rural areas, and sees the paddy fields that yield more than 2 million metric tons of rice a year, the plantations that represent the second-largest sugar production in the free world, the miles upon miles of rows that will provide pineapples for the tables of Europe, America, and some Asian countries, and the endless banana trees, it is well to remember that Cheng Cheng-kung was the first to glimpse this potential of Formosa. In his survey of the island in 1661 he caught ' the vision splendid of the sunlit plains extended ' and all covered with vines and fruits and tea and rice. He it was who outlined the 'Land to the Tiller' programme, on which Sun Yat-sen was later to build, and which today is the secret of Formosa's prosperity, providing its 11 million people with the second-highest standard of living in Asia.

Cheng Cheng-kung would never have claimed to be an economist, but he did know that the basis of prosperity and contentment in any country is the security of its food supply. That was the basis of all his philosophy of life. Further, the only effective guarantee of an adequate food production was the farmer's right to own the land he worked and to take pride in what he could do with it.

Cheng would face a firing-squad if he lived in Communist China today.

Having set the foundation of agricultural development in Formosa, he turned his attention to foreign trade. Soon the island would have foodstuffs to sell to other countries, and the transport for these would have to be provided. His existing fleet was designed for defence purposes and not the carriage of goods. So he began the construction of cargo junks. Soon these were sailing to Japan, the Philippines, Indo-China, Siam, and the Indies. Chen Tien, as Tainan was then named, became the most important port in the western Pacific.

Now that the first plank of his platform, the building-up of Formosa, had been firmly established, Cheng set his mind to the second, the utilization of the island as a base from which to expel the Manchus from China. To this end he looked to the Philippines as a vital stage in the execution of his grand design.

His first move was to send his friend, the Jesuit Ricci, as a special envoy to Manila. The Spanish Governor welcomed him with much pomp and splendour, but the military authorities were not so enthusiastic, especially when they noted that the local Chinese showed such elation over the visit. Perhaps this was some plot to spark off a Chinese rising. So they decided to get in first. The Chinese junks were seized, their masters thrown into gaol, and the Chinese population confined to their own quarters. Retaliation was swift. The Chinese killed a Spanish military officer. This was what the Spanish commander had been waiting for. Immediately the army went into action. The 8,000 infantry and 100 cavalry mowed down the Chinese in and around Manila, and, as the Spanish historian Juan de la Concepción stated, ' had it not been that Manila needed Chinese tradesmen and mechanics, not one of the 13,000 Chinese would have been left alive '.

Ricci, his mission unfulfilled, possibly never even stated to the Governor, left Manila at once to report to Cheng Cheng-kung. On hearing what had happened, Cheng ordered the master of his fleet to prepare for sailing orders to Manila. But the fleet never left Formosan waters, as Cheng had a sudden attack of the illness that had been plaguing him for some years.

Why was Ricci sent to the Philippines?

Doubtless to inform the Governor at Manila that Cheng expected him to pay tribute, knowing all the time that this would be met with a blunt refusal, thus affording Cheng the excuse for attacking the Spaniards there and driving them out of the Philippines as he had expelled the Dutch from Formosa. Probably he would have succeeded, had he not been stricken down at the time, as the poor defences of Manila, like those of the Dutch in Formosa, would have proved no match against the forces of Cheng.

With his son Cheng Ching controlling the south coast of China with his fleet, with his own dominance over Formosa and the Pescadores, the possession of the Philippines would have completed Cheng's plan to gain complete command of the China Sea. In that case he could land a force in south China, another in north China, and thus force the Manchus into an ever-narrowing corridor. A powerful pincer movement would eventually crush the Manchus into dust. And withal, the Mings would be restored in China.

Such was the vision that led Cheng Cheng-kung on.

But it was not to be. On 1 May 1663, he was seized with a return of his illness. Between fits of coughing and spitting of blood, he muttered :

The Great Ming pacified the empire and restored its ancient splendour. How can I meet him in Heaven with my mission unfulfilled ?

Cheng then fell back and died. Probably the cause of death was tuberculosis. He was thirty-nine years of age. Like the Great Macedonian, he ended his young life with much accomplished, but the greatest objective yet unrealized.

The spirit of the Great Cheng has brooded over Formosa ever since. Wherever one wanders in that island today, one is conscious of this, most especially in and around Tainan, where Cheng had his palace, and where still stands the Chekan Tower where, with his councillors, he drew up the blueprints of a progressive Formosa, hard by the Confucian temple he built, with its Wenchang Hall, where he spent long hours in meditation, and at its entrance the giant banyans as silent guardians. And hard by, the plum-tree he planted in 1661, under which his councillors met, after his death, and with their blood-oath formed the ' San Ho Hui ', the secret society, that was to keep alive Cheng's purpose of driving the Manchus from China. That society was to spread from Formosa to south China and, through the years, feed the fires of the resistance, and inspire the greatest of all the champions of Chinese freedom, Sun Yat-sen.

The Hakka of Chui Heng village in Kwangtung was to complete the mission of Cheng Cheng-kung.

Most Western Sinologues have had rather a twisted view of Cheng Cheng-kung. There have been a few exceptions. One of these was J. W. Davidson, who lived in Formosa during the early years of the Japanese occupation. In his *The Island of Formosa*, published in 1903, he wrote :

Koxinga was perhaps the most remarkable character that modern history exhibits in the Orient. Holding one of the highest military commands in China at the age of twenty-two and dying while still under forty, his greatst exploits were accomplished during that period of life when others are ordinarily engaged in study and in preparation for the great deeds they hope to accomplish when they have arrived at perfect maturity.

In his private life, he was frugal and modest in his wants. He was proud of the authority vested in him, but does not appear to have used that authority tyrannically ; otherwise he could not have secured and preserved the willing loyalty that his immediate followers afforded him. He trained his subjects in various industries and enforced agricultural labour on his officers and men.

With his own hands Koxinga carved out a kingdom for himself and provided a safe refuge for all loyal followers of the Ming dynasty, against which the haughty Emperor of China, with his boasted nine countries, could not prevail.

Truly, this was the work of no ordinary man !

Yosaburo Takekoshi, the Japanese historian, concurred in this estimate of Cheng Cheng-kung :

Inheriting tact and talent from his father and a sound judgement and daring from his mother, he [Cheng Cheng-kung] was full of great ambitions roused by the tendencies of the age, and proved himself to be a hero, gifted with great governing and organizing powers. His deeds in Formosa proved him a statesman of no ordinary mould. He was the leading spirit of the Government and he alone gave life and vigour to the whole institution.

The image of Cheng Cheng-kung haunted the palaces and Government offices of Peking. If Peking had not taken Formosa seriously in the past, it certainly awoke to reality during Cheng's regime on the island. In 1662 an edict was issued directing all coastal villages to be evacuated and the inhabitants to withdraw inland to a distance not less than fifteen miles. From Shantung to Kwangtung a veritable no-man's-land fringed the Pacific coast of China. Peking feared that the villagers would co-operate with Cheng's men when they landed, for an invasion was regarded as imminent.

This fear was fully justified, as China was passing through one of the most desperate economic periods in its long history. The Manchu conquest of the country had been followed by a veritable flooding from the north as ever-increasing numbers of Manchus entered China as privileged people. Considering themselves a superior race and the Chinese as their chattels, central and eastern China were ravaged to satisfy the demands of the new-comers. Manchu magistrates had been appointed in every district to see that this spoliation was effectively carried out. To aggravate the position, a succession of bad harvests had reduced many parts of the country to famine conditions. Beggary was the order of the day. Wherever hungry Chinese opposed the demands of the Manchus and refused to hand over what small store of rice remained, they were butchered with relentless fury. A private document, *Yangchow Shih Jih Chi*, written by Wang Hsui-ch'u, an eyewitness at the time, has preserved for history a graphic account of happenings in one town.

Here and there on the ground lay small babies who were either trodden under the hooves of their [Manchu] horses or the feet of the soldiers. The ground was stained with blood and covered with mutilated and dismembered bodies, and the sound of sobbing was heard everywhere in the fields. Every gutter and pond was filled with corpses lying one upon another. The blood turned the water to a deep greenish-red colour, and the ponds were filled to the brim.

From the wombs of a thousand Yangchows were born the sons of revenge, who looked across the waters to Formosa for deliverance.

Peking knew this and feared the avenger.

The news of Cheng Cheng-kung's death in 1663 gave Peking a temporary respite from this fear. The Grand Council was summoned and Li Shuai-t'ai, Governor-General of Fukien and Chekiang, was directed to attend. It was decided that he should interview Cheng Ching, son and heir of Cheng Cheng-kung, at Amoy, and suggest terms of agreement. If he would shave his head and grow a pigtail as a sign of his submission to Peking, and hand over his fleet, he would in return be given position and wealth, and the past be forgotten.

Cheng Ching played for time. His father's death had been so sudden that the fleet was not ready for sailing across the Strait of Formosa. Li Shuai-t'ai could return to Peking and inform the Council that its offer was under consideration. Then, with the envoy out of the way, the fleet could be prepared for sailing orders. While Peking was exulting over the prospect of an early and favourable settlement, which would give the Manchus control of the most powerful fleet in eastern waters, Cheng Ching sailed for Formosa. Arriving at the Pescadores, he dispatched messengers to the island to advise the Governor and Council of Ministers that he was about to carry out the terms of his father's will. But before he set out, the messengers returned with the news that his right of succession had been disputed by his uncle Cheng Shih-hsi, on the ground that his son Cheng K'o-tsang, born of a nurse with whom Cheng himself had consorted, could never be accepted in future as a member of the House of Cheng. Indeed, according to the messengers' report, Cheng himself would have been killed by his father for this dishonour to the family had not his generals intervened.

Angered by this news, Cheng Ching decided to use force to gain what he considered his rightful position. However, this was not necessary, as at the sight of his fleet off the coast his uncle recognized his right of succession.

For the next sixteen years the spirit of the great Cheng lived again in Formosa as Cheng Ching dedicated himself to carrying on the work his father had initiated. Migration was encouraged and land was given to each migrant family. The production of more sugar was encouraged and the first plant for its refinement set up. Liberal tax concessions were offered to all who produced salt from sea water. More schools were established under Government control, and the traditional triennial examinations for entrance to the civil service held. Many of the existing levies were abolished and a land tax, the only imposition on the ordinary person, was introduced. Indirect taxes on wine and shipping supplemented the national income. Trade missions visited the Philippines, Siam, and Japan. The English East India Company was invited to enter the Formosan trade and the first English trading-centre set up on the island, though this venture was not a success.

Meanwhile, Cheng had not forgotten his family's pledge, first planned by his grandfather and then formulated by his father, to use Formosa as a base from which to expel the Manchus from China. In 1674 he entered into an alliance with Keng Ching-chung, who had deserted from the Manchus and was preparing an expedition against them. Cheng landed at Amoy, but suspecting Keng of treachery, he decided to go it alone. He did have some success, but after four years of sporadic fighting on land and sea, he was driven from his base at Amoy and forced to retire to Formosa. There he spent the remaining months of his life instructing his illegitimate son, Cheng K'o-tsang in the duties of the high office, which, if his will was carried out, he would have to discharge. In 1681 Cheng Ching died, ' greatly loved and deeply mourned by his people ' as one native historian put it.

With the passing of Cheng Ching, the fortunes of the House of Cheng began to decline. Within two years, palace intrigue, leading to internal dissension, was to hasten its end. The sun was beginning to wester, and all that the Chengs had done for Formosa was to be threatened, not from without so much as from within. The home front was to crack, thus providing the opportunity for which others, outside Formosa, had long waited.

History has yet to assess the true value of the Cheng period. Certain it is that in the years since, and indeed right up to the present day, that period has been the well from which poet, artist, legislator, reformer, and the ordinary peasant has drawn his inspiration. The character of the great Cheng Cheng-kung has been the model that the Formosan Chinese have aspired to emulate. In the history of the island he was the real *chun tzu*, the ideal man. His vision, both of a progressive Formosa and a regenerated Chinese mainland, has been the one bright light, leading on through days of almost despair and nights of thickest gloom those scholars who toiled for the preservation of true Chinese culture, as well as the peasants, who wanted above all else the right to own the land they tilled.

Though dead, the great Cheng has never died.

The Cheng period saw the birth of a real national purpose in Formosa. Previously the population had been just a loose gathering of families, each recognizing the clan authority as embodied in its elders. The Cheng call to nationalism, Chinese nationalism, was the traumatic result of the brutal colonialism of a European power. For the first time in its history the people of the island had been welded into a unity, inspired by a purpose, stemming from the House of Cheng. Such was the popular response that even the wish of the Cheng was invested with hieratic character. And this at the time when mainland China was rent with disorder and cut into pieces with internecine strife.

Economically the Cheng period was, in the words of Formosa's greatest native historian, Lien Heng, the ' age of reconstruction '. Its basis, the land policy, marked a complete revolution in official Chinese thinking, and struck at the very heart of those troubles that had bedevilled the Chinese economy over the centuries. Through the centuries there had been others, such as Wang Mang and Wang An-shih, who had sought to deal with this problem, but they had defeated their best intentions by giving the state too much control. The Cheng policy cut through this bureaucratic direction by allowing each peasant to own the land he tilled as his basic and inalienable right. This involved the cutting-up of estates, often extensive, held by privileged families, which had acquired the land in earlier times. But with resoluteness and decision this was done, with the result that production increased with startling proportions and a general atmosphere of contentment rapidly spread over the island. During this period Formosa was the most peaceful and prosperous part of the Chinese-speaking world.

It was one of the most exciting periods in the history of the Chinese people, with something of the fervour of an Elizabethan era. The spirit, if not the person, of the Ming had been reborn. Among the 400,000 Chinese on the island, the great majority of whom had migrated from the Chinese mainland to escape death by starvation, it was the dawn of a new age.

The arts flourished along with the economic progress. It was the custom, especially among those favoured with an abundance of this world's goods, to have the panels in the walls of their houses adorned with a painting in the classic Chinese style. In the south of Formosa, schools of painting sprang up, at which this panel-painting was taught. Among the Paiwan tribesmen wood-carving reached a degree of excellence not surpassed since, and the pottery of the Amis on the eastern coast was, in the words of one writer, ' evocative in its decoration '. In most towns there was a ' Ch'u Yuan Shih-she ', a poetry club dedicated to the memory of China's first great poet Ch'u Yuan, who had lived in the third century B.C. and was reputed to have formed the first *shih-she*, poetry club. Having poured out his soul in an impassioned poem, the *Li Sao*, lamenting the evils of his time, he drowned himself. The Dragon-Boat Festival had then been instituted by members of the club to symbolize the search for the body of their leader.

The *shih-she* covered a wide range of studies — poetry, philosophy, and literary style. These clubs in Formosa were to become, in later years, centres of resistance against the Japanese. From them were to come the finest of the patriots and freedom-fighters of Formosa, such as Ch'iu Feng-chia and Lien Heng.

In several of the larger cities there were academies with large libraries, to which scholars from all parts of Formosa came to turn the pages of the rare books on the shelves. One of these was the ' Hsiao Yun Hsuan ', established in a village outside the city of Changhua by the Lu family, which had migrated from Kwangtung during the time of Cheng Chih-lung. It was reputed to have 20,000 volumes. This was the academy which in later years Wu Tzu-kuang, the Plato of Formosa, was to make famous. Many of the men who were to play a vital part in the future history of the island, such as Ch'iu Feng-chia, were to be inspired in the pursuit of knowledge by this great teacher, as they wandered through the groves and gardens surrounding the academy. Wu himself, in the grand tradition of those Chinese academicians, which numbered in its long history such teachers as Cha Chi-tso of Chekiang, Tso Tsung-t'ang of Honan, and Wang Ch'ang of Kiangsu, was to leave his mark on the men who were to make the Formosa of the future.

It is a sad reflection that the order set up by the House of Cheng, and which held the promise not only of making Formosa the pride of Asia, but also of changing the course of Chinese history, should have been so short-lived. It did, however, leave behind one permanent result, the effect of which is becoming more and more apparent today. The French Sinologue René Grousset has noted this :

Cheng Cheng-kung is one of the most curious figures in the history of the Far East. He is the first representative of that overseas China, then being born, whose expansion on every shore of the Pacific and

Indian Oceans represents one of the most important happenings of the nineteenth century.

It was doubtless in imitation of the Spanish, Portuguese and Dutch navigators that he conceived the bold idea of building himself a maritime empire in the China seas.

His attempt to do so is of great interest to the historian, being the earliest revelation of something which is by no means apparent in previous history : the maritime and colonial vocation of the Chinese people. Indeed, Cheng Cheng-kung's venture may be said to have started the era of the great emigration of the Chinese, who today are to be found on all the shores of the southern seas, from Cholon to Singapore, and from Batavia to Manila and Hawaii ; it is a movement of immense importance, the ultimate consequence of which cannot yet be estimated.

To the House of Cheng, Formosa was the focal point from which this great venture was planned.

But it was now too late. As with the T'angs and the Mings, the House of Cheng was to destroy itself. Cheng K'o-tsang showed some promise for a few months, but it was only the hectic glow of an expiring age. He was strangled in the grounds of his own garden. Cheng K'o-shuang, who succeeded him, was weak and vacillating. He was content to leave the conduct of affairs to his ambitious father-in-law, Feng Hsi-fan. Corruption soon became rife, and with it rivalry and dissension. The foundations of the House of Cheng were being undermined and the end was inevitable and imminent.

CHAPTER FIVE

The Age of Unrest

PEKING was well aware of what was going on across the Strait of Formosa. Shih Lang saw to that. His scouts on the island, several of them in official positions, kept him informed of the disintegration that was taking place there. In turn, he made sure that this information reached the proper quarters in Peking.

For years, waking and sleeping, Shih had looked forward to the day when he would avenge the deaths of his kinsmen at the hands of the Chengs. As the T'ang poet wrote of another, ' Even in his sleep, he cherished his burning wrath '.

It had not always been so with Shih Lang. There had been times in the past when his brother, his son, and his nephew had served under him as he captained one of the largest flotillas in Cheng Chih-lung's fleet. In those days Cheng the Elder never made any important naval decision without conferring with Shih of Chinchiang, his loyal captain and close confidant. ' The Manchu will never rule over China as long as the Ming standard flies from your mast ', he would assure Cheng in his hours of uncertainty. So close had this comradeship become, so much did Cheng rely on the advice of Shih, that Cheng Cheng-kung strongly resented the presence of Shih at the secret councils of his father. He blamed Shih for influencing his father against acceding to the plan of Emperor Lung Wu that the Cheng fleet should sail north and land men behind the Manchu lines while he, the Emperor, attacked from the south. It was then that Cheng Cheng-kung had confined Shih to his ship when subsequent meetings of the council had been held. The capture of Lung Wu at Tingchow was laid at Shih's door.

When Cheng Chih-lung was taken to Peking after the fall of Foochow, Shih Lang had gone over to the Manchus, who readily accepted the services of such a proficient seaman. They needed men of his experience to take charge of the fleet they were assembling in north Chinese waters. When he heard of this defection, Cheng Cheng-kung put to death Shih's father, brother, son, and nephew. Shih was exacerbated to the point of desperation.

Now an admiral of the Manchu fleet, rising in imperial favour rapidly, and brooding over the deaths of his kinsmen, Shih became possessed of one all-controlling passion — revenge. Good Confucian as he was, he found in the *Li Chi*, the Book of Rites, justification for this one purpose in life. There he read : ' A man may not live under the same sky as the killer of his father.' In spite of the humanizing influence of the Confucian philosophy over the centuries, this elemental instinct for revenge remained ' the most overmastering passion to which the Chinese mind is subject '.

Shih Lang waited and planned.

In 1668 his popularity had reached such a height that he decided to make a move. He submitted a memorial to Emperor K'ang Hsi urging the subjugation of Formosa. But it was shelved. The time was not opportune, as K'ang Hsi, then a minor, was under the complete domination of the regents, who were not interested in the island across the sea. Shih's concern, however, was noted and his interest commended. He was given a post in the Imperial Bodyguard, which he used to the greatest advantage, especially in making contacts. Chief of these was Li Kuang-ti, Chancellor of the Grand Secretariat, who had been instrumental in weakening the power of the regents, thus enabling K'ang Hsi, though still a youth, to take over control. In 1681 Li was summoned to the palace and commissioned to submit a report on Formosa with recommendations. There is reason to believe that Shih Lang collaborated in drawing up both the report and its recommendations.

Shih's hour had now come. Cheng Ching had just died in Formosa and the struggle for power there was in full spate. Cheng Ching had willed his illegitimate son Cheng K'o-tsang as his successor, but his mother had put forward Cheng K'o-shuang, of whose birth there was no doubt, as the rightful heir.

While discord rent Formosa following the strangling of Cheng K'o-tsang, Shih Lang, under imperial orders, prepared his fleet of 300 war-junks to transport 20,000 picked Manchu forces. In July 1683 he sailed from T'ung-shan in Fukien for the Pescadores, where, in a short but decisive battle, he destroyed the entire fleet that had been dispatched from Formosa, under Admiral Liu Kuo-hsuan, to prevent the imperial fleet entering Formosan waters. News of this crushing defeat created panic in Formosa, where already there were popular risings against the corrupt administration of Feng Hsi-fan. In desperation Cheng K'o-shuang asserted himself for once, in a desperate attempt to save his own skin. When Shih's fleet arrived off the coast, Cheng, instead of making any show of resistance, offered surrender.

That was the last of the House of Cheng, which had ruled over Formosa for twenty-two years — few but decisive years.

The revenge of Shih Lang was now complete. But his work was not yet complete. The literati in Peking still clung to the *tsung chu ch'uan* policy that had been so pronounced in Ming times, and Shih had to convince the Court that the security of Fukien, Kwangtung, Chekiang, and Kiangsu could only be maintained if Formosa was integrated into China. As an admiral he was quick to assess the strategic value of the island. His argument won the day, and in that year, 1683, Formosa became for the first time an integral part of the Chinese Empire. A county administration, including Formosa and the Pescadores, under the jurisdiction of the Fukien Provincial Government, was set up, with an inspector-general at Taiwan, as the chief city, now the present Tainan, was named. Three *hsien* or districts were constituted : Taiwan, embracing the area around the capital ; Fengshan, the region to the south of this ; and Chu Lo, now Chiayi, including the remainder of the island.

This position was to remain much the same for the next two hundred years.

During those two centuries Peking must often have regretted listening to the persuasive words of Shih Lang. The warning of the literati was to be vindicated again and again. The island was to move from the status of a county to that of a province in 1885, but it was a slow and painful progress. China herself had to meet the impact of the West, which was to shake her to her very foundations, and at the same time Formosa was to be the battlefield of an unending civil warfare. The remarkable thing is that, under the circumstances, the island made the spectacular progress it did.

Hitherto Formosa had been virtually an unknown land to Peking. Such reports as had been received over the centuries had related to the coastal plains of the west. It was essential, then, that a survey of the island should be carried out. This was initiated in 1714, and three Jesuits, De Mailla, Regis, and Hinderer, were commissioned to carry out the work. The Dutch maps were of little assistance, as they had confined their attention mainly to the south of the island, and the Chengs, who had penetrated to the north and established many villages, some of these across the mountains on the eastern side, had not had a sufficient tenure to embrace the entire island. The three Jesuits travelled from the extreme north to the extreme south, crossed the mountains, and as a result compiled the first comprehensive map of Formosa that we possess. For the first time the potential of the east coast became known. To anyone knowing something of the mountain ranges of the island, this surveying of Formosa at that time must appear a tremendous achievement, calling not only for remarkable powers of physical endurance but also heroism of the highest quality.

This survey was one of the landmarks in the history of the island. Regis was mainly responsible for compiling the map, which showed hitherto unknown land suitable for production, while the comments by De Mailla, especially in connection with the mountain tribesmen, furnished authentic information previously unknown.

The survey and the map that followed had immediate results. They caught the eye of a migrant from Fukien, Wu Sha, who had just arrived in Formosa. Scanning the map, he decided to settle in the north-east, in the area now known as Ilan. So successful was he that large numbers of migrants followed, and within a short time a fourth district was officially constituted. From

H

Ilan, the more adventurous went south along the east coast, settling on the many coastal plains, smaller than those on the west but equally as fertile. The Central Range, running right down the island, is much nearer the east than the west coast, with the result that the available land on the east coast is limited, but gradually, from Suao to Hualien, villages spread out, and, from these, extensions were to reach as far south as Taitung.

In 1760 the first attempt at irrigation was made in the south of the island. It may seem strange that an island of 14,000 square miles in area, ribbed with mountain ranges from which flow fifty rivers and twice that number of rivulets, should require irrigation. It must be noted, however, that these rivers are both short and of irregular flow. The distribution of rainfall is uneven and the torrential downpour during the typhoon season feeds the ocean rather than the soil of Formosa. During the rest of the year the rivers are not only low but often dry. This first venture had to be abandoned for lack of funds. A century was to pass before Shih Shih-pang of Fengshan and Yang Chih-shen of Tainan were to put up large sums of money to construct an efficient irrigation and flood-control system in south Formosa.

With the opening-up of the island and more and more land being brought under production, the economic prosperity of the island reached new levels. Formosa was supplying both China and Japan with sugar and rice, both countries being short of those foodstuffs. Already Formosa was being described as ' the granary of China ' by the *Canton Register*, which in 1833 mentioned ' the 300 junks from Taiwan carrying rice to Fukien, the large number transporting sugar and camphor to Canton '. One historian noted that ' if violent storms prevented the shipment of rice [from Formosa], a scarcity immediately ensued and great distress was felt '.

This prosperity attracted more and more migrants to Formosa. Records kept by Peking give the population of the island in 1811 as 2,003,860, although it is not clear how this figure was arrived at. Still, the migration from the Chinese mainland must have been very considerable. An official census taken seven years later showed an increase of 545,000 through natural increase and migration.

This development, both in population and production, arrested the attention of the Fukien authorities, who were responsible for the administration of Formosa. One immediate result of this was the encouragement given to Formosan-born Chinese to enter the civil service. Cheng Cheng-kung had introduced the examination system earlier, following the Ming practice of adding to the time-honoured literary tests questions of a practical character. The Fukien authorities, in obedience to the Ch'ing directive, eliminated these and confined the tests to the composing of poems and essays. In 1757 Wang Hsien-chieh, born in Formosa, was the first to be appointed to a post in the civil service of the island by the Fukien Government.

A steady stream of official missions now began to visit Formosa. One of these, chiefly of scholars, was led by Yao Ying, a leader of the literati. In collaboration with Fang Tung-shu, he had just published under the title *Yuan-ch'un t'ang pi-chi* a collection of notes on the Confucian classics, written by his grandfather, Yao Fan. Probably the favourable reception given to this work marked him out for leadership of the mission, the purpose of which was to encourage young men throughout Formosa to become proficient in Confucian studies with a view to entering the civil service.

During the period of its stay in Formosa, the members of the mission visited many of the scholars there, seeking their co-operation, and Yao himself was so impressed with all he saw that he expressed a wish to remain on the island. This was welcome news at a time when the Fukien Government was finding it difficult to recruit suitable officials to accept appointments there. Yao was offered and accepted the post of intendant at Taiwan, then the capital of Formosa. This post gave him the opportunity to travel extensively throughout the island and meet those in whom he was most interested — the scholars. It was chiefly to his credit that schools for the study of the Confucian classics were set up in many parts of the island and Confucian temples built.

But Yao noted something else, which he regarded as even more important. This was the growing interest of the literati in the affairs of the island and their concern at the unrest that had prevailed ever since Formosa had come under the jurisdiction of the Chinese mainland. In all his contacts with scholars throughout the island Yao had been deeply impressed with their anxiety about the future, and he was convinced that the future of Formosa would be determined by whatever action the literati might take. On a number of occasions he drew the attention of his superiors to this and later, when he was recalled following the investigation into the *Nerbudda* incident, when British subjects from that ill-fated vessel, wrecked on the shore of south Formosa, were executed by tribesmen, he continued to urge closer co-operation between the Fukien Government and the scholars in Formosa. They would decide the future of the island. But unfortunately his words fell upon deaf ears.

The subsequent history of Formosa was to prove the truth of Yao's observation.

From 1683, when the island had been integrated into China and placed under the control of the Fukien Provincial Government, until 1843, when Yao Ying had been recalled and demoted, the attempt to set up a stable Government in Formosa had been a tragic failure. China was occupied with other pressing problems, both from within and without. The southern provinces, one after another, were raging with revolts, and the impact of the West was shaking the very foundations of Chinese civilization. The way of life which had survived thousands of years was beginning to feel the movement of forces of a new and, to the Chinese, strange order. At the Court of Peking, in the *yamens* of provincial governors, and in the secluded libraries of scholars throughout China, a fear like the cold wind of death was paralysing all effort. The country was confused, and out of the confusion were born many proposed palliatives. Such as were tried ended only in failure, rendering the darkness blacker than before.

Under these circumstances, Peking could give no thought to the island across the sea. The Fukien Government appointed officials, but only for a brief period, only in special cases for more than two years, as the rate of remuneration was so small that officials had to resort to all kinds of corruption to make enough money to live. These practices reacted in intensifying popular resentment and inspiring the spirit of rebellion. During the period 1683–1843 there were fifteen major rebellions in Formosa against the Government.

Government in Formosa was corrupt in every sense of the word. Squeeze was the order of the day, and as the official's tenure of office was strictly limited, he sought in that brief space of time to make a fortune sufficient to enable him to live in comfort for the rest of his life. Each official grade had its own sphere of squeezing and honour lived in dishonour in that no attempt was made to invade another's recognized territory of legalized corruption. The *tao t'ai* (chief magistrate) supplemented his meagre salary with emoluments from the camphor taxes ; the *chih fu* (prefect) received all court fees and a percentage of the salt taxes, which he himself assessed ; the *chih hsien* (district magistrate) took all court fees in secondary cases ; and the *ting* (port controller) was empowered to seize, without question, any private junks for the transport of rice to China, and decided which of these would be commandeered according to the ' escape money ' offered him.

This legalized corruption, extending from the highest officials in the capital to the lowest ranks in the villages, made government impossible. Each man took the law into his own hands, in fact became a law unto himself. All who bore the same name banded together to fight the officials as well as those who bore another name. Family feuds were common as Formosa rapidly became a battlefield on which each clan fought to maintain what it considered its own rights, thus constituting itself into a kind of independent kingdom. It was a reversion to the state of affairs that had existed in China following the downfall of the T'angs, except that instead of five dynasties there were twenty or more. The economy of the island was threatened, and what had promised before the coming of the Ch'ings to be the most prosperous country in Asia now seemed destined to disintegrate

into a land of chaos. Typhoons and epidemics continued the
spoliation which the corruption of officialdom had begun.

The powerful ' San Ho Hui ' saw its opportunity to capitalize
the situation, and with its cry ' Destroy the Ch'ing, restore the
Ming !' began to organize a general revolt. This crusading call
soon rang through towns and villages and echoed among the
distant mountains. Migrants from south China, who had known
something of Ch'ing repression, became the most ardent recruits
of the rising. For a time Hoklos and Hakkas buried their ancient
grievances and formed a common front. The spirit of the Chengs
was reborn and its burning flame spread throughout the whole
island. It seemed that the day of Ch'ing rule in Formosa was
rapidly approaching its doom.

It was then that Peking had another of its rare moments of
serious reflection. Such a one had occurred in 1730 when
Emperor Yung Cheng had ordered that a permanent garrison
be stationed in Formosa and a censor appointed to control the
avarice of officials and restrict their squeeze. But the reformation
had been short-lived, and within a few years corruption had
reverted to its former control. The Ch'ing rule, as expressed
in its representatives in Formosa, was rotten to the core. Now in
1833, with the ' San Ho Hui ' in control of the rising, Peking
panicked, as it was feared that all grain supplies from Formosa
would be cut off, and this at the time when most of China was
in the deadly grips of one of the worst famines in its history.
When the news reached Peking that, after a bloody battle,
Taiwan the capital was in the hands of the rebels and 20,000 of
the imperial forces had been killed, and the remainder of the
garrison had fled into the mountains, Emperor Tao Kuang
immediately ordered a punitive expedition to proceed to Formosa.
After months of bitter fighting, the rising was suppressed. In
announcing the victory of the imperial armies, the *Ching Pao*
(Government Gazette) stated that the Emperor was aware that
official maladministration in Formosa had been the root cause
of the rebellion, that the commanding officer had been dismissed
and punished, and that the Governor of Fukien himself had not
been blameless. Fortunately for him, he had died during the

months of the struggle, otherwise, as the *Ching Pao* said, ' The Emperor would have inflicted on him such a death as would have been a stern warning to all careless governors '.

But this was not the end. The revolt had been quenched but the resentment of the people of Formosa was more bitter than ever. They licked their wounds in sullen silence, waiting for another and more favourable opportunity.

Meanwhile, other problems were pressing hard upon Peking, both from within and from without.

The major domestic issue was the scarcity of land to meet the needs of an ever-increasing population. While the palaces of Peking continued to be enlarged, the land available for tillage by the people decreased. The emperor and the princes lived in a luxury of ever-increasing dimensions, while most of the people were having less and less of the essentials of existence. During the period 1663–1850 the population of China had risen from 60,690,000 to 414,490,000 according to the Peking calculation, and even if this latter figure be regarded as exaggerated, most statisticians regard it as approximately correct. But tillage had not expanded in the proportion needed to feed such a population. In 1663, when the Manchus conquered China, each person represented eleven *mou* of land suitable for cultivation, whereas in 1730, when the population had risen by 25 million, the amount had shrunk to under six *mou* per person. No detailed statistics are available for later periods, but it is not difficult to estimate the privation that must have accompanied the population increase between 1730 and 1850. As a *mou* was only one-sixth of an acre, we can form some idea of the destitution that must have been the lot of the Chinese people at the time the revolt broke out across the sea in Formosa, where food was abundant.

Allowing for the percentage of the population in China not engaged in food production, but who had to be fed, it would appear that the number of people who had to rely on the production of one acre for their food could not have been less than fifteen. It is therefore no wonder that China was in a state of constant unrest, for starvation is ever the food of revolt.

No less pressing was the external problem. Dissatisfied with the conditions under which China permitted trade, Britain had determined to coerce Peking into granting more favourable terms. Desperate for markets, consequent on the Industrial Revolution at home, Britain was prepared to force the issue. But it never seemed to have occurred to London that China was a sovereign nation and at that time Britain had no treaty rights there, which meant that the British, whether traders or otherwise, were in China on sufferance. If Peking was not disposed to grant more liberal terms for trading, then the proper course was for the British to withdraw. But such was not the mood of the time, nor did it suit the arrogant temper of the British and other Europeans, who had little else than contempt for the Chinese, who, on their part, regarded all Europeans as uncivilized.

This complete lack of mutual understanding was the real cause of the friction between Peking and London. The historian can only regard this as most unfortunate, as the Chinese and the British had so much in common. He was a Chinese who wrote that 'mellowness, a sense of humour, conservatism, and the worship of the past' are national characteristics common to both people. What is the British love of compromise but the Western counterpart of the Chinese *chung yung*, the philosophy of the mean? What is the British concept of 'character formed by education' but the Confucian doctrine of the *chun tzu*, the superior man?

Opium was the occasion of the war of 1839–42 and the subsequent years of conflict. These could have been avoided had those on both sides had cooler tempers. The irony of the situation was that the inherent genius of both peoples sought at times to avert the prolongation of the struggle, and negotiations were in reality begun, only to be foiled by the intemperate attitudes of both parties.

Never before nor since, in the history of Sino-British relations, was there such an unnecessary war.

Humiliated and forced to bite the dust, China became so preoccupied with pressure from the West, which Britain's victory had fed to the full, that Formosan affairs were relegated to a minor place in the programme of Peking. Other European nations, seeing China prostrate, considered the time opportune to grasp some of the spoils. The scramble for spheres of influence began and with it Peking's interest in Formosa waned, so that it seemed that there was to be a reversion to the policy of Yang Ti, twenty centuries earlier. Now as then, China was fighting not only for her civilization, but also her for territorial integrity.

But this attitude towards Formosa was to be fraught with danger. In the past the Dutch had capitalized Peking's neglect of Formosa ; now other Western powers were moving in the same direction. The rich land together with the strategic position of Formosa allured the seekers after privilege and fortune. And these were the carriers of a foreign culture and civilization.

This age of unrest in Formosa which we have noted was not without its compensations. Once again, as in the previous history of the Chinese people, a period of political and social upheaval was to bring forth creative activity of a high order in other spheres. The domestic unrest acted as a cleansing agent, stripping away the dead values and revealing beneath these the permanent values of mind and spirit. Unlike the West, which in similar circumstances has invariably sought for some new political philosophy, the Chinese turned to the arts, poetry and painting, for spiritual regeneration. Their hands reached out, in the midst of turmoil, for the brush. The spectacle of conflict led the thinker and the artist to ponder more and more on the eternal harmony between the *yin* and the *yang*. So it was that these seekers after truth left the court and the city to seek seclusion in some mountain monastery or just wander, ' guests of stream, lake, and forest ', listening for the voice. Some of the finest works of the Chinese brush were created at a time when the country was rent with disorder, and in some cases anarchy.

Rich lotus blooms were rising from beds of mud.

This faculty of distilling from national unrest the stimulus of creative activity was, perhaps, the secret of the survival of Chinese civilization, while its contemporaries, at various periods of history, were declining into disintegration. Chinese civilization has outlived them all. Aided by the infiltration of new blood, so the Chinese became the amalgam of many peoples, and this faculty enabled the Chinese to rise above the periodic disturbances and China itself to be in a constant process of rebirth. Possibly no other people, throughout history, has evinced such a genius for regeneration.

Chiang Kee, an outstanding interpreter of China's creative epochs, referred to the time of the ' Warring States ', when the feudal lords were at war with one another and the Chou Dynasty was breaking up in confusion, as the ' heyday of Chinese philosophy ', with ' painting too in the ascendant '. The full blossoming of that age was Confucius, Lao Tzu, Mo Tzu, and other sages. It was one of the most unique and rare chapters in the human story. In the midst of disorder, these men, or should we call them seers, sought to recapture those values that make for personal excellence and social and national harmony.

Centuries later, in the twilight of the T'ang, this same genius asserted itself. Huang Ch'ao and his armies had devastated China from Kwangtung to Szechwan and then spread north through Hopei to Shantung. By the year A.D. 880 China was in fragments, with rival war-lords springing up all over the country, each calling for allegiance to his standard. It was then that Ssu-K'ung T'u, of the Board of Rites, depressed at the sight of his country thus torn apart, retired to his hermit's lodge in the mountains and there wrote his famous poem on Taoism, which was to become not only a model for future poets but was also to have profound influence in the unification of China in the year 960. Possibly no other poem has had such political effects in the history of any country. At the same time, Han Yu and Liu Tsung-yuan were setting a new standard for ' purity of style and felicity of expression ' in Chinese literature, ' rarely surpassed in the prose literature of China '.

More lotus blooms from beds of mud.

In the half-century that followed the fall of the T'ang, as the five powerful groups, having eliminated the other contenders, contended for the mastery of China, artists such as Ching Hao and Kuan T'ung brought forth from their seclusion a new and powerful style in painting, which the Sung artists were later to carry to perfection. Soon the walls of monasteries and temples, which had known nothing but religious paintings, were covered with landscapes, birds, and flowers. The temples and monasteries had become the art galleries of China. The *shuang kou*, double-lined contour treatment, that made this possible had been born at a time when the whole country was seething with civil strife.

That half-century ended with the coming of the Sung and the reunification of China. A new age of enlightenment dawned as the flowers of Chinese culture, first glimpsed in the years of unrest, now came to their full floresence. The arts flourished. China was the first among the nations of the world as custodian of the refined life. Nowhere else, in East or West, was its equal in the spiritualization of all things, from the tiny flower on the mountain-side, the raindrops on the banana leaves, to the songs of the poet and the visions of the philosopher. It was one of the few perfect moments in the life of mankind on this planet.

But it was not to last. Mankind was not capable of maintaining such perfection. It existed in north China for a century and a half (960–1126) and then, under Mongol pressure, the soul of this perfection sought a haven in south China, at Hangchow. But it was only a temporary tenure (1132–1276). Then, as the lights began to dim and the curtain fall on the once splendid scene, to the accompaniment of the war-cries of the advancing Mongols, the guardians of the enlightenment found their way across the seas, to Formosa and Korea. There they hoped to keep alive the secret which in happier times might return to flourish on its native soil. Korea was a promising place of refuge, as the Li Ning school, set up under royal patronage, was already following the grand tradition of Kuo Hsi and his landscapes, of Mei Fei and his paintings of animals, of Hsai Kuei and his rugged seascapes, of Ma Yuan and his silk-poems of the West Lake, and of the Ch'an monks, whose Buddhist paintings were among the finest flowers of the Sung perfection.

The real soul of China lived in exile across the waters.

There were some, however, who would not leave their native soil, but preferred to remain and sound their prophetic notes in the ears of the foreign controller of China. Such a one was

Yeh Shih, who in one of his poems depicted China as a walled garden, the fragrance of which no bolt or bar could shut out. To him, Chinese civilization would survive the Mongol era.

> Yet bolts and bars can't quite shut in
> the spring-time's beauteous pall ;
> A pink-flowered almond-spray peeps out
> athwart the envious wall.

Yeh Shih did not live to welcome the Ming restorer of China's sovereignty in 1368 and the beginning of those three hundred years of prosperity, which, as before, were to be terminated by the foreigner. Again history was to be repeated as scholars fled to Formosa and Japan. In the art renaissance in Japan, led by the monk I-Jan, the soul of China was to live in exile. Meanwhile, in China, Hsu Hsieh, the Hanlin scholar, was writing his story of the *Antique Inkstand*, a splendid bit of imagery and one of the gems of Chinese prose. 'A heavenly robe', one Chinese commentator called it. In this masterpiece Hsu sought refuge from the disasters of the time in reading the records of the past and intellectually communing with the masters of the lost perfection. It was a spiritual exercise, designed to keep aflame lights which had been dimmed, but, as he believed, only for a time. Hsu saw himself, as he mused before his old inkstand, as :

> A man, who, in his wanderings up and down the long avenue of the past, lighting upon some choice fragment, which, in a moment brings him face to face with the immortal dead.
> Of such enjoyment there is no satiety.

Like Keats dreaming before his Grecian urn, Hsu was confident, as he dreamed before his antique inkstand, that the civilization to which he belonged ' cannot fade ', but ' shalt remain, in midst of other woe '.

Such was the conquering vision, through succeeding ages, that enabled the genius of China to persist against all odds, and indeed to flower in fulness, when the land was in tumult or bowed before the conquering sword of the foreign usurper.

It was not surprising then that in Formosa, a Chinese county, the unrest from 1683 onwards was accompanied with a surge of creative activity. Developments on the island were following the historic Chinese pattern. With the failure of the Manchu officials to promote any semblance of ordered government, and with official corruption rampant, the scholars intensified the study of the Confucian classics, each gathering around him a select group of students. The *shih she* became a popular institution in most Formosan towns and larger villages. This was a very old Chinese society, dating back to those early days when the songs Confucius incorporated in the *Shih Ching* (Book of Odes) were first composed. Through the centuries the activities of the *shih she* had ranged over the whole field of culture, from poetry to philosophy, and had become the basis of those literary groups to which the promotion of the study of Chinese culture had owed so much.

The *shih she* now became the focal point of all cultural and patriotic activities throughout Formosa. What the artist felt, what the philosopher thought, and what the patriot dreamed of, were all put into song by the poet. Henceforth the *shih she* was to become one of the most dynamic forces in the history of the island.

Scholars from those groups went north on missions to the Ryukyus, where in 1795 Sho On had established the Kokugaku and Mihira schools for the study of Confucian philosophy. In 1835, due to the inspiring leadership of Sho Iku, a renaissance of learning had spread over Okinawa, the chief island of the group, and this had attracted the attention of scholars in Formosa. For the first time scholars from Formosa and the Ryukyus met together in the city of Naha, the prefectural capital. The year was 1837.

This reaction to the unrest in Formosa was not confined to the Chinese population. Among the mountain tribesmen, who were suffering severely at the hands of the rapacious Manchu officials, side by side with the frequent rebellions were bursts of creative activity. At Tavarong in south Formosa, the Ami tribesmen, having discovered deposits of rich clay, were fashioning vessels of unique design and decorating them with unusual patterns. Among the Paiwan tribesmen, wood-carving reached its highest peak, with the production by the Tarusagius of wooden containers strikingly similar to the famous *hu* of early China, especially during Chou times. Panel carvings, similar to those common among the Maoris of New Zealand, which had been a craft among the Paiwans for centuries, became more delicate and refined, and unlike the earlier specimens were now highly polished.

For the first time these Paiwan wood-carvers paid attention to anatomical details, especially features. If we compare the carved figures of this period with those produced throughout Polynesia at the time, we find in the works of the Formosan tribesmen a true reproduction of the human anatomy, as opposed to the disregard for such in the carvings from Easter Island right across the Pacific to the Maoris in New Zealand. Anthropologist Peter Buck has offered an explanation for this latter attitude :

In Polynesia, most of the human figures were carved to form symbols of their gods, who, with few exceptions, were deified ancestors. Thus it may be that the early craftsmen, while accepting the human form as a motif, purposely refrained from making the images appear too human in detail. The conventional patterns exaggerated some anatomical features and reduced others and each island group developed its own forms.

This humanizing of art in Formosa during the period of unrest had profound sociological implications. Or it may have been the expression of changes already taking place in the attitude of the tribesmen towards the happenings of the time. Hitherto they had relied on their gods for protection ; now the pressure from without, in the form of brutal Manchu officials, was making them realize that the old order had proved ineffective and now real men, heroes, were needed to safeguard the interests and security of the mountain dwellers. The Tarusagiu artist in the Formosan mountain was protesting against oppression, denouncing the powerless gods of his ancestors, and calling for brave men of flesh and blood to lead the tribe. One is reminded of Pythagoras of Rhegion, far back in the fifth century B.C., carving from the block of marble his famous Charioteer as a call for action against the Persian threat which was becoming more and more ominous.

For excellence in craftsmanship and artistic expression, the works of the Tarusagiu family in the Formosan mountains during the early seventeenth century compare most favourably with the best produced on the Chinese mainland at that time. In the Prague Museum there is a carved figure, generally regarded as one of the finest productions from China of the late sixteenth century and probably the work of Wu Tan. This carved statue might easily be mistaken for a Tarusagiu, with its *ch'i-yun sheng-tung*, to borrow the phrase of Hsieh Ho, meaning 'rhythmic vitality'. Both the Chinese statue and the typical Tarusagiu are deathless poems, expressing rhythm as the free and flowing interaction of all parts of the human body; not a catalogue of limbs but an image of life, vibrant and free, one breathing the mountain air of Honan, the other that of the mountains of south Formosa.

Nowhere in the early seventeenth century did the sculptor in wood reach a higher stage of excellence than that attained by the Paiwan artists in Formosa.

Contemporary with this changing pattern in Formosa, schools of story-tellers, the *pobete*, arose on Lanyu, the small island off the south-east coast of Formosa. These raconteurs, in true Homeric fashion, narrated the heroic legends of the past, especially those dealing with the exploits and wanderings of Shiapun Miturid, the Odysseus of the Formosan tribesmen. From somewhere in the remote south, across the waste of great waters, he had led his companions, till they landed on the island he named Botel, now known as Lanyu, the Orchid Island.

In the language of the Yami tribesmen of Lanyu, *pobete* means 'ten mouths'. The narrator tells the stories of many generations of antiquity. It is interesting to note that in the south China name for a story-teller, *k'ai tzu ku chiang*, the key word *ku* 古 is a compound of + meaning 'ten' and □, 'mouths'.

But the most important reaction to the state of political and social unrest was the awakening of the literati to the challenge of the time. They were shocked out of their timelessness to a realization that the future of their civilization was now at stake. The very values for which that civilization had stood through the centuries were now threatened. It was imperative that they emerge from their seclusion and become active in the affairs of state. Henceforth the influence of these literati was to become the most powerful force in the history of Formosa.

Shen Pao-chen, the architect of modern Formosa

CHAPTER SIX

The Literati at Panch'iao

THE Year of the Monkey — 1860.

From their schools and academies, from their retreats in the foothills, and from their huts of reed by the lakeside, the scholars of Formosa wended their way north to Panch'iao at the invitation of Lin Kuo-hua.

Himself born on the island, where his family had been settled for three generations, Lin had followed with a disturbed mind recent developments on the Chinese mainland. In 1857 he had retired into seclusion with his many books, resolved on devoting his remaining years to the study of the history of Formosa. Having selected a site in the open country a few miles south-west of Taipei, he built his house and laid out his extensive garden. The plan set out by the T'ang poet-official, Po Chu-i, and later enlarged by the Chang family of architects in Ming times, was his guide. In the garden were pine-trees with their gnarled trunks and twisted branches. Rocks, worn by wind and water, stood in the miniature lakes like reduced mountains. Small grottoes had holes in them so that the burning perfumes could simulate mountain clouds. Everywhere were small moon-bridges over narrow winding paths. Temples, roofed with porcelain tiles of green and vermilion colour, decked the mountain-side. On the lake a tiny skiff lay anchored in the eternal silence.

These many moon-bridges gave the garden its name, ' Panch'-iao Yuan ', and the village that later sprang up around the estate of Lin Kuo-hua became known as Panch'iao, a name it still bears.

It was not strange that Lin should have invited the scholars of Formosa to meet in his garden to consider the future of the island, for on many occasions vital decisions in the long history

of their ancestral homeland across the water had been made in
such a setting. Was it not in the garden of his academy that
Ch'ien Ch'ien-i had warned the young Cheng Cheng-kung of
the then impending threat to Ming civilization from the north?
Now that ominous clouds were taking shape in the northern sky
above Formosa, what more natural than that Lin should invite
the literati of the island to gather in his garden and seek to
discover their portent?

Unfortunately the literati, throughout China's history, have
never received just treatment at the hands of Western Sinologues.
They have been represented as a privileged class, ultra-
conservative, determined to uphold a rigid Confucian attitude
towards all change, and, in most cases, opponents of all progressive movements. But such an estimate is not true to fact. The
literati, cautious and often arrogant in their approach to change,
were the true custodians of the bases of Chinese culture and
civilization, and they were responsible, in no slight measure, for
the continuance of a civilization, the oldest extant in history. It
should be remembered that the chief opponents of Emperor Shih
Huang Ti's totalitarianism in the third century B.C. were the
literati, who paid the penalty of their daring. More than four
hundred of the scholars of the time were flung into the flames
that destroyed China's bamboo literature. H. G. Creel, in his
Confucius, noted that the literati were ' sole custodians of the
literature and ancient culture ' of China and that they stood for
' relatively mild and even relatively democratic government, as
opposed to harsh and autocratic rule '.

We have no record of the conversations that took place in
the ' Panch'iao Yuan ', but it is not difficult to imagine the
problems discussed. We do know, however, that as the result of
that gathering, the literati of Formosa determined to crusade for
the maintenance of Chinese civilization as they knew it, and to
oppose all external attempts to supplant it with a foreign culture.

That resolve of 1860 in Lin's garden was to bear fruit in 1895.

The concern of the literati in Formosa for the future of Chinese
civilization on the island was quite understandable. They
were well aware of what had happened on the Chinese mainland

during the past twenty years. A number of missions from Fukien had been in Formosa, one of them, in 1838, being composed almost entirely of scholars. Examiners of candidates for the public examinations were in the island regularly, and it is not unlikely that Lin Kuo-hua had invited scholars from the mainland to be his guests at Panch'iao. Withal, then, the literati in Formosa would have been well informed of developments across the Formosan Strait. They would have known of the increasing pressure on China by the West since the Treaty of Nanking in 1842. That was the year of China's deepest humiliation — her main ports forcibly opened to the West, foreign merchants swarming in, and, more ominous still, foreign missionaries, with their strange religion, turning people away from the ancient temples and persuading them that the teaching of Confucius had been superseded.

But the gains of 1842 had not satisfied the voracious appetite of the West. In 1858 the Treaty of Tientsin had further humiliated China and forced her to agree to what the foreigner had called ' the regularization of the opium trade '. Yet it had been this traffic in ' foreign mud ', as the Chinese called the opium landed from British ships, that had led to the war of 1839–42.

China, their ancestral homeland, was indeed biting the dust.

But this was not the worst. The Treaty of Tientsin had brought Formosa within the orbit of the ambitious schemes of the West, with Keelung and Tamsui as ports of call for Western ships. Already Europeans and Americans were setting up consulates and trading-posts in Formosa. Exports from the island, rice, tea, sugar, and camphor, were reaching an all-time level, but the only import was opium, the only commodity in which Western traders were interested. An American named Mooney had been engaged in this trade before the Treaty of Tientsin, and British and American clippers from Hong Kong had kept up his supplies, which were loaded in a hulk off the coast near Anping. Now, with the enforced legalization of this trade, the foreign merchants vied with one another in their extension of this traffic throughout the island.

Such was the situation which the literati discussed in the garden of Lin Kuo-hua at Panch'iao.

But would this nefarious trade be the end of Western plans? Would it mean Western gunboats in the waters of Tamsui and Keelung and Takow? Gunboat diplomacy had already forced the Chinese mainland to its knees once, in 1842. Would the same thing be repeated in Formosa? Did the Western powers have plans to occupy the island, as Hong Kong had been, when the suitable incident for action happened?

The literati had good reason to ask themselves such questions. The historian, surveying all the indications of the time, cannot fail to understand the grave anxiety of those who feared that, at the opportune moment and on suitable pretext, one or more of the Western powers would claim Formosa as the prize of war. No such intention may have existed, but the Chinese mind, unfamiliar with the ways of the West, was not to know this. It had only the experience of the past half-century to guide it.

In 1833 British merchants in China had urged the British Government to occupy Formosa as a ' convenient and desirable acquisition ', and indeed, prior to the war which gave Hong Kong to Britain, the merchants favoured Ningpo or Formosa as the most coveted spot. In 1834, when the charter of the East India Company in respect of the China trade expired, the Company urged the occupation of Formosa, with the proposal that as a Government trade superintendent was to take over control of trade with China, the Company should have exclusive rights in Formosa. But to guarantee this, the island should be occupied. The Company had had a trading-post in Formosa in the seventeenth century, but had withdrawn in 1682 because of the failure of the post to make ' better earnings of the trade of Tywan '. In 1842, shortly after the cession of Hong Kong to Britain, a British vessel, the *Ann*, was wrecked on the Formosan coast and most of its crew murdered by tribesmen. The British Plenipotentiary to China, Sir Henry Pottinger, after interviewing the Chinese Governor of Fukien at Amoy, issued a proclamation which demanded the degrading and punishment of officials in Formosa, and then added this stern warning :

Without this just atonement, Her Britannic Majesty's Plenipotentiary is not prepared to say that the event which has occurred will not be the cause of a further serious misunderstanding, or that it may not even lead to a renewal of hostilities between the two empires . . . .

Peking and the authorities in Formosa could hardly have failed to remember the incidents that preceded the 1839–42 war, which resulted in the British occupation of Hong Kong. Was Formosa now in danger of becoming another Hong Kong ? The Pottinger proclamation of 23 December 1842 was certainly calculated to support such a possibility. At least, the Chinese might reasonably have thought so.

Whatever plans may have been in the official British mind, any idea of the occupation of Formosa was left in abeyance, chiefly out of a desire not to offend Prussia, which itself was manifesting an interest in the island. But the Americans did not see any such obstacle in their way, and in 1852 the American Commissioner in China urged his Government to occupy part of the island. Commissioner Parker's plan won the attention and sympathy of Townsend Harris, the American Envoy to Japan, who suggested that America should purchase Formosa from China. An American merchant in China, Gideon Nye, believed to have been the promoter of this plan, together with other American merchants in China, presented to Commissioner Parker a plan for the ' colonization ' of Formosa, together with an offer of ' willing assistance '.

These Americans were quite honest in their intentions. They were anxious to safeguard the trade routes, as, in the words of Gideon Nye, ' Formosa's eastern shore and southern point in the direct route of commerce between China and California and Japan, should be protected by the United States of America '. Nye had good reason to know how treacherous the waters along the coast of Formosa could be, especially in the typhoon season. One of his own relatives, a passenger on the clipper *Kelpie*, wrecked on the coast of the island, was believed to have reached land, where he was still living among the tribesmen. Added to these considerations, Nye had no confidence in the ability of the

Chinese officials to control the tribesmen, who lived near the coast and at whose mercy crews and passengers of wrecked ships would be. In fact it was the cruelty of the officials that had resulted in the tribesmen regarding all others as natural enemies. Everybody outside the particular tribe was viewed with a murderous intent.

Many a ship and many a brave man found a grave along that uncharted coast, the most dreaded in the Pacific.

Commodore Perry, fresh from his triumph in forcing open the doors of Japan, was interested in the Formosa plan. Determined to find out just what was in it, he sent some of his officers to the island to investigate possibilities. Their report was so favourable that Perry gave the plan his unqualified support. In a dispatch to the Secretary of State, he urged the immediate occupation of Formosa by America.

But America was not in the mood for such a venture. Her own troubles at home were piling up. Civil war was threatening the Union and already the call to arms had been sounded. The plan for the occupation of Formosa was actually placed before the Government but it had to lie upon the table. Already the bugles were sounding on the American front. One can but wonder if Secretary of State William Seward had that plan, as it lay on the table, in mind when he wrote :

Henceforth, European commerce, European politics, and European activity, although becoming actually more intimate, will, nevertheless, sink in importance, while the Pacific Ocean, its shores, its islands, and the vast regions beyond, will become the chief theatre of events in the world's great hereafter.

Prophetic words of one hundred years ago !

Did Lin Kuo-hua and his literati guests, gathered in the garden at Panch'iao, know of these plans ? British and American consulates had been set up at Tamsui and a British vice-consulate at Takow in the south of the island. Foreign merchants were established at the most important ports and the shipping companies were doing a brisk business in the opium trade. Under the provisions of the Convention of Peking, Chinese customs had to pay the indemnities for the war China had just lost, and to collect Formosa's share of these an Englishman was in control of the customs administration on the island.

Was all this just the first step in the occupation of Formosa? The Dutch had landed on the island as traders, but soon became colonizers. Were Britain and America now following the same pattern?

This must have been the thought uppermost in the minds of the literati of Formosa at that historic gathering at Panch'iao in 1860.

To the Chinese, any occupation of their territory meant a direct challenge to their historic Confucian civilization. This was the deep-seated fear behind all Chinese clashes with the West. The trader could be tolerated, but the missionary was regarded as the front line of this offensive. Devoted more passionately than most people to their culture and civilization, which they considered superior to all others, they suspected the bearers of any new ethic or religion from the West.

This suspicion of the real purpose of the Western powers was most pronounced in south China, from which area the Chinese in Formosa had migrated. Antonio Bocarro, Keeper of the Archives at Goa, in his record of the Portuguese settlements in India in 1635, mentioned a strange belief existing at that time in Kwangtung:

As they [the Chinese] have a prophecy that they will one day be conquered by a people with cat's eyes, and the Hollanders have them, they are all the more reluctant to admit the latter in their Kingdoms, and especially since they regard them as being piratical corsairs of the sea, a name which they greatly abominate . . . .

In his manuscript of more than three centuries ago, Bocarro noted the willingness of the south Chinese to trade with foreigners, to take ' Chinese goods in exchange for other things '. It was the fear that the Dutch were not content with this, but were bent on occupying south China once they secured trading-posts, that gave rise to this suspicion of Western intentions. The Portuguese at Macao never made any attempt to abuse the privileges accorded them. They were content with their base at Macao and so won the confidence of the Chinese that they were allowed to carry on their missionary work there freely. Similarly, about the same time, in 1626, the Spaniards in north Formosa confined their activities to the Keelung and Tamsui trading-stations, and never planned any occupation campaign. The Dutch, on the other hand, were no sooner in the island than they began their colonization, with the aid of the missionaries who, from the outset, branded Confucianism as idolatry.

This Chinese suspicion that the West was determined to supplant their civilization with one of foreign origin persisted through the succeeding centuries. It was accentuated at the very time that the literati were meeting in the ' Panch'iao Yuan ' as guests of Lin Kuo-hua. At Nanking, the rebel leader Hung Hsui-ch'uan had established the capital of his *T'ai-p'ing T'ien-kuo*, ' Celestial Kingdom of Peace ', and his armies were within striking distance of Peking itself. Hung had his agents in Formosa. These were inspiring rebellion throughout the island, in the hope of drawing off more imperial forces from the mainland and thus relieving pressure on the armies of Hung. Later, when the notorious adventurer Henry Burgevine joined the T'ai P'ings, he was sent to Formosa, probably to explore the possibility of the island becoming a haven for such T'ai P'ings as could escape in the event of final defeat.

To the Chinese literati, the most objectionable feature of the T'ai P'ing rebellion was the religion of its leaders. These professed to be Christians, and to the literati Christianity was an import from the West. To them, Confucianism and the state were synonymous. Hence the T'ai P'ing rising was simply an attempt to reduce China, already at the mercy of the West militarily, to a state of intellectual colonialism. They themselves were not averse to a revision of Confucianism. Indeed, at the time when the literati of Formosa were meeting in Lin's garden, the enlarged edition of Wei Yuan's great work, *Hai-kuo t'u-chih* (Illustrated Geographical Dictionary of Maritime Countries), was the book of the day. Published in 1852, it enlarged on Wei's earlier thesis of 1844 that China's humiliation under the Treaty of Nanking, which gave Hong Kong to Britain, had been brought about by the ' barbarian religion ' and the ' barbarian opium '.

Now the T'ai P'ing 'followers of the barbarian religion' were
gaining victories and China was on the way to further humiliation.
Wei called for a revision of Confucianism as part of the process
of China putting her own house in order, if her civilization was to
survive. This book galvanized the opposition of the literati to
the T'ai P'ings into dynamic action. Men such as Lo Ping Chang
of the Hanlin Yuan, the Academia Sinica of the time, and Lo Tse
Nan the poet-painter, left their studios to take up arms against the
'followers of the barbarian religion', in the defence of their
Confucian civilization. A. F. Lindley, an Englishman fighting
with the T'ai Pings', stated that 'had the Ti-pings not possessed
Christianity, China would have risen to their standard as one man'.

It was not the reform programme of Hung Hsiu-ch'uan that the
literati opposed, but his religion, which they regarded as simply
a Western instrument for the suppression of Chinese civilization.

At the very time when the literati of Formosa were considering
the threatened challenge to their civilization, Tseng Kuo-fan,
commander-in-chief of the imperial forces in China, was issuing
a proclamation to the literati there to rally to the defence of their
civilization. He called on 'superior men to arise in defence of
the orthodox faith against these southern rebels, who have
adopted the ways of the barbarians and their religion'. The
proclamation ended :

Never until these latter days have such things been — no, not from
the days of creation. At such unorthodox teaching, Confucius and
Mencius must be weeping.

Shall any scholar, then, fold his arms in his sleeves and sit in peace ?

This appeal struck home. China was stirred to its very
foundations. Recruiting drives were the order of the day in
every province. On city walls, in the entrances to monasteries
and temples, sheets were posted calling on the people to rise in
defence of their ancient civilization, 'now threatened by the
religion of the West'. Confucian and Taoist priests acted as
recruiting agents. One of these sheets, which the author has
seen, read thus :

The rebels have burnt the temples of the sages, destroyed the tablets of Confucius, and scattered the pieces on the ground.

Our gods are angry and great disaster will come upon us unless this false foreign religion is rooted out.

Our ancient civilization is now at stake.

Such, then, was the temper of the Chinese literati, both on the Chinese mainland and throughout the county of Formosa. On the mainland they saw the ancient civilization, which had withstood the strains and stresses of many centuries, now challenged by a foreign culture, with its ' strange ' religion, buttressed, as Hsien Jung put it, ' with the fire and thunder of the barbarians ', the cannon of the English. In Formosa it was feared that the same policy was now to be pursued, as the West was suspected of planning to occupy the island and impose its culture and religion on the population.

But the direct challenge came not from the West, but from Japan. For many years Japan had cast covetous eyes in the direction of the island, and the Yahei incident, though now past history, had never been forgotten. Now the first impulses of Meiji imperialism were making themselves felt, and, like wavelets when a stone is thrown into water, they reached out across the sea till they broke upon the Formosan shore.

From the year 1609, when the forces of Iyehisa Shimadzu, the Daimyo of Satsuma, had invaded Okinawa, both China and Japan had received allegiance from the kings of the Liu Ch'iu Islands. It was a common saying among the people, ' China is our father, Japan our mother'. With the dawn of the Meiji era, as ambitions of a mighty destiny in the Far East began to inflame Japanese minds, China's position in the Liu Ch'ius came under review. The dual allegiance must end at once and henceforth the Liu Ch'ius must send no tribute to Peking. The next step was to be the incorporation of Formosa with the chain of Japanese-held islands, reaching from Japan to the most southerly of the Liu Ch'ius.

Japan realized that she must tread cautiously. She did not wish to antagonize the West, on which she was dependent for her modernization. And any war with China might lead to such a rupture. But there was danger in delay, as some Western power might step in and occupy Formosa. Had the Japanese heard of the Harris suggestion that America should purchase the island ? It is likely that they had word of the presence in Formosa of Perry's officers and the extensive examinations they had been engaged in. And those secret plans of the Germans ? Possibly the Japanese had wind of these.

The 1871 incident provided Japan with the pretext for immediate action — not occupation, but a test of foreign reaction. She would see just what London and Washington did or said in respect of the retaliatory action she would take. A fishing vessel from one of the Liu Ch'iu Islands had been driven ashore in a storm off the coast of south Formosa and all the survivors murdered by tribesmen. When a formal complaint was made to Peking, the Chinese repudiated all responsibility. Two years later a similar incident occurred, and Japan again met with the same response from Peking. On the ground that the Chinese were incompetent to deal with such situations and had no real authority in Formosa, Japan decided to take things into her own hands. General Saigo Judo was ordered to lead a punitive expedition to Formosa. This at least would test British and American feeling. If that was not hostile, then the punitive force could remain in Formosa as an army of occupation.

But the reaction was such that Japan decided to stay her hand for the time being. The Press in Britain and America expressed suspicion that Japan was seeking an excuse to involve China in war. Europeans in Shanghai were very outspoken, declaring that Japan planned to occupy Formosa as a stepping-stone for an imperialist movement into the western Pacific. The intervention of the British Minister at Peking, Sir Thomas Wade, was a clear indication that Britain was not prepared to see the incident off the Formosan coast as a *casus belli*. Japan read the warning aright and decided to wait. Terms of settlement were drawn up, probably by Wade, and agreed to.

However indifferent Peking might be towards affairs in Formosa, there was one man who did see the red light. He was Shen Pao-chen. As a member of the literati, Shen's first appointment had been as a compiler of the Hanlin Yuan and then as a censor. His memorials to Emperor Hsien Feng were so highly commended that, from the beginning, he was marked out for a brilliant career. Tseng Kuo-fan regarded him as ' a man of the future '. When China decided to have her own navy in 1867, Shen was appointed Director-General and was entrusted with the responsibility of the task. He built the Naval Academy known as *Ch'iu-shih t'ang i-chu*, and introduced the study of the French language as an aid in naval construction and the study of English to promote knowledge of navigation. He sent picked students to England and France for further training. Unfortunately, Shen had to contend with the powerful group at Court, which had little interest in naval affairs and succeeded in whittling down the funds Shen needed to carry out his programme. He resigned in 1874.

When, later that year, the agreement settling the Formosan affair was signed, Shen urged Peking to take Formosa more seriously. He offered his services as leader on a mission of inspection of the island to see just what was wrong there, as he warned Peking that there would be further trouble with Japan. His offer being accepted, Shen went to Formosa and spent some months in his investigation. On his return to the mainland, he submitted his report to the Emperor.

This was the first detailed account of conditions in Formosa, and the first plan for the development of the island since the time of Cheng Cheng-kung. It would well have been captioned ' The Blueprints of Expansion '. In it, Shen urged that Formosa, then a county, should be raised to the status of a province. The presence of a governor on the island would not only spur on development but would also show to Japan and the West that Formosa was indeed part of China. Along with this, the whole system of government in the island should be overhauled. Education facilities should be extended to include the mountain tribes. Along the coast, at selected places, a chain of fortresses should be constructed. A communications system was imperative, not only between different points on the island, but also between Formosa and the mainland of China. Until such times as a governor could be stationed on the island, the Inspector-General of Fukien province should spend part of each year in Formosa.

As usual, Peking received Shen's report and recommendations and promptly pigeon-holed them. He was thanked and, again as usual, given a worthy appointment, as Governor-General of Kiangsu–Kiangsi–Anhwei. Much the same procedure as in 1668 when Shih Lang was rewarded for his interest in Formosa by receiving appointment in the Imperial Bodyguard. Peking had a charming way of silencing disturbing voices without giving offence. The plain truth is that in 1875 Peking did not want to be worried over the fate of Formosa, in spite of the recent humiliation she had suffered at the hands of the Japanese.

China continued to bite the dust.

But in Formosa there were men who thought otherwise. Chief of these were the literati, who feared that a foreign occupation of the island was now only a matter of time. The visit of Shen Pao-chen had been an inspiration and they supported his proposals to the last item. Although Peking made no move on Shen's major proposals, the Fukien authorities did display interest and set up new administrative units. This had one very important result: it noted for the first time that the northern sectors of Formosa were equal in importance with those in the south. Hitherto the concentration of interest, even during the Cheng regime, had been around Taiwan, the chief city of south Formosa; henceforth north Formosa was to receive equal consideration. This move in 1875 was, within a few years, to result in the removal of the central administration from Tainan in the south, as Taiwan City came to be called, to Taipei in the north.

Shen Pao-chen did not live to see his plan put into operation, but he must be remembered as the real architect of modern Formosa.

CHAPTER SEVEN

Liu Ming-ch'uan the Master Builder

As Shen Pao-chen was the architect of the modernization of Formosa, so was Liu Ming-ch'uan its master builder.

In the whole panorama of Chinese history, no career was more colourful and fascinating than that of the farm boy of Anhwei who became the first Governor of Formosa.

Liu's rise from the lowest to the highest station was no mere accident. No magic wand brushed aside the obstacles that impeded his ascent. No stroke of chance pointed the way to the summit. From the outset, his native ability, together with an inflexible courage, singled him out from others. Free from the traditional conservatism of his age and with a profound appreciation of both the culture and material progress of the West, he followed, in spite of opposition from Peking — at times intense — his vision of a modernized Formosa. But that opposition was eventually to destroy him.

Liu Ming-ch'uan began his career as a freebooter. Tilling the ancestral land soon wearied him. He preferred adventure. Perhaps this was a strain in the Liu blood. Many centuries earlier a Liu had abandoned his farm in Kiangsu to establish the Han Dynasty, and a later Liu had left the land to sell straw sandals on his way to the establishment of the Sung Dynasty.

Leaving the ancestral home, the young Liu travelled to the city of Luchow, arriving there at the time when Governor-General T'ao Chu was dealing a body blow at the small group of merchants who had monopolized the salt trade. They had succeeded in safeguarding their position by claiming, and securing, hereditary rights. T'ao Chu determined to end this by directing that any merchant could deal in salt, provided he bought his supplies from the Government with payments in advance.

The idea appealed to the eighteen-year-old Liu.   Gathering around him a number of similarly-minded young men, and securing supplies with forged permits, Liu went into business. To silence any honest trader who might be inclined to expose his illicit dealings, Liu armed the members of his group, and named them the ' Ming-tzu Chun ', the Band of Fiery Insurgents.   The very title was enough to strike terror into the hearts of any who dared to talk too freely.   Within two years, the salt trade of Luchow and the surrounding district was in the hands of Liu Ming-ch'uan and the ' Ming-tzu Chun '.

Already Liu was showing his mettle.

In 1854, with the T'ai P'ing rebels advancing on Luchow, Liu saw his opportunity to advance his fortune.   The garrison at Luchow was small and hopeless against any attack by the rebels. So Liu called on the Governor-General and offered the services of the ' Ming-tzu Chun ' as a volunteer force, which, he assured T'ao Chu, he could speedily augment into a fighting force.   The offer was readily accepted, and for the next seven years the ' Ming-tzu Chun ' won distinction in campaigns against the T'ai P'ings.   Chief of these was at the decisive battle of Susung, when Liu led his men against Ch'en Yu-ch'eng, nicknamed 'Ssu Yen Kou ', ' Four-eyed Dog ', because of the two dark spots under his eyes, one of the most ferocious of the rebel leaders. In 1858, by a strange stroke of fate, Liu, whose name meant a ' battle-axe ', was present at Luchow to witness the execution of Ch'en Yu-ch'eng with a battle-axe.

In 1862 the strategic moment in opportunity arrived.   The rebels were overrunning Anhwei and Li Hung-chang had been ordered to recruit an army to resist them before he proceeded to take up his post as Governor of Kiangsu.   Liu decided to merge the ' Ming-tzu Chun ' with this new army, which was known as the ' Huai Chun '.   He soon won the attention of Li Hung-chang, who saw in him a man of the future.   Beginning as a major, Liu rose rapidly in commands and from that time on he never looked back.   Military honours followed in quick succession, the ' Bataru ', the D.S.O. of China, the ' Yellow Riding Jacket ', a highly coveted honour, and then commander-in-chief of the

forces in Chihli. When the T'ai P'ings were destroyed and the
marauding bands known as the ' Nien Fei ' were disturbing the
country, Liu was sent to suppress them. His success brought
him the further honour, Baron of the First Class.

Rarely had such honours crowned such a young head. Liu
was then thirty-one years of age.

Weary of soldiering, Liu retired to his native Anhwei, built
his ' Ta Ch'ien Shan Fang ', ' Large Secluded Mountain House ',
with its extensive garden and many waterfalls. Among the pines
with their gnarled trunks and twisted branches, the miniature
mountains of rock polished by wind and storm, grottoes in
which he burned the perfumes that filled the garden with their
cloud-like smoke, pungent with its aroma, and in the centre the
lake with its tiny boat beside a marble bridge, moored lightly
so that when artificial breezes stirred the water, the frail craft
moved from side to side in metronomic rhythm, Liu wandered
with his guests, poets and artists, or just walked alone and
dreamed of the battles he had fought and won. For eleven years
he enjoyed the idyllic life of his mountain retreat.

In 1880 came the summons he could not disobey. And the
disturber of his dream was none other than Li Hung-chang. Liu
must proceed to Peking immediately. Arriving at the capital,
Liu soon understood the reason for the peremptory summons.
The treaty signed at Livadia on the Black Sea had shot up the
temperature at Peking to fever heat. The Chinese envoy who
signed for China had already been handed over to the ' Hsing
Pu ' (Board of Punishments). But the damage had been done.
Russia had agreed to return to China that part of northern Sin-
kiang occupied in 1871, but had refused to give up command of
the passes through the T'ien Shan range into Turkestan. Li Hung-
chang was quick to realize that Russia had gained a tactical victory,
and that what China needed was a strategist. Liu Ming-ch'uan was
the man. Li remembered his brilliant manœuvre, which had won
the battle at Changchow sixteen years earlier and at a time when it
seemed that nothing could hold back the T'ai P'ing rebels.

Liu understood at a glance the Russian purpose. Control of
the mountain passes would not only cut China off from her

Liu Ming-ch'uan, first Chinese Governor of Formosa

dominions beyond, but would also enable Russia to flood into China at any time. He recalled that it was at one of those passes, now held by Russia, that General Li Ling, with 5,000 men, had held back the Hiung-nu hordes until his numbers were reduced to 400 and the pass was choked with the bodies of the slain. It was only when sheer exhaustion defeated the defenders of the pass that the invaders swarmed through into China over the bodies of her gallant dead. That was two thousand years ago, in the days of Emperor Han Wu Ti.

Tenghi Pass had been China's Thermopylae.

Liu lost no time in getting to grips with the problem. China's great weakness was lack of transportation facilities. He drew up his plan for the construction of railways linking Peking with the north and with the north-west. Mobility of movement was the basis of the plan. But the entrenched forces of conservatism in Peking opposed the plan, although Kuo Sung-tao, who had been in London and Paris, strongly supported it.

Bitterly disappointed, Liu left Peking and returned to his garden among the hills of Anhwei.

The next three years were to be the most decisive in the life of Liu Ming-ch'uan. Though he did not then know it, they were to prepare him for the supreme mission of his life, across the water in Formosa.

Liu had returned from Peking at the time when the clash of cultures, following on the Treaty of Tientsin and the Convention of Peking, was moving to its climax. These assured the Christian missionaries that they ' shall in no case be interfered with or molested '. Most of these missionaries, flooding into China, were products of Evangelical Revival, and in spite of their many virtues were both intolerant and narrow-minded. The Chinese were ' idolaters ' and ' pagans ', who in turn thought of the Christians' God as a European, Christ as a white man, and the church as an alien institution. The view expressed by Westermann in his *Africa and Christianity* was very much the same as that vigorously held by Protestant missionaries in China at that time :

However anxious a missionary may be to appreciate and to retain indigenous social and moral values, in the case of religion he has to

K

admit and even to emphasize that the religion he teaches is opposed to the existing one and the one has to cede to the other.

To the literati in China, this was a challenge to their basic culture, for to them Confucianism and religion were inseparably bound together. Tseng Kuo-fan and Li Hung-chang both favoured the adoption of the scientific methods of the West and encouraged the sending of Chinese students abroad to study these. Hsueh Fu-ch'eng in his *Ch'ou-yang ch'u-i* and Wang T'ao in his *pien-fa* campaign for reform urged that the scientific methods of the West should be incorporated within the Confucian structure. The work of these and others were soon to be embodied in K'ang Yu-wei's epoch-making *K'ung Tzu kai-chih k'ao*, which set forth Confucius as a reformer and Confucianism as a way of life that was capable of embracing new methods and continually carrying out a process of self-reformation. China could be most successfully modernized, not by adopting the religion and civilization of the West, but by so reforming Confucianism that it would answer all the questionings, not only of China, but of mankind. Confucius must become the true missionary.

It is highly significant that a similar upsurge is taking place today among the different ethnic religions in Africa and other places as a challenge to Christianity, conceived as a European cult. These peoples are digging deep into their own past to find some answer to those threats, which, to them, have been imported from the West, such as Communism, which they regard as a Western product.

A reformed Confucianism, absorbing the best and the most modern that the West had to offer China, was the all-important subject that engaged the attention of the literati, who met at Liu's ' Ta Ch'ien Shan Fang ' among the mountains of Anhwei. It was at this time that the challenge from the West took a new form. For the past twenty years France had been biting into South-east Asia. In 1863 she had extended her protectorate over Cambodia. In 1867 she had annexed three provinces of Annam. Then Garnier, Rocher, and others had suggested that the time had come to tap the rich mineral resources of the

Chinese province of Yunnan. This had led to war with China. As Britain had declared the neutrality of Hong Kong, France decided to acquire a naval base in Formosa from which China could be attacked.

Peking once again turned to Liu Ming-ch'uan. He was appointed Governor of Fukien, with instructions to take over the defence of Formosa. In spite of the difficulty in receiving supplies, as the French Navy controlled the Strait of Formosa, Liu's strategy was more than a match for the French superiority in equipment. On 4 August 1884 he drove back the French at Keelung, even when the land batteries had been silenced, and on 3 March 1885 he held Taipei in the face of a massive assault by French marines. Defeated, the French withdrew to the Pescadores, and all that remained of their Formosan venture was a monument set up on a lonely outpost in the Pescadores. But it did serve one purpose. It aroused Peking, which hitherto had looked upon the island as ' a place of banishment, to which subordinate officials, who must be provided with posts, but were unfitted for responsible administrative work, might be relegated ', as one authority stated at the time.

The result was that Formosa was created a province of China, with Liu Ming-ch'uan its first governor. Shen Pao's dream had come true.

This was Liu's great opportunity. He would build up Formosa into a modern, progressive Confucian state. Free from the deadening hands of the ultra-conservatives of Peking, he would adopt the modern ideas and methods of Western science and industry within the framework of Confucianism. In this way the civilization of China would meet the challenge of the West.

This was a formidable task, and he knew it. The problems were tremendous and the temptations most inviting. There was little unity in the island, where various wealthy families held sway over different areas, content only with building up and conserving their own interests. There was no modern transport, industries were small and inefficient, and education lacked co-ordination. At the same time, there was the grave temptation to live the easy life of an official in an island of unsurpassed beauty and abundance of food. To carry through his plan of modernization, which would mean the dispossessing of some of their inherited rights and the interference, to a greater or lesser degree, in the lives of all, called for firm action, strength of character, and resoluteness of will. Many a man of lesser stature would have flinched from the task.

Liu's first move was to travel over most of Formosa and see for himself the actual state of affairs, meet the leading families, and acquaint himself with the nature of the country. On his return to Taiwan, the capital in the south, his plans had begun to take shape.

He was convinced that the seat of government was in the wrong place. From 1624 this had been in the south, but Liu decided that it must be nearer the centre of the island. After inspecting various sites, he settled on the spot where Taipei now stands. There had been a small town there for years, and the surrounding country was such as to allow for speedy and extensive enlargement. As the name of the former capital in the south, Taiwan, was the same as that of the island itself, to save confusion it was changed to Tainan.

Taipei was to be the symbol of the new China. Not vast palaces, roofed with ornate and richly coloured porcelain tiles, and a long string of elaborate and luxurious official residences. Rather a city throbbing with modernity, from which would radiate the spirit of progress. As the nerve-centre of a vigorous and progressive province its influence would spread to the mainland and lead the ancestral homeland into the modern age. Such was the vision of Liu Ming-ch'uan when, in 1887, he switched on the first electric light in Taipei, the first city in the Chinese world to be electrified.

But a progressive Formosa must be prepared to defend itself. Liu had known from experience the greed of the West for colonial empire. Had he not himself but recently driven out the French? Then, to the north, were the Japanese, who only a few years before the French assault had planned to take over the island. Liu was well aware that the Formosa he had in mind would make the foreigner even more keen to possess it. By the end of 1887 Formosa boasted an arsenal in Western style, with batteries at five strategic ports. Orders were placed abroad for supplies of heavy modern armament from Armstrong of England and Krupp of Germany. Around Taipei a massive wall was constructed, on which heavy guns were mounted.

History had shown that the Pescadores were the gateway to Formosa. So a naval base was built there.

But Liu knew that a modern defence system meant much more than armaments. He remembered his experience in Peking in 1880 when he had submitted his plan of railway construction, so that troops could be moved speedily to the north and north-west. That plan had been rejected, but in Formosa he was in control, and he was determined that nothing should stand in the way of his design for Formosa.

First, there was the problem of communications. In 1876, Ting Jih-ch'ang, Governor of Fukien, a man of progressive ideas, had laid down a telegraph line from Taiwan, then the capital, to Changhua in the centre of the coastal plain. Liu extended this to Taipei and then north to the port of Keelung. A school for the training of telegraph operators was established in Taipei. To link Formosa with the Pescadores, the outer rim of Formosan defences, a cable was set down between Tainan and Dome Bay in the Pescadores. Emanuel Hansen, a Danish engineer, was then engaged to continue this cable from Dome Bay to Sharp Peak, at the mouth of the River Min in Fukien province on the Chinese mainland.

Liu then turned his attention to transport. As on the mainland of China, Formosa had no transport system, with the result that there was little interchange between the people of different towns and villages and no means of moving troops rapidly from one place to another. In Formosa, as on the Chinese mainland, there was not a single mile of railway. Popular belief in *feng shui*, which some of the educated shared, opposed any disturbance of the ground such as the building of a railway line would entail, as this might offend the spirits that controlled the lives of the people. A railway, like a mine, could bring irreparable harm. And the building of a railway in Formosa would involve much blasting and innumerable tunnels through the mountains.

However, Liu went ahead and engaged engineers from Europe to survey the proposed track. When these arrived, there was uproar. 'Lung Wang', the dragon, who guarded the graves and sent the rain, would be disturbed with the blasting, and who could tell what might happen if he showed his anger. Without rain the crops would fail and the people die of hunger. In their graves there would be no peace, for 'Lung Wang' would withdraw his protection. When Peking gave its consent to the project, fears began to subside, and the engineers went on with their survey. In 1889, after many hazards, with tunnels collapsing and embankments being washed away, the first train ran from Taipei to Keelung. So jubilant were the people with this achievement that all opposition died down and Liu moved on to his next project, the building of roads. In 1892 the plan for main highways, which Shen Pao-chen had drawn up in 1874, was materializing.

Encouraged by these successes, Liu began to look at the industries of the island. Camphor and tea were the two products that engaged his attention particularly. At that time world chemists were deeply interested in camphor as an ingredient of celluloid, smokeless explosives, and other compounds. For years, indeed as far back as the end of the fifteenth century, camphor forests covered large sectors of the mountains and were extending down into the plains. Among the earliest references to Formosa in Chinese records there was mention of *chang*, but it is not clear whether this signified the tree or the crystallized product. Liu saw the opportunity to make Formosa the world's greatest supplier of camphor, and before he left the island he was to see the camphor export trade reach its highest figure, 6,916,000 lb. This was never exceeded in later history.

He gave a similar stimulus to tea production. He introduced regulations prohibiting dealers from importing inferior leaf into Formosa, mixing it with genuine Formosan leaf, and exporting the mixture as pure 'Oolong' tea. The only answer to this practice was to bring more land under production and thus increase the amount of leaf available for export. As a result of the increased number of plantations, the annual increase of production during Liu's administration averaged 500,000 lb., and before he left Formosa the annual production had reached 20 million lb.

The vessels purchased in 1888 for the transport of Formosan products to the markets of the Chinese mainland, South-East Asia, and as far afield as India were only a provisional expedient. Formosa must build her own ships. Already Liu had drawn up his plans for the construction of yards at several ports. These, however, had not a high priority, as other matters were considered of more immediate importance.

One of these was education. Liu was determined that whilst Formosa must learn from the West the latest methods in the economic development of the island and its defences, she must remain loyal to her basic Confucian way of life. He never accepted the idea that a superiority in industrial and scientific progress was a mark of a superior civilization. On the contrary, he visualized a modernized industrial state in which the individual was guided by the Confucian ethic as the highest achievement of mankind. To this end, education, based on the Confucian philosophy, yet ready to accept the best that the West had to offer, must be the right of everybody in Formosa, including the tribesmen in the mountains. Such a Confucian background would act as a corrective to that extremism in thought and practice that were accompanying the industrial and scientific age in the West.

The public examination system was retained, but the scope of the tests enlarged. He took advantage of the edict of Emperor Kuang Hsu in 1878 that the memorials of the Governor of Fukien in 1869 and that of Li Hung-chang in 1875 be granted. The former provided for a test in mathematics and the latter for a test in scientific knowledge at the public examinations. The tests in Confucian philosophy were retained, but these included the comments and criticisms of the candidate. This latter had been introduced during the later years of the Ming Dynasty, and Cheng Cheng-kung had introduced this test in comment and criticism at the examination in Formosa, but the Ch'ings had cut it out when they occupied the island in 1683. Liu's plan for the education of the mountain tribesmen was a modest one, but it was not a marked success.

There was a greater degree of intellectual freedom in Formosa at that time than on the Chinese mainland. Criticism of the Government was common, especially at the puppet-shows given in honour of those students who had won distinction at the public examinations. Marionettes lampooned the Governor and the officials of his administration in a way that would never have been tolerated in Peking. Liu never attempted any repression of this student expression.

The Confucian temples throughout Formosa were enlarged, and such as had fallen into disrepair were renovated at Government expense. Three of these were closely linked with the Chinese mainland, as the funds for their restoration were supplied from the Court of Peking. These were the Tainan Temple, built in the Cheng Cheng-kung period by Chen Yung-hua and enlarged by Emperor K'ang Hsi in 1690, the Hsinchu Temple, built in 1817 by order of Emperor Chia Ch'ing, and the Taipei Temple, erected during the reign of Emperor Hsien Feng in 1854. The first two stand today as Liu renovated them, the last was destroyed during the Japanese invasion of 1895. On its site a new temple was built in 1925.

As one wanders through the temples at Hsinchu and Tainan, one breathes again the atmosphere of the time of Liu Ming-ch'uan. Lingering in the courts and side-halls, in admiration of the massive beams that swing down, uniting heaven and earth, marvelling at the rhythm in wood that joins in perfect harmony the *yang* and the *yin*, whilst brooding over all is the solemn hush of a devotion both breathless and profound, both timeless and shapeless, one can but wonder at the limited vision of the Western missionary who passed by these same temples in the days of Liu Ming-ch'uan and wrote :

The heathenism of Formosa is of the same kind as the heathenism of China. It is the same poisonous mixture, the same dark, damning nightmare.

The original element was Confucianism.

I know the poison of its sweets, the fatal flash of its light, and the stagnant fetor of its life.

The same missionary remarked on the ' tawdry images in the temples of these idolaters '. Perhaps no more tawdry than one sees in some Christian churches in modern Spain.

As might have been expected, the enterprising programme of Liu's administration cost money, a lot of money. This meant added taxation. The people of Formosa welcomed the modernization of their island, but they resented having to face the bill. They protested, often in a violent manner. But, and this was a tribute to Liu's liberal-mindedness, they were never punished for their protests. On one of his visits to Tainan, the protestors held him a house-prisoner in his *yamen* for some days. Liu never returned to Tainan, nor did the protestors go to gaol. Had such things happened on the Chinese mainland, they would have lost their heads. In Taipei the protests took a different form. On walls everywhere throughout the capital there appeared sheets on which *chu chih chao*, bamboo-twig ditties, were written satirizing Liu and his administration. Crowds gathered to read and laugh. On the day following the proclamation doubling the salt tax, this ditty appeared on the walls of Liu's office :

> Already were the people
> In a state of dire distress,
> And cries and sighs to Heaven,
> All their miseries express.
> What cared the money-grabbers ?
> Their illicit gains to swell,
> They bleed their victims once again
> By doubling the gabelle.

But the satirists were not always content to slip out at night and paste their *chu chih chao* on the wall. On one occasion, when Liu gave a party to honour his mother's birthday, they gathered at the gate of the official residence, and handed to each departing guest this sheet :

> The mandarins have been to call
> On Liu Ming ch'uan's mama,

And now they all return,
As they complete the la-di-da.

Sometimes the satirist's brush had a poisoned tip. Captain
T'ao, one of Liu's chief advisers, was to feel this :

An evil notoriety is this same Captain T'ao,
They hold him in no affection down at Pilam anyhow ;
He made a pretty penny by his private *likin* fee,
And showed us all that laws are made for other folk than he.

Liu took all these protests in good part. He could afford to do
so, for the results of his work were becoming more and more
apparent. Formosa was rapidly becoming the most modern
and progressive province of China. Large numbers of intellectuals were being attracted to the island, encouraged to do so
by the liberalism of Governor Liu. They saw Formosa as a
modern state, applying the latest scientific methods of the West,
yet retaining its ancient Confucian foundation.

But this success was arousing the bitter opposition of the more
conservative officials at Peking, who opposed all change, and
who had been marshalling their forces for years in readiness for
the day when they could strike at Liu. They had defeated Kuo
Sung-tao, who had returned from Europe with his plan for the
modernization of China, yet in the province of Formosa Liu had
actually put such a plan into operation. And to aggravate the
position, many of the literati were crossing over to Formosa and
supporting him. Fortune was on the side of these recalcitrants,
for it was reported that Liu, a victim of malaria for some years,
was now seriously ill.

In 1891 they struck. Liu Ming-ch'uan was ordered to return to
the Chinese mainland. He accepted his dismissal calmly, for he
was now too ill to fight back. He sought retirement in his
beloved ' Ta Ch'ien Shan Fang ', which he had not seen for
years. There, in the company of his friends, he walked through
his garden, dreaming of the island across the water. Formosa,
like the trees around him, was growing stronger day by day —
not the stunted and dying wood that Peking was. The chess-
board was his favourite relaxation. With his closest friend,

Ting Tsu, he would spend hour after hour at chess. In 1896 he played his last game. As he sat at the table, news came of the cession of Formosa to Japan. The Treaty of Shimonoseki had checkmated him.

Historians of the West have never given Liu Ming-ch'uan his rightful place. W. A. Pickering, the English shipping agent, who saw much of Liu's work in Formosa at first hand, regarded him as an ' enlightened man '. But that was scant praise. He was much more. He was a genius, something of a prophet, who lived before his time. In some ways he was ahead, not only of thinkers in China, but also of those in the West. When Liu was Governor of Formosa, it was the prevailing idea, not only in China but also in Europe, that the civilization of the West and Christianity were one and the same. The missionaries in Formosa and indeed throughout the whole of China ' conceived the civilization of the West, its political institutions, its philosophy, arts, and sciences as the products of the Christian religion, and equally needed by the Chinese '. There were a few, only a few, among the Jesuits, and the outstanding Timothy Richard, who did not accept the view that the adoption of Western scientific methods and the technology of the West by China necessarily meant the acceptance of Christianity as Western theologians interpreted it. But these were in a marked minority.

Liu Ming-ch'uan did not accept the prevailing position. To him it constituted a challenge to Chinese culture and civilization. He was as eager to retain Confucian civilization as he was to adopt the scientific processes and technological practices of the West. He visualized a resurgent Confucian China equipped with all the latest scientific and industrial knowledge, and this was the dynamic vision that enabled him to effect the transformation of Formosa. It was on the foundations he laid that Japan was able, during its occupation of the island, to modernize Formosa still further, without, at the same time, adopting the Western interpretation of Christianity.

Seen through Chinese eyes, Liu's position was quite logical. Chinese civilization, based on Confucianism, had survived the centuries, the dynastic changes, some of these violent, and had accommodated itself to all the fluctuations of human thought. It had often been attacked, but it had survived. Foreign philosophies had gained a footing in China, only to be absorbed by that of the Great Sage. Had Liu had a knowledge of the outer world and its history, he would have been strengthened in his conviction and found much to support the position he had taken up. He would have known that in his own day the population held together by Confucianist China was greater than that ever held under one Government, with the possible exception of the then British Empire.

It was the Confucian element in Chinese civilization that gave it a unique place among the civilizations that history has recorded. Indeed, no other civilization that has existed on this planet, including our own, emphasized, as Confucianism did, that human society could prosper only as men preserved correct relations with each other and with the world about them. It set forth, as the chief purpose of the state, the education of the individual in moral character. To achieve this end, character was the first requirement for service in the government. That this was not always attained, and that there were many glaring lapses, does not lessen the excellence of Confucian civilization.

It was resilient and possessed an inherent genius to meet the demands of succeeding centuries. Far from being a fossilized system, as many Western writers would have us believe, for twenty-four centuries before the time of Liu Ming-ch'uan it showed itself capable of reformation and adaptation. Confucius himself advocated and assisted in bringing about such social and political reforms that he was one of the greatest, if not the greatest, of Chinese revolutionaries. As H. G. Creel, in his *Confucius*, noted, 'Within a few centuries after his death, hereditary aristocracy had virtually ceased to exist in China, and Confucius had contributed more than any other man to its destruction.' The guardians of the civilization based upon his principles were equally revolutionary through succeeding centuries, in spite of intensive opposition both by those who claimed to be Confucians and those who opposed it.

Liu Ming-ch'uan was such a guardian. He refused to believe

that the adoption of Western science and technology involved with it the acceptance of Western civilization, with its politics, form of government, and religion. China needed the former but not the latter.

It is highly significant that in recent years there are voices in the West, and some of them missionary voices, echoing something of the same thought that possessed the mind of the Governor of Formosa sixty years and more ago. Dr. Max Warren is such a one :

Everywhere there is a desperate search for some inner basis of security. Particularly in Asia, but not only there, the peoples are seeking to find this psychic security by digging deep into their own past. This is at once an expression of their revolt against the West and one explanation of the renaissance of the great ethnic religions. In a new way these ancient religions are themselves becoming missionary. No longer content to be on the defensive, they are offering themselves as answers to the questionings of mankind.

The portraits of Liu Ming Ch'uan show a man of almost monkish appearance. Always he is looking upwards. On every feature is the impress of dedication. There is, over all, the mark of austerity. Here is a man with a purpose, a Confucian purpose, who not only imposed on himself adherence to a rigorous life-plan, but required the same from all his officials. Like the Great Sage himself, Liu believed that the reformation of the state and indeed civilization itself must proceed from the centre, the individual, to the circumference, and not, as so many Western doctrinaires have proclaimed, from the circumference to the centre. The individual renovates society, not the reverse.

This was true Confucianism, the motive power in the life and administration of Liu Ming-ch'uan in Formosa. Liu Ming-ch'uan would have had no sympathy with Socialism.

CHAPTER EIGHT

The First Asian Republic

LIU MING-CH'UAN'S departure from Formosa in 1891 was the signal for the march of 'Nippon Seishin'. Shao Yu-lien, sent by Peking to administer the affairs of the island, was a weak man who cared more for the easy life than for maintaining the defences which Liu had built up. His successor T'ang Ching-sung, though possessing many admirable qualities, was not equal to the task of governorship.

Meanwhile the spirit of aggression, born of Meiji imperialism, was sweeping over Japan. With the increasing influence of Westernism, she feared for her own identity, her national self, her cultural unity, and her very independence. This fear resurrected her former Asian ambitions and these soon opened up a glorious vista for the assertion of Japan's place and power in the world.

Paranoia Nipponica became the supreme Japanese impulse.

For many years Korea and Formosa had been among these ambitions. Back in 1592 and again in 1597 Hideyoshi had led fruitless expeditions to Korea. In 1592 Hideyoshi had been urged to take over the northern portion of Formosa, and his advisers had actually renamed the island 'Takasago' because of the similarity between some of its scenery with that around Takasago in Japan. When Commodore Perry forced open the doors of Japan in 1853, the Emperor emerged from his seclusion at Kyoto, and with him came the ambitions which had been closeted for many years.

The occupation of Korea and Formosa and their incorporation into Greater Japan now became authentic imperatives. As for the latter, Okuma Shigenabu had already spied out the land in 1874.

One spokesman of this Greater Japan, who urged this occupation of Korea and Formosa as the first steps in the realization of Japan's imperial ambitions, was Yoshida Shoin. He called on Japan to return to her traditional aim of dominating Asia to the exclusion of the West, but with the weapons gained from the West. A vigorous opponent of the shogunate, which he regarded as standing in the way of Japan's role in the world, he had been thrown into prison, where he wrote his *Record of a Dark-Room Prisoner*, a book which was to have a profound influence in shaping Japanese foreign policy. Count Ito, the framer of Japan's first constitution, and many leading samurai, as Saigo, were deeply impressed by it. Yoshida himself summarized this *Mein Kampf* thus:

Hokkaido must have its clan lords; Kamchatka and the Kuriles must be occupied; Korea must pay tribute to our country as formerly; Formosa together with the Liu Ch'iu Islands must become part of Japan.

It was now only a question of timing, of finding the occasion for action. This came in 1894 when the Tong Hake, a secret society in Korea, attempted to take over control of that country. As China had suzerainty over Korea, she answered an appeal from the ruler there, and Chinese forces were sent into the country to quell the rebellion. Japan, not to be checkmated, did likewise, so that Chinese and Japanese armies were soon face to face. This soon led to blows which developed into open war, as Japan secretly hoped it would. The struggle was short-lived, and by the Treaty of Shimonoseki, which terminated hostilities, China was further humiliated. Korea was declared independent, which state was soon to be converted into annexation by Japan, and Formosa was to be ceded to Japan.

But the cession of Formosa to Japan was not to be as easy as the victors imagined. Peking had been forced, once again, to bite the dust, but the people of Formosa had yet to be reckoned with. They had followed the brief course of the struggle in Korea, and as soon as hostilities had ended and it was known what demands Japan was making, a deputation of officials and literati left Formosa for Peking. There they made it clear that under no circumstances would Formosa accept Japanese rule. Peking was stirred as never before over the future of the island. A group of officials who had served in Fukien and Kwangtung offered to purchase Formosa so as to keep it out of Japanese hands, and a number of Westerners living in the capital volunteered their finanical assistance. When the news of Japanese demands, especially in regard to Formosa, spread throughout south China, popular resentment rose to fever heat. An English woman, resident in China at the time, described this in these words :

All along the Yangtse Valley, and especially in far distant Szechuan, I had not believed the people capable of so much feeling about a public event as high and low showed over the cession of Formosa. Tearful questions and incredulity, then a silence that was worse than tears, was the way in which the information was generally received. After which, the visitor would take leave only very perfunctorily, going through the usual forms of politeness. Not a word more, only an air of being crushed, absolutely crushed under the blow that the Emperor had given up Formosa, that pearl of the Chinese crown.

Mrs. Archibald Little's description of Formosa as ' that pearl of the Chinese crown ' was, in itself, most illuminating, as indicating the popular concept of that island throughout south China and indeed west China in 1894.

But the treaty had not yet been ratified. Peking played for time. If Japan gained Formosa and the Pescadores, she might use these as a base for an all-out attack on the Chinese mainland. Had not Hideyoshi boasted in 1597 :

I intend to bring the whole of China under my rule. When I have effected this, Japan, Korea, and China will be one. I shall do this as easily as a man rolls up a piece of matting and carries it under his arm.

This grand design, announced by Hideyoshi at the shrine of Yoritimo at Tsurugoaka, might be the ambition of ' Nippon Seishen ' in 1894. If so, then it was imperative that some way be found to keep Formosa and the Perscadores out of the clutches of Japan. Already Korea was as good as a Japanese possession. That part of the plan had been accomplished. With Formosa and the Pescadores ceded to Japan, the giant Japanese pincers could crush China completely.

To circumvent such a purpose, Peking invited Britain to take over Formosa, as it was hoped, temporarily. Foreign Secretary Lord Kimberley, on behalf of the Rosebery Government, rejected the offer. Hearing of this, a French fleet sailed into Makung harbour in the Pescadores, and the commanding officer offered to take over those islands as a caretaker Government. When this offer was passed on to Liu Yung-fu, commander of the forces in south Formosa, it was flatly rejected. Remembering his experiences in Annam, where he had fought the French, he branded the offer as a ' cloak to conceal some treacherous motive '.

No course now remained for Peking but to send a delegation to Japan to discuss terms. Emperor Kuang Hsu directed Li Hung-chang, its leader, to delay as long as possible any agreement to cede Formosa to Japan. But the Japanese negotiators, Count Ito and Viscount Mutsu, were adamant from the start. Formosa and the Pescadores must be handed over. Nothing short of this would be accepted. ' After I had reached Japan, everyone heard that Japan was bent upon obtaining possession of the island ', recorded Li. He raised all the difficulties he could contrive : ' Formosa is full of malaria and the people have to use opium as a prophylactic ' ; ' Omit Formosa from the treaty until you have taken it ' ; ' Why be in such a hurry about Formosa when it is actually in your mouth ?' ; ' Two hundred millions [indemnity] are enough to appease your appetite for a time.' But such tactics were unavailing. Li ratified the treaty.

When the news reached China, the whole country was in uproar. Every governor and provincial commander memorialized the Throne to reject the cession of Formosa to Japan. Funds for the renewal of the war were guaranteed. Had it not been for the protection afforded by the Dowager Empress Tzu Hsi, Li Hung-chang would have lost his head on his return to China.

Then it was that Formosa acted. On 23 May 1895, T'ang Ching-sung, Governor of Formosa, proclaimed Formosa an

L

independent republic. ' Taiwan Min-chu Kuo ' was born. The declaration read :

Declaration of Independence of the Republic of Taiwan.

The Japanese have insulted China by annexing our territory of Taiwan. The People of Taiwan, in vain, have appealed to the Throne. Now, the Japanese are about to arrive.

If we, the People of Taiwan, permit them to land, Taiwan will become the land of savages and barbarians. If, on the other hand, we resist, our state of weakness will not be for long, as Foreign Powers have assured us that Taiwan must establish its independence before they will assist us.

Therefore, we, the People of Taiwan, are determined to die rather than be subdued by the Japanese. This decision is irrevocable.

The leaders of the People of Taiwan, in Council, have decided to constitute Taiwan, a Republic State, and all administration, hence-forth, will be in the hands of officials, elected by the People of Taiwan.

T'ang Ching-sung, Governor of Taiwan, has been appointed President of the Republic of Taiwan.

The official ceremony of inauguration of the Republic will take place on the second day of the fifth moon at the *ssu* hour, at which, all persons, those of rank, merchants, farmers, artisans, and tradesmen, will assemble at the Tuan Fang Hall.

This is a Declaration of the People of Taiwan.

President T'ang's first official act, after the ceremony had been held, was to dispatch to all viceroys and governors throughout China a message informing them of the establishment of the republic, emphasizing that ' The Republic of Taiwan recognizes the suzerainty of the Emperor of China and stands in the relation of a tributary State to China '.

Where was this republic born ? In whose mind did this determination to set up the first Asian republic originate ? This question is not just an academic exercise. On the contrary, it is of the greatest importance in any summing-up of the present position in Formosa as well as in forming any estimate of the island's future.

The official Japanese view, as expressed by Yosaburo Take-koshi in his *Japanese Rule in Formosa*, was that ' this plan was almost certainly originated in Peking or Tientsin ', and James

Davidson, who was in Formosa about that time, maintained in his *The Island of Formosa* that 'the republic was the work of officials, from first to last'. But we now know that neither of these views was correct. The decision to establish a republic in Formosa was made by the literati in the 'Mu-tan Shih She' at Taipei. The first mention of a republic was in the 'sixteen characters' message, which they sent to Emperor Kuang Hsu :

The literati and people of Taiwan are resolved to resist subjection to Japan. They will declare Taiwan an independent republic under the suzerainty of the sacred Ch'ing Dynasty.

The wall-sheets that appeared throughout Taipei emanated from the Mu-tan Shih She. One of these, pasted on the front of all the public buildings, had this :

China has been insulted by the Japanese dwarfs, who are the enemies of Taiwan. We, the literati, and all the people, must now unite to resist these barbarians, if they attempt to land in Taiwan. Whoever is sympathetic with these dwarfs, let him be killed.

It is true that the republic received both financial and military support from south China, as well as massive moral support, but the decisive step which launched the republic was taken by the literati. When, later, the Japanese succeeded in crushing it in north Formosa, the republican Government in south Formosa was continued by the one hundred literati, who elected Liu Yung-fu as their leader.

Rarely has history recorded such a phenomenon, with poets, artists, and writers taking over the affairs of government in the cause of the preservation of a culture which they considered in danger. Plato dreamed of a state governed by philosophers and Confucius visualized a state controlled by *chun tzu*, noted for their high moral character. The members of the Mu-tan Shih She were, at least some of them, philosophers; all were Confucians and champions of the Confucian way of life. Each, in his own way, by prose, by poetry, by art, was pledged to maintain the culture and civilization which had been the genius of China through the centuries. They knew little, if anything, of politics as we in our age have come to know that term. They were the guardians of a culture, the custodians of a civilization, not the demagogues of an ideology or the spokesmen of a class creed. And they could never forget that Confucius himself had quoted from the *Book of Poetry* more often than from any other classic. Had he not said that ' The Odes serve to stimulate the mind, are an aid to self-examination, and set forth the most important duties ?'

Perhaps our own civilization might have a more secure guarantee of perpetuity if government were in the hands of our literati, and not entrusted to the care of politicians.

The central figure in the Mu-tan Shih She at Taipei was Ch'iu Feng-chia. Born near Changhua, in a family the ancestors of which had migrated from Kwangtung province about the year 1680, he had come under the influence of that great scholar Wu Tzu-kuang, who inspired him with the ideals which were to be the guiding lights of his subsequent career. At the age of twenty-three he attracted the attention of T'ang Ching-sung, who had been appointed to Formosa as Inspector of Finances. As a student at the Hai-tung Academy at Tainan, where prospective candidates for the public service were trained, Ch'iu created a record by qualifying in all the tests before he was thirty years of age. Indeed, he topped the list. His first appointment was as Secretary of the Board of Works, one of the most important departments in Formosa. Then in 1891, when T'ang had been transferred to Taipei as Treasurer, he took Ch'iu with him as his assistant. At the time there was a *shih she* in the capital, but it functioned very spasmodically. The literati met at times, but the artist, the poet, and the writer made little attempt to relate his work to the needs of the people and the welfare of the island. T'ang noted this and urged Ch'iu to interest himself in the club and try to galvanize it into more dynamic action. Ch'iu needed little urging. He succeeded in disbanding the group and establishing a new *shih she* with the title ' Mu-tan Shih she ', the ' Peony Poets' Club ', a name borrowed from the famous group of Hangchow to which Su Tung-po and Huang Ting-chien had belonged in the days of Sung. It had been named after the *mu-tan*, the cream peonies that grew profusely along the banks of the West Lake.

Soon the Mu-tan Shih She at Taipei became not merely a meeting-place for the literati, where they could discuss their writings and their arts, but also the centre of resistance to anything that might threaten the civilization of which they were a part. With the increasing impacts from the West at the time, such threats, in the minds of the literati in Formosa, were many. No longer did the artists of Taipei meet just to talk of their dreams, the poets to compare their calligraphy, and the writers to discuss their points of view; all now had a national purpose, and the spirit of true culture-guardianship was injected into all their proceedings. In 1894, with China and Japan at war over Korea, the Mu-tan Shih She became the dynamic centre in Formosa. Then, in the following year, when the Japanese demands involving their island became known, the members of the club decided to take action and inform Emperor Kuang Hsu of their decision to declare the island a republic.

Not that this plan to resist was confined to the literati. The statements by Davidson and Japanese historians that the establishment of the republic and the decision to maintain it lacked popular support were not in keeping with the facts. Japanese accounts of the fighting when they landed in north Formosa mentioned the bravery of the Hakkas, who 'formed the rank and file of the opposing forces and who fought with a bravery that we were compelled to admire'. Hardly the action of men who had no stomach for the contest, and who could easily have surrendered or escaped into the mountains. The Shueh Shan range, with its innumerable caves, would have provided a haven for the entire resistance forces.

The people of Formosa were as eager as the literati to defend their civilization and tear up the Treaty of Shimonoseki and throw the fragments into the sea. Even the Taiyal tribesmen played a role of distinction in one battle in north Formosa, and later, in south Formosa, the Bunums from the mountains wiped out a Japanese force converging on the city of Tainan. The entire population of the island, Hoklos and Hakkas, and the tribesmen of the mountains, men and women alike, were united in the one effort to drive back the Japanese invader. When that failed, there lived on in their minds and hearts a bitter resentment, which deepened as the years of the Japanese occupation passed by. In fact, the period of that occupation was one series of revolts and uprisings by men called in the Japanese records 'brigands', but who were patriots whose sole purpose was to expel the Japanese from Formosa.

But to return to Ch'iu Feng-chia. During the struggle in north Formosa, which lasted only for weeks, the Formosan forces being no match for the better-equipped Japanese, supported by a powerful navy, Ch'iu travelled throughout the northern section of the island, establishing food-centres for the troops, strengthening the national morale, and impressing on one and all just what the struggle really meant. When T'ang Ching-sung fled from Formosa, the whole burden of carrying on the war rested on Ch'iu. Faced with overwhelming enemy forces, he realized that only military assistance from the Chinese mainland could save Formosa, and such help would be difficult to obtain, as the Japanese Navy led by the flagship *Matsushima*, controlled the waters of the Strait of Formosa. In these desperate circumstances Ch'iu crossed over to the Chinese mainland to contact the one man who could assist the cause of Formosa. He was Chang Chih-tung, then Governor-General at Nanking. Chang had played an important part in sending both recruits and supplies to the army during the recent war in Korea, and had been a bitter opponent of the ratification of the Shimonoseki Treaty. He had vigorously supported the establishment of the Republic of Formosa. Ch'iu fondly hoped that Chang might find some way of transporting men and munitions to north Formosa.

By the time Ch'iu reached Nanking the resistance campaign in north Formosa had collapsed. He never returned to the island, but was to play an important part in the revolutionary movement on the Chinese mainland, first as Director of Education in the Kwangtung Government led by Hu Han-min, and later as one of the delegates to the Nanking Conference, and then as a member of the Administrative Committee of the Republic of China set up in 1911. His last post was as an official of the Central Government of the Republic in 1912.

Chiu Feng-chia had named his son, born in Formosa, Nien T'ai, meaning 'in memory of Taiwan'. Ch'iu Nien T'ai is today a member of the Government of Formosa. His father's dream has been realized.

The Japanese found south Formosa a much harder nut to crack. It had been comparatively easy, in spite of their losses, to crush the resistance in the north, but in the south it was to be quite a different matter. There they were to meet opposition that was to test to the full their equipment and military technique supplied by the West. There were historic reasons for this.

All the sentiments and loyalties that people everywhere associate with their capital city were invested in Tainan, which for centuries had been the symbol of China to the people of Formosa, the living reminder of their homeland and the graves of their ancestors. This was a deep-seated devotion, irrespective of who might sit on the Dragon Throne. China was greater than any clan or any emperor. To the people of Formosa, Tainan was China. True, the capital Taipei was in Japanese hands, but Taipei was a modern city, without history, without any historic past. It had been declared the capital less than ten years earlier, whereas Tainan had been gazetted as such nearly three hundred years ago. Japanese troops parading the streets of Taipei might be a sign of the present, but to permit them, a people without any ancient history, upstarts and dwarfs, to take over Tainan would be an insult to their ancestors and the greatest sacrilege.

Over all brooded the spirit of the Great Cheng. Cheng Cheng-kung had lived in Tainan and from there his liberating armies had expelled the foreign Dutch. Surely now, in the day of dire peril, his spirit would devise some means of expelling this latest foreigner from the north. As each day brought news of the advancing Japanese, as darkness darker than night descended on Tainan, thousands thronged the street in front of the Temple of Cheng in their efforts to get into the building and light a votive candle before the image of the great hero.

Day and night the temple doors remained open. Day and

night one unbroken supplication rose from the troubled heart of
Tainan, that Cheng would once again come to the rescue of his
beloved island.   The spirit of the great deliverer infected
everybody, and even the farmers from the surrounding country-
side, who had fashioned their rude farming tools into weapons
of defence, flocked into the city.   Little did they dream how
ineffective these would be against the modern war machine of
the Japanese.   The ' San Ho Hui ', which had been formed by the
followers of Cheng Cheng-kung in 1664 and had been increasing
in numbers through the years, fanned the flames of popular
enthusiasm.   Their former slogan, ' Destroy the Manchu !', had
now become ' Destroy the Northern Dwarf !'

During the first week of September 1895 tension reached its
height.   It was then that the literati of the Tainan district, one
hundred of them, met to consider the position.   This assembly on
17 September in the Kaiyuan Temple in an outer part of Tainan
was one of the most important happenings in the history of
Formosa.   In the city itself excitement was seething as more and
more country people flocked in to hear the latest news.   Men of
the mountains were there too, fierce Bunum tribesmen.   Meanwhile, in suburban quietness, and surrounded with relics of the
Great Cheng, whose proclamation, issued in 1661, announcing
the expulsion of the Dutch from Formosa, hung on the wall, the
one hundred literati discussed the situation.   Something must
be done, for there was the grave risk of the existing tension
leading to chaos, in which case Tainan, and that meant south
Formosa, would defeat itself.   The dwarfs from the north would
not need to fire a shot.

Wall-sheets which appeared some days later suggest that the
long history of Japanese designs on Formosa was the subject
discussed by the literati.   In 1593 Hideyoshi had planned the
conquest of the south of the island and encouraged the merchants
of Kyoto and Nagasaki to open trading stations at Anping and
Wan Nien (Fengshan) to prepare the way for his armed attack
by acting as intelligence agents.   Then in 1609, Iyeyasu, the first
Tokugawa shogun, had dispatched Murayama to conquer south
Formosa.   With his 4,000 troops, he had landed just south of

Anping, but had been routed by a combined force of Chinese and tribesmen from the mountains. In 1874 a large Japanese fleet had arrived off the south Formosan coast to avenge, so the Japanese said, the execution of shipwrecked Japanese sailors by Formosan tribesmen three years earlier. But even the British Commissioner of the Maritime Customs, Henry Edgar, had said that ' an expedition of such a nature was hardly necessary to deal with a few tribesmen '. It was reported that British intervention had at that time prevented a Japanese take-over of the island. The literati firmly believed that Americans had planned this Japanese venture. In a letter from the Governor of Fukien to the American Consul at Amoy, dated 14 November 1874, the *Tao T'ai* (Administrator) of Tainan District has been quoted as complaining that ' this expedition has been planned by the former American Consul at Amoy, General Le Gendre, also one named Cassel, with others assisting '. Commander Cassel and Lieutenant Wasson, both of the American Navy, were with the Japanese fleet that sailed for Formosa. Now the Japanese, with the most powerful fleet ever seen in Formosan waters, were bombarding the island, while Japanese armies had overrun the northern portion of the island and were marching south. Already Changhua had fallen.

The literati were unanimous in agreeing that something must be done at once. The resistance in the north had not been well organized. T'ang Ching-sung had fled and Ch'iu Feng-chia was on the Chinese mainland seeking armed assistance. But even if his campaign proved successful and troops from the mainland could succeed in getting through the Japanese naval blockade, they would be too late to save Tainan and south Formosa. Some immediate action was imperative. The republic must continue in spite of the failure in the north. Some public announcement must be made to this effect without delay.

The one hundred literati decided to constitute themselves the Government and appoint Liu Yung-fu, commander of the forces in south Formosa, President of the Republic.

Immediately this was agreed, the literati went to Liu's headquarters, informed him of their decision, and on his acceptance of the official seal they had prepared, issued the following proclamation :

This independent Republic of Taiwan maintains its allegiance to the Emperor of China. The Government of the Republic of Taiwan will be conducted in unison with the Government at Peking. We shall work together as 'Twin Mountains'. When the dwarfs have been driven out of Taiwan, once more will Taiwan return to China and place itself under the direction of the Emperor.

This announcement had the immediate effect of transmuting the tension throughout south Formosa into a popular enthusiasm to wage a victorious war against the advancing Japanese. Thus was emphasized the truth that the guardianship of civilization is in the hands of a few. Earlier history had shown this, and the subsequent history of the world has demonstrated the same again and again. The human herd is never the custodian of the civilization it enjoys, in spite of all the boasts of democracy. Nor are the politicians, with their bureaucracies of professional advisers, of economists, statisticians, and the like. Not once but many times has civilization been saved and its continuance been secured by the select minds, the one hundred.

An Executive Council, consisting of seven of the literati, was constituted and commissioned to draw up the policy of the republic and devise means by which it could be carried out. Having done this, the literati retired from active participation in the Government, but maintained a watchful eye on all developments. Others, more accustomed to routine and administrative matters, took over.

This is not the place for a detailed statement of the war-time measures of the republic, except to mention that for the first time in history a state lottery was set up to provide funds for the conduct of the war and the first regular postal system in Formosa was introduced. A private system had operated previously, but to keep a check on all correspondence, especially such as was leaving the island, all letters had to carry a Government stamp. This was a form of censorship.

Never before, in the long history of the Chinese people, had such a close alliance existed between the Government and the governed. An assurance was given that when the Japanese had been driven out of Formosa, a programme of railway construction, the opening of mines, and the most attractive incentives to production and trade would be given. The lethargy which had characterized officialdom since the departure of Liu Ming-ch'uan in 1891 gave place to a new national spirit, which was evidenced throughout south Formosa. Men, women, even the children, rallied to the cause. The daughters of President Liu went into the mountains, recruiting the tribesmen, and actually led them into battle. While the famous ' Black Flags ', who had fought with Liu against the French in Annam, fought against the combined forces of Prince Fushimi and General Nogi, these Formosan tribesmen engaged in a flanking attack with their strange torpedoes. The author has seen posters that appeared in Tainan during those desperate days, depicting the flight of the Japanese pursued by these tribesmen. One of these showed a group of Japanese breaking open a long bamboo tube which the tribesmen had propelled from their powerful bows. Out of the tube a swarm of wasps was so tormenting the Japanese that they writhed in pain on the battlefield.

Such were the torpedo tubes of the men of the Formosan mountains.

But it was an unequal combat. More Japanese were arriving and the Formosan warriors were short of munitions. Fearing that the Japanese would exact severe penalties from the people of south Formosa if the struggle continued, and knowing that he could not hold out much longer, Liu decided on surrender. Through the British Consul he asked for an armistice so that terms of surrender could be discussed. These were that himself and his ' Black Flags ' be allowed to return to China and that Formosa be handed over to Japan on the understanding that, after two years, the people of the island be allowed to decide whether or not they would become Japanese subjects. He wanted to get the best he could for the people. With his Jeffersonian concept, he believed in the right, the inalienable right, of the governed. But he feared from the outset that his terms would never be accepted. Japan had her own plans for Formosa. History was to prove him right.

Liu escaped to China on board the British ship *Thales*, disguised as an ordinary passenger among the 1,400 refugees, with a child in his arms. There he died in 1917, a copy of the *Ch'ien Chia Shih*, the famous collection of T'ang and Sung poems, by his side and open at the page on which was brushed the poem :

> Some, like a heap of grass, in wild confusion turn,
> O'er earth and heaven, their glaring flames would burn ;
> But some, like steady fires of coal would glow,
> And their surroundings cheer with warmth but little show.

Liu Yung-fu was of the first, a ' glaring flame ', at times wild and confused. In Tainan he had been nicknamed ' T'angt'u ' because of his staccato speech and disregard for ceremony. In his earlier campaigning against the French in Annam he had been known as the ' Black Warrior ' and his troops as the ' Black Flags ', from the small triangular black flag, on which was the figure of a tortoise, which each had attached to his horse's mane. Like Alexander the Great, Liu had his Bucephalus, which none but himself had ever ridden. He had called it ' T'u ' after the famous steed ' of colour like glowing charcoal, with not a hair of another colour ', which Lu Fu rode in his exploits, 'crossing rivers, ascending mountains as if they were plains, and travelling a thousand *li* a day '. Lu Fu was the ' irresistible ' spearman in Lo Kuan-chung's great ' Romance of the Three Kingdoms ', the *San Kuo Chih Yen I*.

In 1881, when France occupied Hanoi in her campaign to gain an entry into the rich mineral province of Yunnan, Chang Chih-tung, then Governor-General of Kwangtung–Kwangsi, encouraged Liu Yung-fu and his ' Black Flags ', at that time a band of banditti, to attack the French. They succeeded in driving the French out of Hanoi, in which battle the French commander, Henri-Laurent Rivière, was killed. But Liu was not able to hold the city for long, and the arrival of large French reinforcements regained the Annamese capital. Peking's refusal to honour the secret agreement which Li Hung-chang had made with the French in 1885, under which all Chinese troops were to be withdrawn from Annam, led the French to retaliate. They attacked Foochow and crossed the Strait of Formosa and bombarded Keelung in north Formosa. These were not just retaliatory acts occasioned by Peking's bad faith over Annam; they were designed to offset Britain's growing influence in China.

After a period of convalescence, during which the ' Black Flags ' healed their wounds and rested their horses, Liu decided to offer his force to Peking, to be integrated into the regular army. From then on, for several years, Liu and his ' Black Flags ' had been used against the French in the Yuling mountains, separating the Chinese province of Kwangsi from Tongking, and in suppressing revolts in Kwangsi and Yunnan provinces.

The rider of the black horse was well on his way to the top of the mountain. Liu Yung-fu, former bandit leader, was now the favourite of Peking.

In 1893 Chang Chih-tung recommended his appointment as Commander of the southern defences of Formosa. Liu and his ' Black Flags ' had arrived at Tainan at the time when developments in Korea, which culminated in the Sino-Japanese war of 1894, were becoming ominous for Formosa. His instructions were to build up the defences of Formosa so that the island could become a bastion of defence against any plans to occupy Formosa by Japan or the West.

These had now proved ineffective and the Republic of Formosa had been destroyed. But the spirit which had inspired its creation lived on in the minds and hearts of the people of the island. It was deathless, but long and bitter years were ahead. The greater part of Tainan, symbol of the Formosan attachment to the Chinese mainland, was in ruins, but one day the phoenix must arise from the ashes. Japanese occupation was to be powerless to suppress that love of freedom, born in the far-off days of Cheng Cheng-kung, and kept alive through the years by the songs of the poets, the brushes of the painters, and for a few short months by the ill-fated ' Taiwan Min-chu Kuo '.

Western historians of China who have mentioned Formosa, and these have been few, have been disposed to ignore the existence of that republic. Evidently they judged it by the length of its life rather than by its deeper significance. It is true that it operated for only a few months, and that it regarded itself as a caretaker for the Emperor in Peking. It is also true that the presidents, T'ang Ching-sung and Liu Yung-fu, had been elected not by the people, but by a group of literati. But it was a time of grave emergency. Also, it must be noted that whilst these literati were agreed that, during the crisis, the Government must act as a caretaker for the Emperor in Peking, they were sharply divided as to the future. The older among them favoured reform, but the younger were on the side of revolution. They were convinced that the existing monarchical system in China had been impotent in the face of the increasing challenge from both Japan and the West. They saw revolution and not reformation as the need of the future. China needed not a physician but a surgeon, for China was very sick.

This revolutionary spirit of the younger literati infected the youth of Formosa. As Chang Chi-yun noted in his *A History of Taiwan* :

Such an independent spirit can be traced back to the pioneer fathers who would not submit to Manchu rule. They fled the mainland and established themselves on this island [Taiwan] where they could enjoy freedom and from which, they hoped, they would fight back and bring freedom to their mother country. Such a patriotism and love of freedom, as the guiding principle of all the pioneers, had passed on to their descendants, so that there were few Taiwanese who were not brought up in a revolutionary spirit.

On the Chinese mainland a similar division was to exist for years. There were to be reformers of varying degrees of radicalism, with missionary support and counsel. Emperor Kuang Hsu himself was to lend support for this reformation. Sun Yat-sen, however, did not believe that doses of Western physic would ever heal China. He demanded surgery, the cutting out of the monarchy and all that went with it — revolution and the establishment of a republic.

Was there any connection between the manifesto issued by the Hsing Chung Hui, the revolutionary group set up by Sun Yat-sen in Honolulu, and the republic established in Formosa? The manifesto, issued on 24 November 1894, stated that the aim of the Hsing Chung Hui was 'the establishment of a republican government in China'. This was just six months before the republic was proclaimed in Formosa. It is a fact of history that Sun Yat-sen, who had moved the headquarters of the Hsing Chung Hui to Hong Kong in February 1895, planned an armed assault on Canton as the signal for the revolutionary uprising aimed at setting up a republic in China, during the same month as the republic in Formosa collapsed, October 1895.

That attempt was to prove a tragic failure, but sixteen years later success was to be assured and the Republic of China established, with its capital at Nanking.

During those years the full story of the Republic of Formosa crossed the Formosa Strait to south China. From Fukien to Szechwan it circulated, flaming the spirit of revolt. Mrs. Archibald Little, in China at the time, noted that whereas ' the populace of Peking appeared to be in total ignorance of what was going on ', in south China, especially in far distant Szechwan, ' I had not believed the people capable of so much feeling '. She was referring to the failure of the Republic of Formosa. Refugees from Formosa flocked to south China, one ship conveying no less than 1,400 of these. The stories of these refugees, each of whom had fought in the republican armies, men and women, would have helped to spread the flames of revolt throughout south China, and thus make possible the victory of 1911. Indeed, it might be said that the Republic of China, inaugurated at Nanking in 1911, had been born in Formosa in 1895.

It is well to remember this, for it may be that what is happening in Formosa today may be a pointer to the ultimate solution of the present China problem.

CHAPTER NINE

The Japanese Occupation

FORMOSA was now a Japanese colony, after 212 years as part of the Chinese Empire. After the first ten years of Japanese occupation, the Japanese historian, Yosaburo Takekoshi, published his account of the position in Formosa:

> When Formosa first came into our possession, and we, Japanese, commenced to colonize it, we were ourselves anxious as to what the result would be. As it was our first attempt, we naturally made some mistakes; but, notwithstanding these mistakes, good work has been done. Peace has been restored, order prevails, the productive power of the island has increased, the Government is respected and trusted, and on every hand are seen evidences of life and prosperity....

> When Viscount Kodama took office, he called together all the leading men in the island who held Chinese degrees, and held a meeting in Taihoku [Taipei] for the encouragement of learning. In this way he manifested his respect for the learned, and also attested his purpose to devote himself to the development of culture and enlightenment in the island, leaving no stone unturned to adapt himself to the manners and customs of the natives and to pacify the disturbed minds of the people.

Today, in 1965, with all the available material for our examination, we are able to see to what extent this programme was carried out during the fifty years of Japanese occupation and to discover just what the Japanese purpose in Formosa really was. At the same time, the spirit of the people of Formosa will reveal itself.

Japanese occupation of Formosa was designed, from the outset, to be the first step in a campaign of imperialist expansion.

For centuries Japan had been dependent on China. From the despised Middle Kingdom she had borrowed her religion,

Ch'iu Feng-chia, founder of the Republic of Formosa in 1895.

Lien Heng, anthologist of the Japanese occupation period.

writing, music, architecture, even her cooking. When she decided to build a capital city, her builders were sent to the T'ang capital in Shensi to draw their plans, and Nara and Kyoto became mere imitations of Ch'ang-an. Gradually this dependence on China appeared to Japanese scholars as a wound on the body of their country.

Then, from 1853, the year Commodore Perry and his American fleet appeared in Uraga Bay, Japan had turned her eyes towards the West, with its ships of war, its guns, and its technology. She began to imitate the West. To the scholars of Japan, this new dependence, this time on the West, intensified the sense of inferiority. The wounds on the body of Japan were aggravated. They began to fester.

Out of this sense of national inferiority, first to China and then to the West, was born a megalomania which saw Japan as the divine country, to which all others would bow the knee, and from which a new civilization, a synthesis of Japanese culture and Western technology, would spread throughout the seven seas, 'To conquer the world and embrace the universe as our State', as General Araki was later to write in his *Problems of Japan in the Showa Era*. To this end, he added :

Our Imperial morality, which is the embodiment of the combination of the true spirit of the Japanese State with the great ideals of the Japanese people, must be preached and spread over the whole world. All obstacles standing in the path of this must be resolutely removed even if it is necessary to apply real force.

The occupation of Formosa in 1895 was the first move towards this end. It was the first medicament for the healing of Japan's historic wounds.

But the lust of empire has always been to expand. The tragedy of the Japanese occupation of Formosa was destined to be seen not only on the island itself, in the lives of the people there, but years later, when, from bases in south Formosa, Japanese bombers were to blast Allied cities and bases throughout the Pacific.

From the outset, Japanese migration to Formosa was not encouraged. She was constantly complaining of population pressure at home, but with the exception of a small number who

M

settled in Formosa as farmers, the Japanese in Formosa were
either in the armed forces, in Government service, or directors of
industrial enterprises. Migrants from China were not admitted,
for, as Yosaburo Takekoshi stated, ' They would make the island
altogether too Chinese ', a thing Japan did not want. It would
have proved a serious obstacle to Japanese plans.

These plans called for the economic development of the island.
To achieve this, the Chinese population was regimented in the
most ruthless manner, which would have shocked even a doctrinaire Western Socialist. All industries were controlled by the
Government, which was concerned only with the exploitation
of the island. This, combined with the abject subjection of the
population and the construction of military bases, was the
Japanese purpose in Formosa. Lest land-hungry farmers in
Japan be disposed to settle in the island, all official pronounce-
ments in Japan relating to Formosa emphasized the ' excessive
heat ' of the climate, and the Emperor, in congratulating the
Governor-General on his achievements, made mention of the
' hot and most unfavourable climate ' of Formosa.

Japan was determined to spare her own people the system she
was enforcing on the people of Formosa.

During the occupation years the island made remarkable
economic progress. This was made possible by the plans which
Liu Ming-ch'uan had drawn up when he was Governor. The
Japanese followed these and extended them. The land survey
in 1909 resulted in large areas coming under sugar production,
which contributed largely to Formosa's achieving economic
solvency by 1915 and contributing 100 million yen annually
to the Government in Tokyo. During the First World War,
when all foreign enterprises were ousted from Formosa, the
textile, chemical, and machinery industries made startling progress
and Formosa was well on the way to becoming one of the most
advanced regions in East Asia. To meet the needs of war in
1931, when Sino-Japanese hostilities began, Formosa became a
valuable base for heavy industries. The power plant erected at
the Sun Moon Lake made cheap and abundant power available,
and the economic prosperity of the island reached new record

heights. In 1938, most of the 1·2 million tons of rice produced in Formosa went to Japan, and of the 1·46 million tons of sugar produced, 1 million tons were shipped to Japan. In all, 90 per cent of all Formosan production for export went to Japan.

The Japanese plan was working. In 1941, just before Japan entered the Second World War, official statistics showed that for every 18 Chinese in Formosa there was a Japanese official, either connected with the administration, or a farm-production supervisor, or an industrial director, or an export agent. Regimentation always spawns a multitude of officials.

But what of the people?

The Japanese plan for Formosa had to be discriminatory. Its success depended on this. Accordingly, the Japanese, like all the champions of regimentation everywhere, imposed heavy taxation. The host of officials had to be maintained and the heavy cost of the armed forces met. The capitation tax applied not only to every member of the Chinese farmer's family but also his pigs, dogs, cats, geese, and chickens. This, together with the land tax, had the desired effect. Unable to meet the demands, the farmer had to surrender his right to the land, which soon became the property of the Government. From then on, the farmer became the tenant, producing rice and sugar for the tables of Japan, whilst he and his family lived on sweet potatoes. This confiscation led to corruption. Many highly placed Japanese became owners of land on which the Chinese farmer worked as a tenant. He had been taxed out of his land, in much the same way in which foreigners were taxed out of their business holdings in China in more recent years by the Communists.

From the outset it was made clear that the Chinese in Formosa were a conquered people and therefore could not claim any political rights.

If the Japanese Empire should venture to apply the [Japanese] Constitution to Formosa, the only result will be commotion and disorder. Japanese and Formosans would enjoy equal civic and political rights and it would be impossible to discriminate between the ruling and the conquered races . . . .

Such a course must be postponed until the Formosan sense of

loyalty towards the home country [Japan] has been more fully deepened and strengthened.

The Japanese writer of those words admitted that ' the Formosan Chinese have no love for Japan, and to give them the privileges of our Constitution would be to teach them to rise up in revolt against us '. Hardly a compliment to the Japanese Constitution !

All education was designed to further the imperialist purpose of Japan. The ' unique and divine culture of Japan ', to quote the phrase common in Japan at the time, and used so frequently later by Baron Hiranuma, must be embraced by the people of Formosa, who, according to Yosaburo Takekoshi, were ' satisfied simply to send their children to the village teacher's house to be taught merely to read the books of Confucius and Mencius '. All this had to be changed, as he recorded :

It was under such conditions as these that the Government opened schools and began to teach the people the Japanese language, which they despised, and Japanese history, which they had no wish to learn.

No attempt was made to disguise the basic purpose of the Japanese authorities. This was to assimilate the people of Formosa with the Japanese so that they could be instruments in furthering the grand design of Japan.

When civil administration was introduced, the authorities adopted the assimilation idea. Government schools were opened in fifteen districts. In these, Japanese language and history were the principal studies and all graduates were employed as interpreters.

For specialized education, normal schools were established where selected students were trained in trades and crafts essential to the success of Japanese expansion. The more proficient among these went to Japan for further instruction. All instruction in these normal schools was in Japanese.

The doors to a general advanced education were closed to the native-born Formosans. A university was established at Taihoku, the capital, but it was for Japanese students, and few Formosans passed through its doors. Its benefits were for the sons of the master race. Only one Formosan ever succeeded in attaining the status of a lecturer, and his work was strictly limited.

A Spanish priest, Bartolomé Martinez, who lived in Formosa for forty years, most of them during the Japanese occupation, assured H. A. Franck during his visit to the island in 1925 that the educational policy of Japan in Formosa was 'designed to elevate the Japanese and maintain the subject status of the Formosans ':

Primary schools for the Japanese and the Formosans are separate, but the Formosan children must learn Japanese, since teachers are forbidden to teach in the Formosan language. No Formosan child can go to a government school unless he can speak Japanese, and, according to a new ruling, no more private schools can be opened. There are still a few tutor schools, but even in these, Japanese must be taught.

He affirmed further that ' the more stupid Japanese always gets any available government position first, can rise higher, and is paid from fifty to eighty per cent more for the same work than a Formosan '.

This Spanish priest must not be confused with the first Bartolomé Martinez, the ' Apostle to Formosa ' of the seventeenth century, after whom he had been named.

As there was little hope of the adult population learning to speak Japanese, at least the names of their towns and villages must bear Japanese names. So it was that every settlement throughout the island, from the largest city to the smallest aboriginal village in the mountains, was renamed. Henceforth it was to bear the mark of the divine conqueror and fly the flag of the Rising Sun. There were some villages which defied the order and continued to fly the republican flag, a yellow tiger on a blue background, but summary action ended that ' insult to our divine emblem ', as one Japanese record had it.

Formosa was looked upon as ' a southern wilderness ', to quote Yosaburo Takekoshi. Hence the people who lived there had no claim to be treated in the same way as the superior and highly civilized Japanese. There was one law for an offending Japanese, another for a Formosan. A British scientist, who spent several years in Formosa during the Japanese occupation, has placed on record a vivid description of the treatment of the Formosans :

During my residence in Formosa I personally saw instances of the most hideous cruelty on the part of the Japanese toward the Chinese-Formosans, and of barbaric torture, officially inflicted, as punishment for the most trivial offences.

It seems probable that, under the dominance of the Japanese, the Aborigines of Formosa will, in a few decades, or, at the longest, in a century or two, have ceased to exist as a people.

In her summing-up of the prospects in Formosa under Japanese rule, that scientist, Janet McGovern, put her finger on the basic cause of the problem, the Japanese belief in their superior culture and their appointed mission to spread this throughout the world :

No race, whatever its virility or potentiality for development, can long survive the military despotism of a conquering people ; especially when that conquering people is consistently ruthless in the methods its adopts for crushing out the racial individualities of the peoples whom it conquers.

But there was a force, working beneath the surface in Formosa, which Japanese ruthlessness could not destroy. The first Governor-General, Count Kabayama, had reported to the Emperor in Tokyo that ' the island is now pacified ', and his successors, probably to win favour at court, continued to repeat this report. But the fact is that Formosa was never pacified, from the day the Japanese occupied the island in 1895 until they left in 1945. The author has examined all the available Japanese records of the period of the occupation, and these show that from 1895 to 1920 the number of persons arrested for attempts to overthrow the Japanese was never less than 8,200 in any year ; that from 1921 to 1930 the lowest figure for any year was 6,500 ; and from 1931 to 1940 the number was never below 3,450 in any one year. During the entire occupation there were nineteen major uprisings, all brutally suppressed.

The Formosans involved in these activities were officially

branded as ' brigands ', but they have ever been remembered among the people of the island as patriots, fighting for the freedom of Formosa against one of the most brutal despotisms in history.

Behind all these risings were the literati, who, from their *shih she*, spread throughout the island, kept alive the spirit of resistance and the soul of freedom. That soul, crushed but never subdued, expressed itself in poetry. By day the people toiled and sweated under the watchful eyes of their Japanese masters, but at night their choicest sons gathered in their poets' clubs to talk and sing of the coming revolution.

Lien Heng of Tainan, who lived through the greater part of the occupation years, collected many of these songs as he wandered from town to town, and gave them to the world in his *Flowers of Taiwan*. Some of the poems in this anthology remind one of the nocturnes of Chopin, filled with sighs and sadness, laments for the passing of the freedom once enjoyed, now that ' the Japanese rule, with iron hand, the people of Taiwan '. In other poems we can see the peering of wistful eyes across the water to the Chinese mainland, where the new republic had been established.

> The mainland has, at last, been recovered,
> But, alas, Taiwan still suffers under foreign bondage.

These were poems of protest, outpourings of rebellious souls. The Formosan body had been bound, but not the Formosan mind. The Japanese had not yet learnt the art of *hsi-nao*, the technique of brain-washing. They had subdued the land, but not the minds of its people, who continued to express their love of freedom in their songs. One day the brushes of the literati were to prove more powerful than the swords of the Japanese jackbooters.

This hope was set forth in the poems of the dawn, which fill the greater part of Lien Heng's anthology, songs of the ' brigands', from one end of Formosa to the other. In the early years of the Japanese occupation the ' Brotherhood of the Free ', formed by Lin Ho-wan, Lin Shao-hua, and Lin Shao-tsun, in Giran, the present Ilan, had one of these songs as their ' Marseillaise ', and later the ' Army of the Night ' at Hozan, now Fengshan, in south Formosa, was to march into battle and drive back the picked troops of the Japanese singing one of these songs of the dawn.

' If a man were permitted to make all the ballads, he need not care who should make the laws ', wrote Andrew Fletcher of Saltoun, a century earlier. So it was with Formosa and the songs that Lien Heng collected, the songs the literati had written, during the dark night of the Japanese occupation of the island. In villages and towns these songs became the secret strength of the people. They enabled them to endure the pains of unspeakable wounds and suffer hardships of innumerable wrongs.

This power of the poet in Formosa, singing his crusade and assuming the true leadership of his people, found an echo, far to the south, in the Australian Bernard O'Dowd :

They tell you the poet is useless and empty the sound of his lyre,
That science has made him a phantom and thinned to a shadow his fire :
Yet reformer has never demolished a dungeon or den of the foe
But the flame of the soul of the poet pulsated in every blow.
When, comrades, we thrill to the message of speaker in highway or hall,
The voice of the poet is reaching the silenter poet in all ;
And again, as of old, when the flames are to leap up the turrets of
          Wrong,
Shall the torch of the New Revolution be lit from the words of a song.

The words of a song !

The words of the songs of the literati in Formosa, an island described at the time by an American visitor ' as strictly under Japanese exploitation as its people are politically under the rule of Japanese militarists ', pointed the way to the Cairo Declaration of 1943 and its reaffirmation at Potsdam in 1945. This, in turn, cleared the way for the Sino-Japanese Peace Treaty later that year, under which Japan renounced all right, title, and claim to Formosa and the Pescadores.

The Japanese occupation had ended. Gained by the sword, it was lost by the sword. Formosa returned as a province of China.

The despots gone, the literati emerged from the seclusion of the *shih she* to join the populace in their songs of victory and liberation. Gone was the frustration and silent the protests. The new song rang through the island, from Keelung to Hengchun and from Changhua to Hwalien, till the distant mountains echoed the strains :

> San Min Chu I, our aim shall be,
> To found a free land, with world peace our stand.
> Lead on, Comrades, vanguards you are,
> Hold fast your aim, by sun and star.
> Earnest and brave, your country to save,
> One heart, one soul, one mind, one goal.

It was Sun Yat-sen's battle hymn of the Republic of China.

Only a few would not sing it, those whom the defeated Japanese had inspired to resist the return of Formosa to China.

CHAPTER TEN

Sun Yat-sen and Formosa

In September of the year 1900, a stranger, a Chinese, had arrived in Taihoku, capital of the Japanese colony of Formosa. For his times, he was a much-travelled man. He knew America and had been in London where he had had a most dramatic experience. The Chinese Legation had actually kidnapped him, with the idea of returning him to China to be dealt with as a rebel. A good English friend had rescued him. Then he had almost lived at the British Museum. On his daily walk from the cheap boarding-house to the museum he had had to pass through slums, which made him think hard. There seemed to be a great disparity between the social theories of the time and actual conditions. It had seemed to him that Britain, like China, had her liberal Chang Chih-tung and her radical K'ang Yu-wei, professed reformers, but without any panacea for their country's ills.

Leaving Britain he had visited several European countries and then crossed to Canada on his way to Japan. From there he had gone to Hong Kong, then the headquarters of the ' Hsing Chung Hui ', the secret revolutionary society he had formed in Honolulu back in 1894. But the authorities in Hong Kong were not happy with his presence on the island. Peking had made it clear to the British that it would regard any permit to this ' rebel ' to remain in Hong Kong as an unfriendly act. So he had had to return to Japan. From there he had gone south to Formosa. The Japanese had made no objection to that.

The two months that Sun Yat-sen spent in Formosa were to be among the most decisive of his life. A virtual refugee, a wanderer in many lands and among many peoples, he was now among his own, among Chinese, whose own experiences made it easy for them to understand his plans.

In the *Pictorial Biography of Sun Yat-sen*, published by the Historical Archives Commission in Formosa, there is a drawing of Sun Yat-sen, with the caption ' Dr. Sun on the seashore of Taiwan, looking towards the Chinese mainland '. The editor, Chia-luen Lo, states that this was done by an artist according to the detailed description given by those present at the time. Sun Yat-sen stands on a large rock, binoculars in hand, as the succession of waves rolls shoreward, looking towards the west. There is a sadness on his face, the look of a baffled man. Yet behind the sadness, one glimpses a calculating mind, planning something. Perhaps a vision of what that homeland beyond the turbulent water will yet be. Significantly, he is looking south-west, to Kwangtung and Fukien. Yes, he can see something, for out of the sadness there is developing a fixed stare. Sun Yat-sen has seen something.

It is not difficult to diagnose the mind of that watcher on the Tamsui shore, as the events of the past moved in panorama before his inner eye. The very island on which he stood had for centuries been the centre of the revolutionary spirit. The flames of revolt had been kept burning by the zeal of the ' San Ho Hui ', the secret society formed by the followers of Cheng Cheng-kung after his death. From its headquarters in Formosa, this organization had inspired the creation of similar groups, with a revolutionary purpose, in Fukien, Kwangtung, and Kwangsi on the Chinese mainland. Here he was, on the very spot of this power-house, meeting and talking with the men who supplied the dynamism of this ever-expanding campaign.

During the centuries of Manchu rule in Formosa, the ' San Ho Hui ' had worked underground, ready to surface at any opportune moment. Such a time had been in 1721, when Chu I-kwei had staged a revolt, and again in 1786, when Lin Shuang-wen had nearly succeeded. Then there had been the Lin–Wang campaign of 1813, which could have changed the history of his country had not Lin acted ahead of the date agreed on. Lin Ch'ing was to advance on Peking, while Wang K'ung and Ko K'uang marched on the Manchu garrison at Tamsui. Lin's premature move gave Peking time to warn the Tamsui garrison, with the result that the revolutionaries, who had spread the revolt from Tainan to Changhua, found themselves faced with a formidable force at Tamsui, well equipped and ready for battle. Sun Yat-sen, when a boy, had heard the full story from the village school-teacher.

But the most vivid sight of all, as he peered across the water, was of himself in 1872, then a six-year-old boy, in the Chui Heng village tea-house, into which he would creep to hear the tales of the T'ai P'ing veterans and especially those told by one ' old man, whose fascinating story never tired one with the retelling '. These old farmers, chatting over the prices of their farm products and reminiscing over their past exploits, had been on the long march from Kwangsi to Nanking, following the standard of Hung Hsui-ch'uan, and had climbed the walls of the burning Nanking to escape the avenging swords of the Manchus. To the boy Sun Tai-cheong, as he was then named, these old men were the real heroes. Later he was to learn how the story of the Hakkas' prosperity in Formosa had been one of the inspirations that led Hung Hsui-ch'uan on, over mountains and rivers, right to Nanking itself, and how, when faced with the prospect of defeat, he had sent Henry Burgevine across to Formosa to enlist assistance.

Little could he have dreamed that day, as he stood at Tamsui, looking across the waters of the Strait of Formosa, that one day, as Provisional President of the Republic of China, he would pray before the tomb of Chu Yuan-chang, and in his prayer to the spirit of the Great Ming mention the ' worthy campaign ' of Hung Hsui ch'uan, the leader of those Hakka farmers, whose stories had so drawn him each day to the village tea-house twenty-eight years earlier.

Then there was the bitter memory of the failure in 1895, exacerbated by the humiliations which his country had since suffered. Germany has seized Kiaochow Bay and forced Peking to grant a 99-year lease ; Russia had secured a 25-year lease of Dairen and Port Arthur ; France was demanding a similar lease of Kwangchow Bay and an assurance that Hainan Island would never be handed over ; and Britain, not content with Weihaiwei and a 99-year lease of the Kowloon peninsula, had wrested from Peking a guarantee that no other Power be granted a sphere of influence in the Yangtze area.

China, his country, was being carved up as the great powers sat around the feasting-table brandishing their swords. And all the time Peking submitted.

There was but one redeeming spark in the vision that passed before the eye of Sun Yat-sen that day on the Formosan shore. The secret presses in Shanghai, Hong Kong, and Macao, beyond the reach of Peking and its prohibitions, were rolling out their revolutionary literature. Here, at least, was hope for the future.

As he returned from Tamsui to the city, passing through the many groups of Japanese soldiers and officials, all of whom symbolized the despotism under which his people sweated in Formosa, his mind was made up. It was now the time for action. And there must not be a second failure.

At a conference with leaders of the ' San Ho Hui ', Sun Yat-sen outlined his campaign. He himself would take supreme command. He arranged for supplies of arms from Japan, and a number of Japanese officers in Formosa were ready to assist in the campaign. Cheng Shih-liang was on his way from Japan to Fukien to direct operations in that province, and Li Kiang-jo was already in Kwangtung. The uprising would begin simultaneously in both provinces as soon as he, Sun Yat-sen, received advice that the arms from Japan had arrived. He would then proceed to south China with the trained personnel.

When the plan was outlined to the literati, the younger members were jubilant, as they had favoured a complete break with the Manchu Government five years earlier when the republic had been set up. They considered that the humiliations China had suffered at the hands of foreign powers were the result of the impotence of Peking to safeguard China's rights. Unless the Manchu was deposed and a republican Government established, which could gain the confidence of the people, in a short time China would be so parcelled out among the powers that only a small area in the north would still remain to the Chinese.

Fired by the enthusiasm of Sun Yat-sen, the ' San Ho Hui ' and the literati in Formosa saw victory as certain. Then China would stand firm and demand from the powers the abolition of all the unequal treaties and the return of their ill-gotten gains. No longer would China bite the dust, but would claim her place as an equal among the nations of the modern world.

Meanwhile, Cheng, who had arrived at Amoy, and Li in Kwangtung, waited for the signal from Formosa to begin operations. But that word did not come. Sun Yat-sen had been informed that a change of Government in Japan had resulted in a decision that all support for the revolutionary movement in China must cease. That meant no arms from Japan, and no officers from Formosa. Unaware of this decision and impatient with the delay, Cheng and Li decided to launch the rising on their own account. At the outset, this promised success. A writer in *Outlook*, a Mr. E. Lynch, described what he saw :

When I went through Southern China in October [1900] for the purpose of seeing something of the rebellion, which was in progress there near Canton, I was perpetually hearing of Sun Yat-sen. He was the organiser, the invisible leader, the strange mysterious personality, whose power was working in all. Sometimes, one heard that he was in Formosa, sometimes in Hongkong in disguise, and sometimes in a district close to that in which the rebellion was in progress, and which would shortly flare up in insurrection.

This mystery surrounding the whereabouts of Sun Yat-sen was quite understandable, as he had never left Formosa. He knew, then, that the second venture was doomed to failure. Nor was he surprised when he received the heart-breaking news that Cheng and Li had failed. Once again the revolutionary spirit had to master the agony of a munitionless retreat.

Sun Yat-sen left Formosa to continue his wanderings in search of that aid that would make his campaign for a free China triumphant, if not in his day, then at some time in the future. He refused to admit defeat. His unconquerable spirit, dedicated to the one republican objective, was confident of victory sooner or later. Throughout the eleven years that were to transpire before his vision was realized, Formosa was to be his source of inspiration. His two months there had put iron into his blood and steeled his spirit so that he was able to rise above all disappointments and become more convinced than ever of ultimate victory. Formosa saved Sun Yat-sen. So certain was he now that he would achieve his ambition and reach his goal, that he began to plan the reconstruction of China after the revolution. It was shortly after he left Formosa that he began to work on his ' San Min Chu I ' (Three People's Principles), which he outlined for the first time in Belgium in 1905.

Sun Yat-sen never forgot Formosa, where, as a baffled man, he had found both inspiration and healing. In 1911, when success crowned his long struggle, he revisited the island, then again in 1918, and yet again in 1924, the year before his death.

It may be that the final estimate of Sun Yat-sen has yet to be written. To the Western mind there are so many irreconcilables in his record. On the other hand, these may all find their explanation in the *yang–yin* philosophy of the Chinese mind. However, his influence over the Chinese people everywhere remains second only to that of Confucius. Even the Communists have honoured his memory, although they have twisted his political and economic teachings. That he was able to reach such stature among Chinese everywhere was due largely to the impact Formosa had on him. It is conceivable that had he not visited that island in 1900, his subsequent career, though it would have continued, might not have been so rewarding.

Sun Yat-sen, known to the Chinese as the ' Father of the Republic ', had his spiritual baptism in Formosa.

What, then, was the secret of that Formosan influence over Sun Yat-sen? Wherein was its magic power? What did it possess that was not to be found, in any striking measure, either in China or among the Chinese communities throughout the world which he visited? Possibly this was the large number of literati in Formosa, who favoured not reformation but revolution. In China the scholars, or a large number of them, were on the side of reform, and just two years before Sun Yat-sen arrived in Formosa they had launched their reform campaign, which won the sympathy of the Emperor Kuang Hsu. The literati in south

China, especially, were all for reform. The Europeans in China, especially the missionaries, exercised a not inconsiderable influence on this reform campaign. But in Formosa the position was entirely different. Though under Japanese domination, the literati there were still Chinese and they followed the movement in China very closely. Some of the older among them were with the reformers, but the great majority were of a revolutionary mind. They did not consider that any reformation, however drastic, could save China. Nothing short of revolution could effect this. This was precisely what Sun Yat-sen had come to believe. His long hours spent in the British Museum had persuaded him that revolution in China, leading to the overthrow of the Manchu monarchy and the establishment of a republic, was the only answer to his country's problems.

Sun Yat-sen sensed, from the moment he landed in Formosa, that he had more in common with the literati there than with those on the Chinese mainland.

This revolutionary temper of the literati in Formosa is not difficult to understand. In one sense it was un-Chinese, for in the long history of China there had been many rebellions, but few attempts at revolution. But the position of the literati in Formosa was unique. Whereas the bulk of the migrants from south China to Formosa had gone to that island for economic reasons, the literati had migrated for an entirely different reason. They had sought freedom from the intellectual serfdom that the Ch'ing emperors, from the time of K'ang Hsi, had imposed on all scholars. To suppress any criticism of the dynasty, both K'ang Hsi and Yung Cheng had ordered books by scholars to be burnt. This campaign of suppression had reached its peak in 1786, when the rising in Formosa led by Lin Shuang-wen had challenged the authority of Ch'ien Lung over that island. Fu Kang-an, Governor of Fukien, had sent 10,000 picked troops across to Formosa to quell the rebellion, but they had met with such popular opposition that Ch'ien Lung decided on a nation-wide assault on the literati.

This was done in a subtle manner. He would compile a compendium of Chinese literature, with reference to ' every

Chen Cheng, pioneer of land reform in Formosa

known work of antiquity, as well as everything in print, from the pen of well-known authors and poets, to be collected, revised, and reprinted at the expense of the government '. This *Ssu-k'u Ch'uan Shu* would be the glory of his reign. Everybody possessing a rare book was invited to send it to Peking, for loan or sale. On the surface this seemed a most praiseworthy enterprise, but subsequent events revealed the Emperor's real purpose, which was to discover the names of those literati who were opposed to the ruling dynasty. The inquisition that followed led not only to the burning of thousands of books and the execution of many scholars, but also the flight of hundreds of the literati across the sea to Formosa. By the year 1800 that island had become the haven, the place of refuge, for thousands of the best Chinese scholars.

These literati passed on their legacy of freedom of thought to the men who had set up the Republic of Formosa in 1895 and who welcomed Sun Yat-sen in 1900.

Ch'ien Lung's method was not new. Back in 213 B.C., Emperor Shih Huang Ti had adopted a similar device. On the advice of his chief adviser, the infamous Li Ssu, he had arranged a brilliant assembly, to which the leaders of the literati were invited. During the proceedings these had been invited to speak openly, if they had any ideas for the improvement of affairs. One responded and expressed his mind freely, with the result that he was summarily executed. He had fallen into the same trap as Mao Tse-tung was to set centuries later with his ' Let a Hundred Flowers Bloom ' proposal.

The literati in Formosa in 1900 who talked with Sun Yat-sen knew that the one revolution that had promised most success in the past, the T'ai P'ing, had failed mainly because its leader, Hung Hsui-ch'uan, had not attempted to gain the support of the literati. His armies had won battles and extended their rule over a large area of China, but as the T'ai P'ing leaders knew nothing of the art of government, the revolution was doomed to defeat. They had not realized that, throughout the long history of China, government had been in the hands of such as qualified at the public examinations. In the minds of the literati of Formosa,

N

no armed revolution could be effective without the support of scholars to take over when the armies had completed their task.

This philosophy was the source of the inspiration which Sun Yat-sen found in Formosa. It was to shape the whole future of his revolutionary thinking. Whatever misgivings or hesitations may have disturbed his mind were all resolved during his visit to Formosa. The literati there had put steel into his soul.

When he left the island he was a transfigured man, and the influence of those literati was to remain with him for the rest of his days. It was a compelling impulse from which he could not escape. The very presence on the Chinese mainland of Chi'iu Feng-chia, the scholar who had been the inspiration of the short-lived Republic of Formosa five years earlier, was in itself sufficient to ensure this.

Once again, Formosa had set the pattern that the Chinese mainland was to follow. In 1887 Taipei had been the first Chinese city to be electrified ; in 1889 the first Chinese railway was in operation in Formosa ; in 1895 the first republic in Chinese history had been set up there ; now, in 1900, Sun Yat-sen, who eleven years later was to establish the republic on the Chinese mainland, learned the secret of success in Formosa.

If, as Friedrich von Schlegel wrote, ' Der Historiker ist ein rückwärts gekehrter Prophet ' — the historian is a prophet with his face turned backwards — we confidently hope that the history of the Chinese mainland in the not too distant future will be as that of Formosa today.

CHAPTER ELEVEN

Formosa since 1945

FORMOSA reverted to China in 1945, but it was not an easy return. There were various reasons for this.

The Japanese, aware of the decisions of the Cairo Conference of 1943, knew that defeat in war meant the handing-over to China of 'Manchuria, Formosa, and the Pescadores'. The moment they realized that defeat was inevitable, they set in motion their plan to make the return of Chinese control as difficult as possible. A similar plan operated in Indonesia to hamper the return of the Dutch. Local independence movements were organized, and selected men, trained by the Japanese, were entrusted with the campaign. In Formosa this campaign was carried out with remarkable thoroughness and attention to detail. Japan was determined to make one final attempt, whatever the cost, to prevent the island becoming again an integral part of China. When defeat did come, and the Japanese left Formosa, these Formosans, with arms supplied by the Japanese, roamed the island, fanning the flames of revolt against the return to China, and claiming independence for Formosa. They were few in number, and when they failed to gain popular support they left for Japan, where they carried on their campaign, which still continues, but with diminishing virulence.

Their brief activity in Formosa was assisted by a small number of disaffected Formosans who, having fled from the ruthless oppression of Japanese colonialism to China in past years, now returned in the hope of receiving posts of authority in the island. Disgruntled and disappointed in not realizing their ambitions, they joined up with the Japanese-inspired independence movement, and they, too, eventually found their way to Japan. At times an echo of their bitterness can he heard from the pages of certain periodicals in America and elsewhere.

The situation in Formosa created by these two groups was aggravated by the unfortunate choice of Chen Yi as Governor of Formosa. This was one of the biggest blunders made by the Chinese Government. From the outset, Chen Yi showed himself to be nothing less than a Chinese reincarnation of one of those Japanese despots whom the people of Formosa knew only too well. Chu Chia-hua, Minister of Education in the regained province, reported that ' Chen Yi, from the beginning, never tried to win the goodwill of the people, and his misrule, together with his arrogant personality, brought about public indignation and the subsequent uprising '. His dismissal won popular support for the Chinese Government, and from that time the independence movement began to peter out. At no time had it been popular. The disturbance of February 1947 had been directed not against the Chinese Government, but against the despotic rule of Chen Yi.

Hard pressed by the Communists, the Chinese Government moved in 1949 to the province of Formosa. This was not an unprecedented act, as a similar thing had happened on many occasions in the past history of China. In the time of the Chou, when the capital in the valley of the Wei had been attacked by marauding tribesmen, ancestors of the Hsiung Nu, the administration had moved to Honan province ; in 1127, when the Mongols overran north China, Kao Sung had moved the Government from Honan province to Chekiang province ; in 1403, when Nanking had fallen, the Ming Emperor Yung Lo moved north to the ' metropolitan province ' of Peking ; and as late as 1898, as foreign pressure against Peking increased, the Chinese Government moved to the province of Jehol. But as with the movement to Formosa in 1949, the Government remained on Chinese soil.

It is significant that most of these movements of the seat of Government synchronized with attempts to set up rival administrations, as in 1949 when the Communists established their Government in Peking. Since then the world has been divided as to which is now the legal Chinese Government, although it is not clear just how legality is to be defined. By the sword ? Or by the will of the governed? If by the latter, then the historian must point out that the Government now operating in Formosa province was originally elected by the Chinese people, although circumstances do not make it possible for this Government to receive a renewal of mandate. Also, it was this Government which signed the Peace Treaty with Japan in 1952, which recognized Formosa as an integral part of China. On the other hand the Government in Peking has never received a democratic mandate from the people, as it has never sought one. Such is the register of history, whatever the politicians of the world may decide upon.

Since 1949 Formosa has emerged from a state of colonialism to one of outstanding progress in all fields of human endeavour. Most observers who have studied the position there at close quarters agree that the standard of living is now the second highest in the whole of Asia. This achievement has been brought about by three men — Chiang Kai-shek, the late Chen Cheng,[1] and Chang Chi-yun. This is no triumvirate in the Roman manner, devoted mainly to the arts of war. On the contrary, these three have devoted their time and talents to the development of Formosa and the enrichment of the lives of its people. As one of these reminded the author, the immediate objective is to transform the island into 'a model Chinese province'.

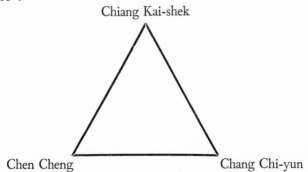

Chiang Kai-shek

Chen Cheng   Chang Chi-yun

At the apex of the triangle is Chiang Kai-shek, of all world leaders the least understood and in consequence the most grossly

[1] Chen Cheng died in 1965 as this book was going to press.

misrepresented. The author has been privileged to come close
to him over the years, and to see him as he really is and to discover
wherein lies the secret of this remarkable man.

His very name is rich with meaning. When Wu Wang,
founder of the Chou Dynasty, died in 1115 B.C., he was succeeded
by the young Emperor Cheng under the regency of his uncle
the Duke of Chou. To the third son of the duke, named Pai-ling,
the Emperor gave an estate in Honan known as ' Chiang '. As
was the custom, his descendants took as their family name that
of the estate. Hence they became known in history as ' Chiangs '.
During the Han Dynasty a branch of the family migrated south
to Chekiang province, settling at Taichou. In the Yuan Dynasty,
when the Mongols swept into south China, the Chiang family
was forced to move along the River Yen, seeking refuge. This
they found at Chikow in the district of Fenghua. It was there,
after many generations, in 1887, that the boy was born, who
was to become famous in the history of his country. His official
name was ' Chung-cheng ', meaning ' rightness ', and his first
name ' Kai-shek '.

' Kai-shek ' signifies ' hard rock ', and what better name to give
to the lad, who was one day to live through turbulent years which
demanded supreme courage and indomitable resolution !

> Iron dug from central gloom,
> And heated hot with burning fears,
> And dipped in baths of hissing tears,
> And battered with the shocks of doom
> To shape and use.

It was as though Destiny was fashioning this man in the forge
of life by hard and bitter experiences for the master task ahead, in
Formosa. There, on that island, thanks to his genius and
inspiration, China has been reborn, a rebirth that might well
excite the wonder of all who care to look, and inspire the pen of
the historian as he observes the oldest civilization extant now in
process of revival, as it links its ancient culture with modern
techniques. For the first time in history, a ' culture ' civilization
and a ' technique ' civilization are meeting and coalescing. Out
of the process may come something new for China and mankind,

saving the West itself from technological suicide. It may be that in the future, when history makes up its book, this Chinese in Formosa, Chiang Kai-shek, will be noted and the names of others, now on the world stage, not even mentioned. Perhaps, in that day, thanks largely to his efforts, China will be the greatest of all the world powers and the leader of the new civilization.

What, then, is the secret of this man, who has wrought such a transformation in the history of the Chinese people? By what means has he been able, in the brief space of sixteen years, to effect such a bloodless revolution, that a previously little-known island has now become a showpiece in Asia?

Chiang is a man of the mountains. Born in the high country around Chikow, and profoundly influenced by a Buddhist mother (although he himself is a Methodist), something of those mountains has entered his soul. He lives apart. With whom he communes in the rarefied air of the heights we do not know. What plans take shape there, we can only guess. One cannot meet him without being conscious that he is no ordinary man. No host of secretaries and officials surrounds him. No battery of telephones clutters his table. Rather a strange mystique, that one does not associate with the demagogic leaders of other countries. And from him there flows down to those in charge of the political, economic, and cultural activities of Formosa an inspiration, as life-giving water from the mountains of Formosa into the plains. When he enters his office each morning, attends a public function, or inspects some new enterprise, he meets the ordinary people and converses with them. Among national leaders, there is none so remote and, at the same time, so close to his people.

This man has discovered something which has eluded others. Most leaders of our Western democracies, with an eye ever on the next election, and their horizons limited by the space of four or five years, have dedicated themselves to the winning of votes. The state of the party is their major concern. The political grind leaves little time for thought and contemplation, long-term planning and creative endeavour. As a result democracy tends to lose its soul as the leader seeks to please rather than guide the herd. Opposed to this, the dictators, whose numbers are on the

increase, impose on their people a slavish obedience, destroying
in the process all initiative and stifling all progress. Between
these extremes there is another way which few discover, a way of
retaining the spirit of true democracy without being levelled by
the machine.

Chiang appears to have found this way.

As a man of the mountains, he, like Elijah, has heard a ' still
small voice '. Living in the elevated country of the spirit, he is an
ardent believer in spiritual determinism. Long ago he rejected
the philosophy of economic determinism which the Communists
preached and practised and which the West denounced but
nevertheless followed. He is convinced that history is fashioned
by spiritual rather than economic forces. This is why he has
been a lifelong opponent of Marxism. As far back as 1923, after
his visit to Russia, where he made a close study of both the
apparatus and the results of Communism, he reported to Sun
Yat-sen that any co-operation with Russia would be not only
inadvisable but would certainly result in spiritual annihilation.
The danger, as he saw it, was not in the field of politics, economics,
or even ideology, but rather in the realm of basic Chinese values.
He seemed to have seen what Heinrich Heine had glimpsed
eighty years earlier :

Wild and gloomy times come roaring on, and the prophet who
would write a new Apocalypse, must imagine new beasts, and these
so terrible, that the old symbols of St. John, as compared to them,
will seem like soft doves and amorets. The gods hide their faces out
of pity for mankind, their nurslings for so many years, and, perhaps,
out of fear for their own fate.

The future has an odour as of Russian leather, blood, blasphemy,
and much beating with the knout. I advise our descendants to come
into the world with thick skins.

While Chiang was making his report to Sun Yat-sen, some in
the West, who professed to be ' experts ' on Russian affairs,
were talking of the ' Russian reformers ' just as later they were to
classify the Chinese Communist leaders as ' agrarian reformers '.

This concept of spiritual determinism found expression
immediately Chiang arrived in Formosa. While elsewhere in

the free world men talked of peace as the greatest of all values, he placed the emphasis on freedom. Everybody in Formosa, including the aborigines in the mountains, must be free. Under Japanese rule the people of the island had neither political nor economic rights. These were the preserves of the privileged race, the Japanese. But this great adventure in freedom has justified itself. An experiment it was, but it has paid the highest dividends in terms of human progress and happiness. He must have known that sooner or later the defence forces would be composed almost entirely of Formosans, who, if they wished, would be able to take over control. That no attempt to do so had been made speaks well for the Chiang dictum that ' freedom is the basis of peace, domestic and international. Where there is freedom, there is little danger of internal strife and the greater possibility of international peace.'

Chiang's address to the youth of Formosa had something of a Greek ring about it :

Youth of Taiwan !

This is a bright age ; also it could be a dark age. It is a time for creation ; also it could be a time of destruction. Our future, whether blessed or doomed, glorious or disgraceful, hinges on how we decide to conduct ourselves.

At such a time, you should rededicate yourselves to the great cause, always remembering that spiritual weapons are more effective than military ones.

Chiang put into words what, many centuries earlier, Myron had sought to express in his famous Diskobolos. When that great sculptor set out to immortalize the triumph of freedom over the threat of slavery at Salamis in 480 B.C., he did not seek a soldier or one of the sailors of Themistocles' fleet in the marble, but rather a disc-thrower, for his was the attitude which expressed with complete fidelity the concentration of the Athenian will upon the supreme effort for freedom. Eyes fixed on the path of aim. The centre of gravity exactly over the supporting foot. The left arm and leg acting as counterpoise. Perfect concentration. Absolute self-surrender. Spiritual dedication set forth in marble.

This is what Chiang was saying to the youth of Formosa.

There is a prevailing picture of this man, among many who should know better, as what one writer called ' A Philoctetes, licking his wounds in exile on an island in the sea '. Philoctetes, in the Sophoclean tragedy, had been banished to the island of Lemnos, where, ' sick of a consuming wound and pierced through and through by the destroying viper's venomous fangs ', he was doomed to languish in vain hope of return to his native Greece. But Chiang is not in exile. He remains on Chinese soil. Even his enemies, the Communists, admit this. Formosa is as much a part of China as Kwangtung or Shantung. It is testimony to the courage of the man that, when hard-pressed, he did not flee from China to Switzerland or Portugal to live out his life in peace, as he could have done, but preferred to remain in a Chinese province. And far from licking his wounds, he sees always a renovated China in the future, modelled on the province of Formosa. Indeed, the plans for the rehabilitation of the Chinese mainland have already reached the blueprint stage.

Chiang believes that Formosa is the symbol of the New China which one day will eventuate, when the surgery of time has done its work. He has seen the fulfilment of the age-long Formosan dream, born in days when Cheng Chih-lung ferried migrants across to the island from the mainland, over which the sun of the Mings was beginning to wester and only a few distant peaks retained the hectic glow of its expiring life. Cheng Cheng-kung had revived that dream for a brief period. But it had never died ; it lived on in the songs of the Formosan people, songs which revealed a promise of the dawn through the dark night of foreign occupation. In 1949 it became a living thing, a radiant reality. Flaming in the forehead of the morning, the new day dawned, as the poet sang of the ending of

> That long drip of human tears,
> Which people, old in tragedy,
> Had left upon the centuried years.

Whether or not he shall see this dawn break over the rest of China, the mainland, is a matter of conjecture. It may be that Chiang will never again tread the soil of the mainland. But, whenever and however, the renewal of the Chinese mainland comes about, and that regeneration must surely happen, Chiang will be remembered as the spirit of its inspiration. His name will live on through the centuries. In a very real sense he has already reached his goal. His retreat from the mainland has been transformed into a triumphant advance by demonstrating that the Chinese people, when free, can within the space of a few years take their place among the most progressive peoples of the world, without the surrender of their historic values.

This is more important for the future of China than any personal return of Chiang Kai-shek to the Chinese mainland, to the accompaniment of blaring trumpets and a sea of flag-waving. There are greater victories than those won by arms, and Chiang has gained one of these. His transformation of the province of Formosa will yet prove to be a more powerful weapon than all the might represented by army, navy, and air force. It may not be so spectacular, but it will be both more effective and more enduring.

The dynamic influence of Chiang Kai-shek has percolated down to Chen Cheng on the one side of the triangle and to Chang Chi-yun on the other. The former has been responsible for administration and reform, the latter for the direction of education and cultural activities in general. The former has cared for the body of Formosa, the latter for the development of its mind and soul.

Chen Cheng, as Governor of Formosa directing the domestic affairs of the island, and later as Premier of the National Government, proved himself no ordinary man. Physically a small man, of lesser height than the ordinary Chinese, he rose in real stature far above most others in Formosa, with a vision of what China should and can be in the modern world, and an inflexible determination that this must be realized. He it was who led the Chinese province of Formosa into the new age. As Governor and then as Premier he manifested the genius of harmonizing the activities of the different political parties and directing these towards the one objective, the building-up of Formosa into a modern and model Chinese province. Contrary to the prevailing impression in many places, there are three different parties in Formosa, the Kuomintang or National Party, the Democratic Socialist Party, much like the Labour Party in British countries, and the Young China Party, which emphasizes the necessity of a strict rule of law and the extension of private enterprise. In both the Provincial and National Governments all three parties are represented. The differences are really matters of mechanics, as all three share the same basic aims. Chen Cheng proved his statesmanship in preventing any serious clash between the parties, and was successful in guiding them towards the common national purpose. He knew from the outset that each had its contribution to offer, and he accepted this. More than that, he never forgot that each party had been born of conditions prevailing on the Chinese mainland before 1949. With this in mind, his policy was one of synthesis, with his eye ever on the national purpose rather than the fate of any party, even the one to which he himself belonged.

At the present time, the heads of local government in the chief cities of Formosa are Democratic Socialists ; in the Provincial Assembly all three parties have elected members ; in the National Assembly there are 56 elected Democratic Socialists and 85 elected Young China members. The growing strength of these minority parties is gradually reducing the strength and power of the Kuomintang, the National Party, as more intellectuals, businessmen, and even officials join their ranks. Out of this process and this healthy democratic rivalry, government in Formosa moves closer and closer to the ideal of a free country. Universal suffrage has operated for years and today Formosa has the Government, local and national, that the people of the island want.

When it is remembered that prior to 1949 the people of Formosa had no political rights, it is a tribute, largely to Chen Cheng, that the present enlightened situation exists. That the transition from political serfdom to political liberty has been carried out in a peaceful manner is witness to his vision and splendid courage. In other Asian countries, and indeed outside Asia, such a transition has been brought about only after bloody revolution, leading in some cases to the bankruptcy of the national economy.

In Formosa the recognition of the individual's right to full political freedom has resulted in the building-up of an economy without parallel, save in the case of Japan, in any other part of

Asia. It is true that America has given massive assistance, but this is not peculiar to Formosa, as American aid has gone to many other countries. But in no other country receiving American aid have such dividends in economic growth and human progress been apparent as in the case of Formosa, where within the next three years not one more American dollar for economic assistance will be required.

The *United Nations Bulletin of Statistics* shows what the Chinese can accomplish, when free :

Index Numbers of Industrial Production

Country	1952	1953	1954	1955	1956	1957	1958	1959	1960	1961	1962	1963
1. China — Taiwan	100	124	133	148	155	177	190	215	245	270	305	336
2. Argentina	100	99	107	117	117	120	124	110	114	126	118	—
3. Belgium	100	99	105	115	122	122	115	120	128	133	141	149
4. Canada	100	106	106	117	128	129	128	138	138	143	155	163
5. France	100	101	111	121	133	145	151	153	166	175	186	195
6. Germany, Fed. Rep.	100	110	123	141	153	161	166	178	198	209	219	226
7. India	100	102	109	118	123	129	134	145	161	172	184	—
8. Italy	100	110	120	132	140	150	156	173	200	222	243	265
9. Japan	100	120	130	140	175	201	203	252	317	378	408	444
10. Netherlands	100	110	121	130	137	140	140	153	174	176	182	—
11. Pakistan	100	128	164	206	242	256	275	308	327	347	412	—
12. Philippines	100	114	127	143	166	179	193	208	216	230	243	—
13. United Kingdom	100	105	112	118	119	121	120	126	134	137	138	142
14. United States	100	109	102	115	119	119	111	125	129	130	140	147

No sweated labour was responsible for this production. Trade-union officials from Australia, who visited factories and other industrial plants in Formosa, were impressed with the human side of production. In their report they stated :

Everywhere we went there was a complete air of freedom and contentment.

As a lot of the industry is decentralized, all factories have housing facilities, which are family units for their employees, and are provided free of charge. When an employee is not provided with a free house or apartment, he is paid extra to cover his rental in the adjoining town. In many cases, the Trade Unions provide houses for their members as part of their welfare programme. In Keelung, the Union of Dockworkers has built 250 family units and plans to increase these to 600 units to cover all its members. . . .

Most factories are self-contained communities. A tobacco factory at Sung Shan provides bathrooms, a very large assembly hall, and a separate and equally large lunchroom. There is a cafeteria where a two-course meal can be purchased. Also, there is a reading room, a change room, a barber shop, a tailor, laundry facilities, a shoemaker, a co-operative store which sells groceries, clothing, radios, bicycles, etc. . . . It has its own baseball ground, tennis courts, its own hospital facilities, providing a doctor, dentist, and medicine, free, for the employee and his family. For the women employees, who are married, with young children, a nursery, complete with mothercraft nurses is provided.

These trade-union officials visited a cement factory to find the clinic staffed by twelve doctors, two dentists, an operating room, and a separate women's section, with women doctors. Also a kindergarten equal to any of a similar size in Australia.

Provision for insurance covering 'accident, disability, death, and old age' won the admiration of those visiting Australian trade unionists, including, as they noted 'free hospitalization'. Also, they concluded that the provisions for collective bargaining are 'similar to those made by American and European Labour Unions, with their employers, and including clauses for working hours, leave of absence, holidays, and safety measures'.

Over the past ten years the author has visited many of these industrial plants to find that in Formosa everything is not subordinated to economic interests and the national ledger; not determined simply by the rate of industrial production or the barometer of the export market. Human considerations are a most important factor in the industrial life of the island.

But Chen Cheng's greatest achievement was in land reform. This has been not only the most forward move in Asia for centuries, as it has solved the basic problem of unrest, but is without parallel in any other country of the world. It is unique in history. Not even in the West, with all its social progress, has such a reform been carried out. No wonder the emergent countries of Africa as well as several Asian countries seeking an answer to this land problem are looking, not to the West, but to Formosa. Missions from these countries have visited Formosa to study the mechanics of this reform and investigate its results.

In turn, agricultural experts from Formosa have gone to Africa in an advisory capacity, and some are there at the present time.

In view of this greatest of all social revolutions, this land reform, initiated by Chen Cheng, calls for detailed examination.

As a young man, though committed to a military career, he had wrestled with this problem in his own mind. He had come to realize that Tung Chung-chu's diagnosis two thousand years ago that ' the poor have not even enough land to stand on because the land owned by the rich stretches from one end of the country to the other' had been true of China all through the centuries. And such doctrinaire remedies as those of Wang Mang of the Han Dynasty and Wang An-shih of the Sung had been ineffectual. Something more radical was needed. The years of unrest caused by food-shortages continued to outnumber the years of peace. As a young man in his twenties he had enthused over the ' Min Sheng' proposals of Sun Yat-sen, one of which claimed the right of the farmer to own the land he tilled. As Governor of Hupeh province in 1939 he had taken the first step in implementing Sun Yat-sen's policy by enforcing a 25 per cent reduction in farm rents, but the growing disturbances throughout China provoked by Japan made it impossible for him to proceed further in land reform. He had to devote his time and service to war and put his land-reform programme into cold storage.

The year 1949 brought him his great opportunity. As Governor of Formosa, he could proceed without distraction. He would carry out a land-reform policy in Formosa, which would be the blueprint for a future reform on the mainland of China also. But first a thorough survey of land tenure in Formosa must be carried out. What this revealed might well have dulled the enthusiasm of the most determined reformer, but not Chen Cheng. He was made of other stuff and sterner. He looked upon the results of that survey as a challenge, which he was resolved to accept.

The survey showed that such families as claimed ownership of land could not produce proof of such, and in the cases of tenancy, which included the great majority of the farming population, no written contracts existed. The oral contracts, as far as they could be understood, provided for eviction at the will of the professed landlord. In seven districts, the average annual rental was as high as 57 per cent of the main crop. There were districts where the annual rent had to be paid in advance, the landlord fixing the expected value of the non-existent crop. To meet this demand and provide himself and family with a roof, the farmer had to resort to the money-lender, thus putting himself at the mercy of two tyrants, the landlord demanding the greater part of the crop as he himself estimated it, and the money-lender demanding exorbitant interest.

These landowners, who claimed the land although they had nothing to support their claim, were men who had found favour with the Japanese during their occupation of Formosa. These were used by Japanese to win over the support of the people. They were virtually agents of the Japanese, who, by oral agreements, permitted them the use of the land. When the Japanese left, they claimed ownership. The survey showed that 80 per cent of the farmers were tenants, the remaining 20 per cent claimants to ownership.

Chen Cheng was quick to realize that any sudden and complete change would create chaos and promote disturbance. Under the existing conditions at that time, this latter was to be avoided at all costs. Also, tenancy complications were such that time was needed to sort them out. The reform must be gradual and in stages.

The first stage of the reform was the fixation of the maximum rent. The percentage of 37·5 per cent of the main crop, which the Central Government of China had decreed back in 1930, but was unable to carry out owing to the threat of war with Japan, was adopted, and the law enforcing it promulgated in April 1949. Under the provisions of this law, all rentals above that figure had to be reduced, any lower were to remain as they were, and all attempts to secure advance payments were to end. All leases had to be in writing and for a period not less than six years, with the proviso that the tenant could renew unless the owner intended to cultivate the land himself. The lease could be cancelled if the tenant was in arrears for two years. A board was set up to settle any disputes arising between owners and tenants.

Chang Chi-yun, former Minister of Education and now Director of the
Institute of Advanced Chinese Studies

The effect of this first remedial stage was soon apparent. Like a photographic positive being taken out of the immersion, the Formosa of the future was taking shape, dimly perhaps, but still the lines were clear. Two years after the maximum rental had been fixed, an inspection team travelled throughout Formosa to observe results.

Everywhere we went, we saw newly built or newly repaired houses on the farms. The women and children were better dressed. There was a general improvement in the food which was eaten. Those whose main article of consumption has been sweet potatoes are now eating polished rice.

Official figures, compiled four years after this maximum rental had been fixed, showed that rice production had increased 47 per cent and the average income of the farmers by 81 per cent. Everywhere there was a new spirit. Hitherto life had been one long drudgery; now things were different. Cattle bought with the increased income were referred to as ' 37·5 cattle ', the new farm-house was a ' 37·5 house ', even the brides were ' 37·5 brides '. Indeed, the only ones not jubilant over the beginning of the new order were the Communist subversives who had infiltrated into the island. The former conditions of the farming families had been a most promising field for their exploitation, as maggots feed on rotten wood, but the reform programme was to be their death-blow.

In June 1951 the second stage of the reform was announced. This was made possible by the unqualified success of the first stage. Many farmers now had sufficient money to place deposits on land they wanted to purchase.

This second stage was the opening-up for sale of all public land suitable for agricultural purposes. During the Japanese occupation of Formosa, 430,000 acres of public land had been earmarked by the Government. Several large Japanese organizations had been commissioned, it was reported, to settle Japanese migrants on these lands, which represented about 20 per cent of the arable land in Formosa. Few of these settlers ever arrived ; in fact it is doubtful if the Japanese authorities wanted them. What did happen was that the organizations sold these lands to

o

Japanese officials, Japanese corporations, and Japanese retired military men. These, in turn, let their holdings to Formosan farmers. The average rental was 55 per cent of the total production.

The Chen Cheng plan of 1951, which offered these lands for sale, the existing tenants having the first option, reserved for public purposes such portions as were required for water conservation, schools, hospitals, etc. The remaining land was then subdivided into farms within what was known as the ' maximum allowable area '. This allowable area was not constant, as the soil of the island differs considerably in different regions. But as the population was increasing rapidly and the agricultural land was limited, it was essential that some limit be placed on the area of land any farmer could own. This limit was determined by the nature of the soil and the estimated cost of maintaining a family of six persons. The price to be paid by the prospective owner was 2·5 times the total annual yield of the main crop, this to be paid in ten annual payments, without interest, not in money but in farm products, thus saving the purchaser from the results of currency fluctuations.

The number of farmers who purchased land was given officially as 139,688.

So successful was this second stage of the land-reform programme that at the end of 1952 Chen Cheng gave an indication of what the third and final stage would be :

By taking the initiative in the sale of public lands, the Government has set an example for private landowners. This has served as a harbinger for the compulsory purchase of privately held farm land for resale to farmers and therefore paved the way to the realization of the land-to-the-tiller ideal.

In January 1953 this final stage was announced. To avoid the inevitable bargaining which would take place if the landholders dealt with prospective buyers, the Government purchased all the privately held land and offered it for sale to farmers. The former owner was permitted to retain any area, within the allowable maximum size, if he intended to live on it and farm it.

To avoid all risk of inflation, these former owners were not paid in cash but in bonds, land bonds and Government enterprises stock. The former, representing 70 per cent of the price due to them, were payable in kind, which could be converted into cash at the market value of the goods ; the latter, representing the remaining 30 per cent of the price due to them, related to such Government industries as the Cement Corporation, the Paper and Pulp Corporation, the Mining Corporation, and the Forestry Development Corporation.

In this way two results were achieved. The tenant farmer became the owner of the land he tilled, and the Government-controlled industries and enterprises gradually began to pass into the hands of private enterprise, represented by thousands of ordinary people.

The purchase of farm land by 193,823 families under this third provision of the reform policy brought the total number of families settled on farms of their own to over 400,000, with, of course, the aid of the Land Bank.

But even this figure, impressive as it is, does not convey the full significance of this revolution in land ownership. When the maximum allowable area was determined, the basis of computation was the area needed to support a family of six persons. On this estimate, which was very conservative, the number of persons affected by this land reform was 2·5 million. Probably the figure was nearer 3 million, as many Chinese families comprise more than four children.

This was probably the most enterprising and massive land reform ever carried out. To plan such a vast scheme was in itself an achievement. At one time 2,234 official investigators were at work. No less than 2·1 million plots of land were inspected. As no written agreements had existed between owner and tenant, one can only imagine the innumerable interviews that must have transpired. Yet it was a bloodless revolution, with all parties concerned satisfied with the outcome. The author has seen the pride stamped on the face of a Formosan farmer, born an economic slave, then a harassed tenant farmer, and now the owner of his own farm, as he showed his title to the soil he worked. And, significantly, he had just returned from the village school, where he had recorded his vote in the provincial elections. Economically and politically he was now a free man.

Chen Cheng's land reform brought a new life to Formosa. As we examine the statistics we begin to discover just how far-reaching this new life really is. Before the land-reform policy was initiated the percentage of children attending schools was 72 ; today it is 96. Not one member of a farming family was in the Provincial Assembly ; now there are four. 10,648 teachers and other officials are from farming families, whereas previously the number never reached 3,000. And, most important of all, whereas formerly the tenant farmer had no say in rural organizations, today 6,700 are on such bodies.

An English scientist visiting Formosa during the Japanese occupation noted that ' all the land of agricultural value in the island has passed from the hands of the Chinese-Formosans into those of their Japanese conquerors by force or extortion '. Now, in 1965, every farmer in Formosa either owns the land he tills or is in process of doing so. Landlordism in respect of agricultural land is a thing of the past. Can any other country in the world equal this ?

The following index numbers of food production, compiled by the Food and Agriculture Organization of the United Nations, are clear evidence of what Chen Cheng's land reform has mean in terms of Formosan production :

Country	1952–1953	1953–1954	1954–1955	1955–1956	1956–1957	1957–1958	1958–1959	1959–1960	1960–1961	1961–1962	1962–1963
China — Taiwan	100	108	115	118	127	134	142	139	147	148	155
Argentina	100	96	101	99	108	108	113	103	96	—	—
Burma	100	96	94	95	105	91	107	112	112	112	120
Canada	100	94	70	88	96	81	85	90	94	—	—
Ceylon	100	92	104	114	99	103	107	114	119	128	134
France	100	109	114	114	111	115	115	122	137	—	—
Germany, Fed. Rep.	100	106	106	105	108	111	117	113	131	—	—
India	100	113	113	115	119	118	123	128	132	133	132
Italy	100	113	104	114	113	111	127	127	121	—	—
Japan	100	88	97	118	113	119	120	125	128	128	137
Korea, South	100	141	160	163	151	170	177	178	178	192	174
Netherlands	100	100	102	104	99	107	118	119	131	—	—
Pakistan	100	104	106	98	106	104	104	111	116	117	115
Philippines	100	104	105	107	114	119	120	120	127	132	135
Thailand	100	120	94	118	129	102	118	121	139	148	160
Union of South Africa	100	110	112	115	124	119	124	127	137	—	—
United Kingdom	100	102	103	103	113	110	106	116	122	—	—
United States	100	99	101	104	106	104	112	112	113	—	—

The third member of the triumvirate is Chang Chi-yun, outstanding among the literati in Formosa, and probably the greatest living interpreter of Chinese civilization. Like the Chinese scholar in every age, he considers himself a guardian of the historic values of Chinese culture and civilization, but unlike many scholars of the past, he believes that these values can be harmonized with new knowledge. Accordingly, he has set himself the task of mating in Formosa the ' culture ' values of China with the ' technique ' values of the West. In this endeavour, he reminds us of the words of Isaiah Bowman, a former President of Johns Hopkins University :

> The gains of her [China's] race lead one to hope that statesmen can be found who will bring her internal forces, material and spiritual, into a close working relationship. If they do, China may become one of the great nations of the world.

This is precisely the objective of Chang Chi-yun, who at times uses the same term as was employed by Isaiah Bowman. He once referred to the ' spiritual aspect ' of national welfare, which he regarded as just as important as the ' material aspect '. On another occasion, he expressed the view that ' the world is at the crossroads and in need of spiritual leadership '. Again, when Minister of Education, he stated that ' all education must have a spiritual basis '.

What does this mean ? In our modern parlance, this term has come to have a very wide connotation, ranging from religion to a certain philosophy that admits of no religion. ' Spiritual-mindedness ' is a term that covers a multitude of meanings. But what does it mean to a Chinese scholar and leader of the literati such as Chang Chi-yun ? We must understand this if we are to discover the meaning of Formosa, for this man is one of the three who have made Formosa what it is, and who at the present time are guiding the course of life on that island. Chang Chi-yun is the greatest mental force in Formosa.

We of the West have sectionalized the activities of life. The philosopher, the poet, the man of letters, the artist, the politician, have all been departmentalized, as though there was little, if anything, in common between them. And all these are separate from those we call 'the workers'. Precisely labelled, each carries on his own activity in a world remote from others, and each strives to learn the secret of existence and the purpose of life. The Chinese approach is entirely different. It sees all these as seekers after what Chang Chi-yun calls 'Oneness of Mind and Matter', and again 'Unity of Heaven and Man'. The peasant on his farm, the philosopher in his study, the artist with his brush, the politician in Parliament, the poet in his garden or on the mountain-side, the priest in his temple or church, all are one in the great pilgrimage.

This is what Chang means when he uses the term 'spiritual'. This is the basis from which all Chinese values have developed.

As Minister of Education, Chang set out to give Formosan youth a view of life, not after the Western manner, where there is 'a marked demarcation between God and man', as he said, but in which 'the unity of God and man' will be the fundamentum of all thinking, 'not only to seek the riddle of the universe and the systemization of phenomena, but also to achieve the union of Heaven and man and the universal truth underlying all things'. Thus the application of the latest scientific discoveries and technological processes would be harmonized with the fundamental Chinese values, and as a result the life of the individual and that of the nation would be made whole.

Led on by this vision, Chang Chi-yun laid the foundation of an educational system in Formosa which would do credit to any country. On this his successors at the Ministry of Education have built, following his blueprints. From the age of six years the journey begins, then passes from grade to grade until the university, vocational, or technological institution is reached. This education, from the lowest to the highest grade, is free.

Chang Chi-yun, like Chen Cheng, is a reformer. His great adventure in social reform began in 1954 when he took over direction of education in Formosa. A new social order, inspired by the 'culture–technique' concept which possessed his mind, would be brought into being. This would mean breaking with some things which had barnacled on the way of thinking, but as these were not essentials but excrescences, none should lament their passing. The basic Chinese values would remain.

To understand Chang's reform programme, we must remember that throughout China's long history the literati had always been the cream of Chinese society, the aristocrats — not by birth, for China never had an hereditary aristocracy, but by qualification. A person became an acknowledged member of the literati by qualifying at the competitive examinations. Success in the first of these, which awarded the title of *hsiu ts'ai*, was the key that opened the door into the entrance lobby of the select. Success in the second, the *chu jen*, gave entrance into the hall. Success in the third examination, the *chin shih*, led into the inner circle. Such was the respect paid to these literati, in all grades, that when the son of a poor villager gained his *hsiu ts'ai*, it was permitted his family to hang out a board in front of the house to signify that a member of the literati lived there. Throughout Chinese history these literati were the decisive force in the country. As already noted, they had played a most important part in the history of Formosa. They had been the driving force in establishing the republic back in 1895.

Chang Chi-yun planned to extend this group until it embraced the greater part of the growing population The opportunity must be given to every young man and woman to join the ranks of the literati and become a member of the new aristocracy by educating them in the new culture, the harmonization of China's historic values and those of the present scientific age. This was his vision of the New China and Formosa's role in its realization. It was a bold and daring adventure, but it was made with an eye to the future. So it is that in Formosa today the study of the humanities, based on the Confucian canon, goes side by side with scientific and technological training. The latest figures show that of the total of 51,707 students in the universities in Formosa, 12,958 are doing courses in modern science and technology, 12,070 are studying the humanities, 14,525 are engaged in social science studies, and the remainder in medicine and the fine arts.

Having set the foundations of the education programme, Chang

Chi-yun resigned from the Ministry of Education in 1949 to enter a larger sphere of activity. As Director of the Institute of Advanced Chinese Studies at Yang Ming Shan, near Taipei, he embarked on the ambitious plan of influencing every section of cultural activity throughout Formosa and making these known to the world. Soon, his publication *Chinese Culture* became the most authoritative interpretation of Chinese culture in the English language. At the same time he began the gigantic task of writing, in thirty-two volumes, the *Chinese History of Fifty Centuries*, four volumes of which have already appeared. This promises to be the Chinese Gibbon of the future.

Meanwhile his influence is spreading into every cultural corner of Formosa. It is like the incoming tide, slowly and silently filling every crevice among the rocks. No artist, whether poet or painter or worker in ceramics, can escape it; the historian quotes Chang's interpretations; Ch'i Ju-shan, the greatest figure in Chinese opera, describes him as ' the creative spirit '; one of the leading technologists pays him the tribute of calling him ' China's guide into the future '. It was to Chang Chi-yun that Sir Percival David put the question : ' What is the real purpose of Chinese culture ? '; to which he replied, ' The prime purpose of Chinese culture is to enhance the spiritual values of man '.

This man, influencing the mind of Formosa from his study on the slope of Yang Ming Shan, means more in the long run than all the deliberations of the Legislative Yuan, the speeches of the politicians, the dinners in honour of distinguished visitors, and the endless round of courtesy calls. These things belong to time, but the spiritual force that emanates from Yang Ming Shan is, like China itself, timeless. There is reason to believe that it is already making itself felt in the halls of the legislature, for as one politician remarked to the author, ' Chang is an historian and himself is making history '.

As noted earlier, the poet kept the light of freedom burning through the dark night of Formosa's past. From the *shih she* the sons of liberty sang of the coming dawn. Today, Hsia Chin and his companions of the ' Blue Stars Society ' have been inspired by Chang's vision of the New China. As we read his elegy on the death of Chin Tzu Hao, Shelley's *Adonais* immediately comes to mind :

> As noon rises high, so rises the flame
> That burns the immortal phoenix,
> The martyr moth,
> The sun-flower.

> Rises the lustre, rises the fire,
> That soars and soars and soars
> Towards the sun, towards the God.

> Above the dust, above the praying hands,
> Above all languages, all shapes.
> But soon will it return, falling
> Everywhere like a shower of oracles.

Out of the burning, the New China is beginning to rise — the superfluous of the past in ashes, the basic values stripped of the clinging rubbish of the centuries, and the New China, as seen in Formosa, rising phoenix-like from the flames. This is the vision of Hsia Chin as revealed and interpreted by Chang Chi-yun.

The painters in Formosa are seeing it too. What Hsia Chin put into words, Shiy De Jinn set out in oil upon canvas. His ' Decay ' in 1959 expressed in stark terror, more vividly than words, however eloquent, could ever convey, the desolation of the time, and his ' Fall of a Meteorite ' in 1960, while depicting the blackness of the earth and the depth of the indent, had above it all the blue sky, ribboned with streaks of white cloud. This was the promise of that New China that Chang Chi-yun was already forecasting in his ' culture–technique ' philosophy.

Among the Chinese, more than among any other people in history, the poet and the painter, rather than the politician, have been the true guide to history and the march with destiny. In his essay on the poet-painter Cheng Man-ching, Chang Chi-yun had said that the artist was the true interpreter of Chinese culture in the past and would be the most successful missionary ' in spreading Chinese culture overseas ' and making known ' the spirit that has been alive in Chinese culture for thousands of years '.

It is not surprising, then, that Chang's outlook has not been limited by those narrow horizons that are so marked in other

places. His ' culture–technique ' concept of future civilization
gives him an eclectic approach to religion. ' The greatest freedom
that man can ever enjoy on earth is in the spiritual realm ', he
wrote in his study of *Confucianism and Christianity*, and he is
convinced that ' in this hour, there is no more urgent task than to
permeate Chinese culture with the spirit of historical Christianity'.
In this way he sees the Confucian ideal being attained. In Islam
and Buddhism he sees values complementary to this ideal.

Under the guidance, then, of this Chiang–Chen–Chang
triumvirate, Formosa, after centuries of uncertainty, at times the
spoil of the powers, at others rent with internal strife, but always
dreaming of a brighter future, has now attained its goal. Its
people are free, its economy is sound, and life there is the envy
of others in Asia. From various parts of Africa and Asia
representative missions have gone to Formosa to learn how this
transformation has been brought about. From the Chinese
mainland there is a constant movement of refugees to its
shores.

What, then, is the meaning of Formosa? It was to find the
answer to this question that we set out. From what we have
discovered, we can now conclude that Formosa is the symbol of
what all China can become in the future. It may take many
years, perhaps a century, but then the Chinese, unlike ourselves,
are not the slaves of time. Their history has acclimatized them
to division. At times this extended not over a decade, but over
centuries. An infinite patience, in the face of these divisions, has
been one of their cardinal virtues. The Yangtze River, like the
Strait of Formosa today, was the water of demarcation, dividing
China into two.

But those of us who have lived in China and become conversant
with its history have not lost faith in the eventual renaissance
of the Chinese mainland, the coming of the New China. We
may not see clearly, at the moment, how or when this will come
about, but we are confident that, at some future time, the Chinese
mainland will be as Formosa is today.

In short, Formosa has set the pattern for the China of the
future, and at present can best serve the people of the Chinese

mainland by remaining faithful to that pattern, and, wherever possible, strengthening it.

Contrary to the popular view, neither politics nor economics determine the course of civilization, which is the accumulated product of the spiritual dynamics of a few individuals. Only as we realize this shall we see the true stature of Chiang Kai-shek and grasp the true position of Formosa in the world, especially when we consider that China may well be the greatest world power of the next century.

Such a prospect need not appal us, as a China, with its hundreds of millions, following the Formosan pattern of the ' culture–technique' civilization, would be to the good of Asia and the peace of the world. A most exciting prospect !

Postscript

SUCH has been the transformation of Formosa. A former Japanese slave colony has in the space of a few years become a prosperous island, its people enjoying personal, political, and economic freedom, without parallel elsewhere among the Chinese people, with a standard of living higher than ever previously known in Chinese history, and, as regards land ownership, a condition unequalled in any other part of the world, in East or West. A Chinese province, to which an increasing number of visitors from the emerging countries of Africa are going, seeking an answer to their own problems. An Asian island, on which agricultural production has been so successfully mechanized that, at the present time, teams of its experts are in three of those newly independent African states advising on land reform.

Why, then, did not the Chinese Nationalist Government, now in control of Formosa, and which has brought about this transformation there, carry out similar reforms on the Chinese mainland when it was in power there? Had this been done, the Chinese mainland would not have been Communist as at present.

This question, so often asked, has a direct relevance to the future of Formosa itself.

Few historians would attempt to justify the ineptitude and, in many cases, inefficiency, of the Nationalist Government in China from 1911 up to 1949, especially such as may have lived there during the whole or part of that period. This granted, it is doubtful if any other Government could have acquitted itself any better. Prior to 1911 there was no such thing in China as political consciousness, and little of industrial revolution. In the West there were long periods between the birth of political consciousness, the demand for political and economic rights, and the industrial revolution. Men moved slowly from one to the other. It was a gradual, though painful, process. In China, on the other hand, these three came together. As a result there was internal chaos. At the same time, the threat of invasion from without, by Japan, hung like a pall over the country.

Attempts were made in certain provinces, Hupeh, Hunan, Kwangtung, and Chekiang, to enforce the law promulgated in 1930 fixing the maximum rental that any tenant farmer could be charged by the landlord. But both internal and external conditions made the enforcement of the law extremely difficult. Even among Western countries, the threat of invasion has curtailed certain liberties and led to the postponement of planned reforms.

In all these circumstances, it was impossible for any Government to carry out a transformation, comparable with that which has been effected in Formosa.

Furthermore, the provinces of the Chinese mainland were, to a marked degree, self-contained regions even after the establishment of the Republic. Through the centuries, there had been little intercourse between the peoples even of neighbouring provinces The topography of the country had been largely responsible for this. The Chinese had never possessed a road sense, preferring to dig canals as a means of transport, and the course of these was determined by the physical nature of the land. Each province had its own regional pride, a legacy from the days when it was a separate independent kingdom. In the days when the author lived in Chengtu in western China, he was frequently reminded that Szechwan had once been the Kingdom of Shu. Any sense of Chinese nationalism has been a product of modern times. The feeling of personal independence had always been the major consciousness, as expressed in one of the oldest peasant songs of China :

> I rise at sunrise,
> I rest at sunset,
> I dig my well and drink,
> I till my field and eat ;
> What is the Emperor to me ?

Through the centuries the Chinese represented a civilization rather than a nation. And any attempt to set up an effective central Government was fraught with tremendous difficulties. On the other hand, Formosa, a small island, did not present any such problems to the carrying out of a reform programme. No local hindrances existed, and there was no lack of speedy communications.

However, while recognizing the epic achievements in reform since 1949, Formosa has its problems, which will assume much greater proportions with the years. The future of the island and its relation both to the Chinese mainland and the world will be determined by the attitude of the Nationalist Government to these problems. There can be no excuse for any failure to face these and find a solution. None of the conditions that existed on the Chinese mainland, hampering and obstructing the reform programme in earlier years, are present in Formosa today. Political consciousness is a reality, human rights in every sphere are assured, the industrial revolution is well on the way, and the Sino-American Mutual Defence Pact of 1954 has virtually eliminated any threat of invasion. Under all these circumstances, history will not be kind in its assessment if there is any neglect or lack of courage in dealing with these issues.

Since 1949 the achievements of the Nationalist Government in Formosa deserve the admiration of the free world. What will happen from now on may well determine both the future of Formosa and the Nationalists themselves.

1. Formosa is already an overcrowded island. The pressure of a rapidly increasing population in a comparatively small area must create problems of the most serious nature. Formosa is only 240 miles at its greatest length and 88 miles at its broadest width, the total area being 13,885 square miles. Physiographic conditions are such that a little more than a half of this area is arable and suited to close settlement. Yet during the past ten years the population has increased from 8,128,000 to 11,884,000 and the density of population from 585 to 855 per square mile. During this period births rose from 373,000 in 1953 to 424,000 in 1963, whereas, thanks to the progress of medical science and

its application in Formosa, the deaths in 1963, at 79,000, were the lowest for any year during that period. An increasing birth rate together with a decreasing death rate must soon result in Formosa reaching a saturation stage, if, indeed, this has not been reached already.

The use of the most advanced methods in both agriculture and secondary industry can do something to alleviate this problem, but with 352,000 added to the population each year, something much more radical and effective must be done. Just what this can be presents the Government in Formosa with an extremely difficult problem.

Just how is the present standard of living in Formosa to be maintained? There are parts of Asia where the density of population per square mile is greater than in Formosa, but there the standard of living is much lower. It is difficult to see how Formosa can maintain the existing standard with the present natural increase in its population. The farms are small and cannot be reduced in size, and such untilled land as does exist on the eastern sector of the island is only suited to cattle, certainly not to intensive food production.

At present the people of Formosa are contented and prosperous. But what will happen if or when living standards drop? The hard fact of too many people and too little land will have to be faced.

Of course, in the mind of the Government, the answer is that the regaining of the Chinese mainland will solve the problem. But this is extremely doubtful, for if there was free movement of people between Formosa and the Chinese mainland, the only relief this could possibly afford Formosa would be in the return to the Chinese mainland of those who crossed to Formosa since 1949. This would reduce the pressure for some time, but it would only be temporary.

There are many in Formosa quite aware of this population problem, and the practice of birth-control is encouraged. Lectures on this subject are given in many centres throughout the island, and there are some signs, faint perhaps, that this campaigning is beginning to bear fruit. It may be that, although the

1963 figure of births was the highest for any year since records were kept, the annual rise in the birth rate since the family-planning campaign began has been less than in the preceding period. Since 1959 the annual increase over each preceding year has never exceeded 3,000, and that on one occasion only, whereas in the earlier period it rose to 20,000 in one year (1955) and to 16,000 in 1958.

The number of children under four years in 1963 was 16 per cent of the population, the lowest figure since 1952. This may suggest that the family-planning campaign is becoming effective. However, at the present rate of natural increase, the population will be 14 million in 1970. Formosa cannot possibly support this population on the present standard of living.

Any campaign of family-planning is likely to be resisted by the Chinese, as it appears to strike at the very root of their traditional concept of the family. Among the Chinese, the function of the family has been, throughout the centuries, quite different from that prevalent in the West. A family is responsible for the conduct of its members and is itself a model for the Government, the state itself being regarded as a large family. Those functions associated with the state in the West, such as old-age pensions, unemployment benefits, and sickness benefits, are, to the Chinese, family responsibilities. The family is the one continuous life, reaching back to the ancestors, who, as the founders of the family, must be honoured and revered.

Consequently, any suggestion that the family should be limited immediately meets with opposition. It is considered an insult to the ancestors and a threat to the very foundation of the entire structure of Chinese society. The former of these is the more serious, as the constant watch by the spirits of the ancestors over the affairs of the family is one of the greatest consolations to the Chinese mind. Had not Confucius himself said that ' Civilization began with filial piety ', and much farther back in history, had not Shun been selected as Emperor to succeed Yao because of his devotion to his family ?

In Formosa, it was realized from the outset that any campaign of family-planning must be one of education, as it involved basic

Chiang Kai-shek and the author in 1956

changes in national thinking. To the ordinary Chinese, the economics of the problem were of little account. What did concern him was the attempt to interfere with the stream of life that linked him, through the family, to the ancestors. Hence the approach had to be to the mind rather than to the pocket.

The Government, in fixing the maximum area that a farming family could own, had this population problem in mind. The basis on which this area was determined was the capacity of the land to maintain a family of six persons. When we consider that one in every thirty-five of the population is over sixty-five years of age, and a large number of these are living with their children, this figure of six persons can be divided up as three adults and three children. This lead by the Government has been followed up by Press and radio and clinics set up throughout the island for purposes of consultation and the dissemination of information on family-planning.

Then there is the question of the increasing number of students graduating from the colleges and universities. At present these number 51,700 spread over the different faculties. It is difficult to see how these graduates will find suitable posts. The 5,000 studying agriculture will be hard pressed to find land, the 8,000 prospective engineers will not find it easy to secure engagements, and the 26,000 studying the humanities and social sciences will need to find other fields than public education for a livelihood. It is difficult to see how Formosa can absorb all these.

Perhaps an empty country like Australia could find a place for some of these, as educated Chinese from Formosa would prove worthy migrants to a country desperately in need of population. These Chinese would be of greater value to Australia than some types who have already been welcomed there. They share the same concepts of freedom with Australians, and on examination it will be found that all the values held fervently by Australians are also esteemed by these educated Chinese.

However, this problem of population in Formosa must be faced if the present standard of living is to be maintained and the present state of contentment preserved, for it is as true today as in the time of Han Fei-tzu, who warned China over two thousand

P

years ago that when ' food supply is not sufficient to meet the
needs of an increasing population, there is strife and disorder '.
Even as late as 1894, Sun Yat-sen, in a letter to Li Hung-chang,
remarked on the dangers facing an overpopulated country.

2. The future leadership of Formosa is equally if not indeed
more important. Of the triumvirate that has brought Formosa to
its present prosperity and standing in the world, Chiang Kai-shek
is seventy-seven years of age, Chen Cheng, after resigning the
premiership because of prolonged illness, died in 1965, and
Chang Chi-yun, though the youngest of the three, is more fitted
to be the director of the mind of Formosa than controller of its
affairs. Are there others, of like stature to these three, who in an
emergency could take office and lead Formosa to its goal ? Are
these three irreplaceable ?

This is a question to which no positive answer can be given.
But it must be said that at the moment there does not appear to be
anybody who could be to Formosa what Chiang has been and
still is. His experience before going to Formosa had been unique.
His link with Sun Yat-sen, the idol of free Chinese everywhere,
was not shared with another. His prestige in Formosa has been
and still is solitary in its grandeur, like a towering peak in the
mountains. In peace he has been to Formosa what Churchill
was to Britain in war, a prophet of the undying hope ; not a
prisoner of history, like so many leaders on the world stage at
the moment, but a maker of history. As for Chen Cheng, he
created a momentum that must continue as a powerful impetus
for some time, irrespective of his successors. The foundation he
laid and the structure he built on it must remain unless some
unforeseen disaster overcomes Formosa. Pressure of population
could, however, discount in time some of the benefits of his work.
It was a tragedy that ill health forced his resignation, and finally
killed him. Chang Chi-yun has inspired many others with his
ideal and, provided the Government takes note of the warning
given by the literati, which will be mentioned later, his work
should not fail for want of competent successors.

Formosa is not without men of ability. It remains to be seen, however, whether any of these can measure up to the stature of these three, who have transformed Formosa into her present position. It is thought in some quarters that Formosa is not making the most of its best talent. If so, then a heavy price will have to be paid in the future for this failure.

It may be that the Kuomintang exerts too much influence in the appointments and is still clinging to outmoded ideas. It may be that, as one hears in Taipei, family influence still remains very powerful. One man, a distinguished scholar and diplomat, perhaps the most capable man after the members of the trium-virate, remains without a post, because, it is alleged, he differed with the Kuomintang on an important point of policy. A member of the Foreign Service, who has held important posts abroad, assured the author that there is too much devotion paid to tactics practised on the Chinese mainland in past centuries and too little readiness to break with the past, where basic values are not involved.

If these things are so, then Formosa is not building wisely for the future. It may be that the maintenance of the Legislative Yuan, elected years back on the Chinese mainland and, owing to circumstances, unable to hold an election during the past twenty years, is to some extent responsible for this. Most of its members have grown old in this, the highest legislative organ in Formosa, thus barring the way to younger men, and tending to preserve allegiance to fossilized ideas.

How this Legislative Yuan, which is Formosa's link with the Chinese mainland, can be reformed, is a problem without a solution.

3. The grave risk of Americanization is the most important problem that Formosa has to face. There is no suggestion here that America seeks, as so often stated by Peking, to colonize Formosa. Such a charge is sheer nonsense. Nor is there any evidence that America has ever attempted to impose on Formosa the American way of life. Whatever assistance has been given Formosa has been on the same terms as American aid to Britain and other countries. There have been no hidden strings. At the

same time, any country that has to rely upon another for its physical survival tends, even unconsciously, to emulate the ideas, methods, and ways of life of its protector. This is seen, to some extent, in Australia, where the American way of life is becoming more and more apparent. It is less the case in New Zealand. But in both these countries there is still the counteracting influence of British customs and way of life, very strong in New Zealand, but declining in Australia. In both countries, dependent for their survival on American power, British influence is still a fact.

In Formosa, like Australia and New Zealand a Pacific country and dependent for its survival on America, the danger of Americanization is very real. The contacts with the Western civilization are mainly through Americans. The absence of any other contacts with the West, with the exception of occasional visits by Australians and a few Europeans, is due in part to action by the Nationalist Government in Formosa. However, Western civilization is seen in Formosa according to the American pattern. The danger lies in the ignorance of many officials in Formosa of any Western country outside America. These officials, some of them of high rank, visit America regularly, there is a regular flow of students to American colleges and universities, and an increasing number of Americans visit Formosa each year. To most people in Formosa, including Government officials, the West means America, and Europe, including Britain, is a closed book.

This is no criticism of America, for most Americans themselves would admit that their way of life was just one facet of Western civilization and not necessarily for export. Rather is this condition the result of Formosa's isolation from most Western countries, for which circumstance Formosa, or at least the Nationalist Government there, must bear some of the blame.

Scholars in Formosa were the first to draw the author's attention to this danger of Americanization. On various occasions lecturers at the National University in Taipei expressed their regret that there was not closer cultural contact with Britain. Several Australians who have visited Formosa on a number of occasions were impressed with signs of this Americanization, especially in their dealings with officials.

It is not surprising that members of the literati in Formosa are concerned about the future, as the literati have been the historic guardians of Chinese values in the past, and conspicuously so in Formosa. From the time Yao Ying led the mission of scholars from Fukien province to the island, to the gathering of literati at Panch'iao in 1860, and then to the formation of *shih she* in the cities and villages to keep alive a true devotion to basic Chinese values, the literati have been the custodians of Chinese culture and civilization. Had not the Republic of Formosa been born in the Mu-tan Shih She at Taipei in 1895, and had not a hundred of them formed the Government at Tainan in south Formosa and appointed Liu Yung-fu President to carry on resistance against the Japanese?

It is customary for this isolation of Formosa from most Western countries to be blamed on the West, but the Nationalist Government in Formosa itself must bear some of the blame for this unfortunate position, as a result of which Formosa is the loser. This absolute dependence on America has led to a certain disregard of Britain. It is true that Britain recognizes the Peking Government, but there is no reason why the Nationalist Government should not have a consulate in London. There are many Chinese in Britain who own allegiance to the Government in Formosa and who regret that there is no representative of their Government in Britain. There is a British Consulate in Formosa, which, although it has no official contact with the Nationalist Government there, does have contact with the people of Formosa. And there are fewer British subjects in Formosa than there are Chinese, recognizing the Nationalist Government, living in Britain.

Then there is a much wider issue. There existed, until recently, a number of groups of British students in universities throughout Britain interested in Formosa. These met to hear lectures and then discuss different aspects of the China problem. True to the student mind, they wanted to hear the facts. The academic freedom existing in Formosa, as opposed to the academic slavery in Communist China, made a strong appeal to these students.

Gradually there was building up in these universities a body of opinion favourable to Formosa and based on a knowledge of conditions existing there. As in Britain the universities have, for many years, been the training-ground for the majority of politicians, this awareness of conditions in Formosa and especially the freedom enjoyed by the people there was of the utmost importance. Unfortunately, the Government in Formosa was not interested. It failed to realize that here was an opportunity to create in Britain a new attitude towards Formosa, such as might, in the long run, mean more to that island than the officials there seem to realize.

Communist China has now stepped in to present its case to the students. Peking is taking British students more seriously than Taipei did when it had the opportunity.

Australia could do much to meet the wishes of the literati in Formosa in checking this Americanization of the island. In spite of many aspects of Australian life taking on the American look, the Australian way of life still remains British. A kind of balance has been achieved. And it is a healthy balance. Australia recognizes the Nationalist Government in Formosa and an embassy of the Nationalist Government is established at Canberra. But Australia has not reciprocated by setting up an embassy at Taipei. Ministers of the Australian Government have visited Formosa, a mission led by a former Chief Justice of the Australian High Court went to the island, several trade-union deputations followed, and Australia has always been a staunch champion of the Nationalist Government at the United Nations. Behind all these activities there is a strong popular support of Formosa among the Australian people.

The establishment of an Australian Embassy at Taipei could do much to counteract the danger that the Chinese scholars in Formosa fear. It could lead to closer cultural contacts between Australians and Chinese, an interchange of university professors, and could bring to bear on Chinese officials a British influence which the literati in Formosa are most anxious to see happen. On one occasion a highly placed Chinese official in Formosa sought the assistance of the author in seeking an opportunity to visit Australia for the purpose of giving a series of lectures in Australia on cultural aspects of Formosa. An Australian Embassy at Taipei could have brought this about.

Then there is France. A French surgeon, of considerable standing in his profession, expressed to the author his view that the action of the Nationalist Government in breaking off relations with France when Paris stated its intention of recognizing Peking was a grave mistake. He considered that it would have a profound influence in France if Paris had been forced into the position of having to make the break.

The literati in Formosa fear that this Americanization process could result in defeating the avowed purpose of the island. Confident that the true mission of Formosa is to set the pattern of the China of the future, they fear that the basic Chinese values will be lost and Formosa become just another state. They are concerned over the future of the island as the repository of those values. They see Formosa becoming so Americanized that, with the passage of time, its spiritual mission will cease to exist. On that day, the island will lose its identity with the Chinese mainland.

This concern cannot be dismissed as idle. It is very real. There is a growing body of world opinion that the solution of the China problem lies in the creation of a Formosan state, guaranteed from invasion by the United Nations but completely independent of the Chinese mainland — in short, the world recognition of two Chinas. The literati in Formosa agree with the Nationalist Government in rejecting such a concept. They are unanimous in this rejection. At the same time, many of them fear that this silent Americanization of the island could lead to this end. While the official mind thinks of regaining the Chinese mainland by arms, these literati see forces at work within Formosa which could destroy the true mission of that island by undermining its very foundation. These forces are not evil, but are born out of Formosa's complete reliance on another country for its security.

On the surface this plan for the recognition of two Chinas has much to commend it. To those ignorant of the history of Formosa, it would seem to be a solution of the China problem.

Peking refuses to have anything to do with it, but a change of mind there is not inconceivable. Much would depend on what was offered in exchange for any renunciation of the present claim to Formosa. Peking might regard world recognition and membership of the United Nations as constituting a reasonable exchange.

An independent Formosan state would be an attractive answer to the existing tangle in the minds of many who admire the outstanding progress made there in recent years. The people there enjoy freedom, personal, political, and religious. In the Provincial Government, which administers the domestic affairs of the island, the native-born Formosans are well represented. Also, in the National Government, some important posts are held by men born on the island. Christianity, Buddhism, and Islam flourish side by side, and nothing of that religious antagonism so marked in other parts of Asia exists. The people are happy and contented ; indeed, Formosa is the one section of Asia that enjoys internal peace. No riots occur in the streets. Politicians are never shot. And there are no paupers. Trade flourishes, with Formosa ranking high among the exporters of sugar and the highest in the world in the export of certain canned fruits. The Press is permitted to criticize the Government, provided the security of the island is not endangered. In fact, all the values cherished by free men elsewhere are maintained in Formosa.

Under these circumstances, the recognition of Formosa as a separate state, its security guaranteed, makes a strong appeal to many.

The only objection that can be made to such a plan is the historic meaning of Formosa. Chiang Kai-shek and the Nationalists did not create this, for it existed centuries before their time. They inherited it. In their fidelity to the pattern worked out by other hands and in other times lies their justification for their rejection of this ' Two Chinas ' proposal. In this they have the support of history.

But the Americanization of the official mind in Formosa could destroy this pattern, and this is precisely what many scholars in

Formosa fear. Some of these have not hesitated to express their concern, and state that while the island enjoys increasing economic prosperity, gains security from external aggression, and is accorded status in the councils of the nations, it may lose its soul and thus disregard its historic meaning. The prosperity of the island might even accelerate this tragic failure.

This protest, or warning, call it what we may, is not subversion. There is nothing sinister in this attitude of the literati of Formosa. On the contrary, these men are intensely loyal to the Nationalist Government, but first and foremost they regard themselves as the custodians of Chinese culture and those values that have made Chinese civilization. They do not oppose the adoption of the techniques of a materialistic civilization — indeed, they welcome these, but not at the expense of these values. Their attitude is that of Liu Ming-ch'uan, who, nearly a century ago, made it clear that Western techniques must be transfused with Chinese cultural values so as to produce that ' culture–technique ' civilization of China in the future. And in Formosa, he said, this pattern was to be worked out. This vision of the first Governor of Formosa, back in 1880, later captured the attention of Chang Chi-yun, who has sought to keep it bright before the official eye since 1949.

Perhaps a reappraisal of values in Formosa is imperative. There is too much imitation of the protecting country at present. One might even conclude that Formosa is just an outpost of the American way of life. Such imitation may be regarded as a form of flattery ; it could lead to suicide, to the self-inflicted death of the true meaning of Formosa. It could result in Formosa becoming just another state in Asia.

Such a reappraisal would dispel the idea, common among officials in Formosa, that American and Chinese values are identical. This is what is disturbing the minds of the Chinese scholars. They know that any such idea of identity has no basis in fact. Confucius would never have signed such a document as the American Declaration of Independence. He would have objected to its first postulate, that ' all men are created equal '. Sun Yat-sen would have violently opposed this. But both would have freely assented to the Declaration of Rights, set out in France in 1789, that all men are ' equal in respect of their rights '. This is a very different thing and very Chinese. Nobody knew this better than Sun Yat-sen himself:

> If we pay no attention to the difference of intelligence and ability between individuals, but push down those who distinguish themselves in order to insist upon absolute equality among men, humanity will not advance but retrogress.

This was a reaffirmation of one of the cardinal concepts of the Confucian philosophy of government. Upon this was based the Chinese civil service examination system, which gave to China a governmental structure, which, judging by the number of people it controlled, the length of time it endured, and its record in maintaining order and ensuring justice, compared most favourably with any other ever devised by man. Its genius lay in the Confucian emphasis on personal merit and not external influence as the determining qualification for public office. Formosa would be wise to return to the traditional Chinese standard, which is being overshadowed by the cult of Washington, with its emphasis on the mechanics of government rather than on the capability of the individual. It would be tragic if Formosa exchanged the pattern it has inherited for that of America. This latter could never suit the China of the future, for national values, whatever their success at home, are never exportable with advantage to the recipient.

Confucius made it clear that officials selected for their personal merit are more likely to be efficient than those who gain office through the influence of others. The former will be more disposed to consider themselves servants of the people, whereas authority will rest heavily upon the shoulders of the latter. Perhaps, in this matter, Formosa needs to return to the Confucian values.

One final note. America has made possible the military strength of Formosa, which is considerable. There is, however, the grave danger of mistaking this physical might and the ability to use modern arms for the real meaning of Formosa. Too much prominence is given in publications and at public gatherings to the armed power of Formosa. One hears too much of plans to regain the Chinese mainland as though this was the primary mission of Formosa. The day could arrive when a rising on the Chinese mainland would be a just cause for assistance from Formosa, but it would be fatuous to consider this as an end in itself. To do so might create a China problem more difficult than exists at the moment.

Formosa has been fashioned through the centuries to play a decisive role in the making of the New China. But there are different interpretations of what this role really is. To the Chinese Nationalists, it means the provision of a base from which they hope to launch an assault on the Chinese mainland to do battle with the Communists. At present, the so-called 'split' between Moscow and Peking is adding fervour to this hope. It is believed in high places in Taipei that such an assault would be contained within the limits of a civil war and would not extend beyond China. This, however, is very doubtful, as there is no valid reason for concluding that Moscow would remain impassive in such a conflict. In spite of all the speculations in Formosa, and indeed throughout the West, the things that unite Moscow and Peking are greater and more important than the things that divide them. It could well be that the existing difference is purely tactical, the disagreement between chiefs of staff both of whom have the same objective.

The historic role of Formosa is not to spark off another world war but to set out and maintain the blueprint of what the China of the future can, and, as we confidently hope, will be. This is of much greater importance than the fate of any individual or group, either in Formosa or on the Chinese mainland, for it concerns the future of the hundreds of millions of Chinese and indeed that of the world at large. It is not surprising that Communist tyranny on the Chinese mainland has generated bitter hate in Formosa, as there are few families there without family connections on the mainland, but there is the real danger of this hate, like a thick black cloud, obscuring the vision of Formosa's true role in history.

Under whose leadership this Chinese pattern, now worked out and functioning in Formosa, will be put into operation on the mainland of China, we do not know. Nor in what manner. Nor when. What agony will mark the prelude of its adoption, in the period of transition, we can only imagine, for the task will be tremendous. The years of waiting may be long, but China has already waited a long time, for centuries, and its people have been most patient. They have become inured to timelessness, which has not sapped their power of resilience. Perhaps the liberation will come from within, as has been the case always of effective liberations in the history of mankind. When it does come, the resultant accompaniment of chaos will be only temporary, as Formosa will have the blueprint of reconstruction at hand.

Meanwhile Formosa, as an essential part of China, can best serve the interests of the China of the future and its people by having this blueprint in order and by maintaining the basic values of Chinese civilization, for the New China will have much to contribute to world civilization. That contribution could be decisive in a world inordinately committed to a technological way of life.

It is unfortunate that the major countries of the free world, with one exception, have not appreciated the part played by Formosa in the past history of China. Perhaps this is not surprising, as Western Sinologues have also failed in this direction and taken little note of this. Certain it is that Formosa's role in the future has been mostly ignored. A closer association between these countries and Formosa is now not only most urgently needed, but there should be a united guarantee of the security of the island against any threat of external aggression. At present this has been left to America, a situation which, as already pointed out, is aggravating the most serious problem Formosa has to face. Unless this is solved by some such united guarantee, the role which the centuries have fashioned for Formosa to play in the future could be seriously impaired, if not completely negated.

The waters of the Strait of Formosa flow, not only between

that island and the Chinese mainland, not only between America and Communist China, but through the heart of the world.

Not for the first time in history has a small island pointed the way into the future. In this case the small island has the advantage of being the repository of the values of the oldest civilization extant, values that have withstood the strains and stresses of the centuries and survived the experiments of all the 'isms' from Socialism to totalitarianism, values above all politics, ideologies, and the multifarious economic philosophies that have fuddled the minds of the peoples of the world and continue to do so.

Surely such values warrant preservation at a time when civilization at large seems to have lost its bearings.

But if Formosa is to maintain the pattern of the China of the future and contribute to world civilization, her leaders must listen to those warning voices which have sounded across the years.

In 1887, when the Governor of Formosa, Liu Ming-ch'uan, engaged Western engineers to modernize the island's communications, he urged the population to remain steadfast to their historic Chinese values. To sacrifice these, he said, would be too great a price to pay for modernization.

In 1898, Liang Ch'i-ch'ao, the standard-bearer of the Kang Yu-wei reform crusade on the Chinese mainland, issued a similar appeal :

Our duty is to develop our civilization with that of the West and to supplement Western civilization with ours so as to synthesize and transform them, and in so doing, bring forth a new civilization.

Forty years later, when the Western impact on China was becoming intense, Sa Meng-wu, Ho Ping-sung, and other scholars published their historic memorandum :

We must examine our heritage, weed out what is useless and preserve what is good. It is both right and necessary to absorb Western culture, but not with an attitude of total acceptance. We do not want the dregs.

We must maintain our basic Chinese values, whilst, at the same time, adopting a more critical approach and applying the scientific method. We must examine the past, hold on to the present, and thus create for the future.

In the last conversation which the author had with Hu Shih in Formosa, that outstanding modernist expressed the view that it would be a tragedy if, in the modernization of the island, all the values of the old civilization should disappear. Perhaps he could see the trend of things. He repeated the words he had written years earlier :

The problem is how best to assimilate modern civilization in such a manner as to make it congenial and congruous and continuous with that civilization of our own making.

All these warnings from the past are being echoed by the literati in Formosa today as they see the vision of a ' culture–technique ' civilization obscured by their limited contacts with the West. It is unfortunate that official pique in Taipei has closed the doors to such countries as Britain and France, both of which have so much to offer Formosa, simply because these have recognized Communist China. Added to this is the grave disadvantage that few of the present leaders in Formosa have themselves had any close association with the West other than with America. The result is that they interpret Western civilization in purely American terms.

Such a short-sighted view, with its resultant official policy, is contrary to the real genius of Chinese civilization through the centuries, which enabled China to survive above the wreckage of other cultures because of its insistence on certain basic values other than those of politics or economics.

Formosa now faces the strategic moment in opportunity. It is no longer a problem of physical or economic survival. The 1964 returns show that in that year agricultural production forged ahead by 10 per cent over that of 1963, and industrial production registered an advance of 20 per cent. The favourable trade balance was three times that of the preceding year. Indeed, 1964 marked Formosa as the country with the soundest national economy and the most stable Government in the whole of Asia.

But to those in Formosa who look into the future, beyond the machine, beyond physical and economic security, another and deeper problem is taking shape. This does not take spectacular form, but nevertheless is very real. They fear that as on the mainland of China a foreign way of life has been imposed on an unwilling people, Formosa may, almost unconsciously, become a self-constituted cultural appendage of America. And with the loss of Chinese values.

Will the new leaders in Formosa now have the courage to face this problem ? Will they rise above the limitations imposed by a narrow diplomatic outlook and come to see Western civilization in its broadest dimensions ? Or will they be content with their present myopic vision and continue to look only across the Pacific ? Upon their response to these questions the future of Formosa will depend. Either the island will carry out its historic mission to the China of the future and make a unique contribution to mankind by the development of a new ' culture–technique ' civilization, the foundation of which the Chiang–Chen–Chang triumvirate wisely laid, or become just a prosperous independent state in the western Pacific.

Formosa is now at the crossroads of history. This is the time of decisions.

The last word will not be said by Peking or Washington but by Taipei itself. It is there that the future of Formosa will be determined.

Books Consulted by the Author

Chinese Dynastic Histories

SHEN CHIN-SSU, *Yuan-lu lun*, 1720.

LAN TING-YUAN, *P'ing T'ai chi* (Essays on the Pacification of Formosa), 1723.

HUANG SHU-LIN, *T'ai-hai chih-ch'a lu* (one of the finest descriptive writings on Formosa), 1723.

LIEN HENG, *T'aiwan T'ung-shih* (History of Formosa), Shanghai, 1937.

HEN LIH-WU, *Taiwan Today*, Taipei, 1951.

CHEN CHENG, *Land Reform in Taiwan*, Taipei, 1961.

CHANG CHI-YUN, *The Spirit of Taiwan*, Taipei, 1957.

MURAKAMI, N., *Diary and Correspondence of Richard Cocks*, Tokyo, 1899.

TAKEKOSHI, Y., *Japanese Rule in Formosa*, Tokyo, 1905.

BELLOTTI, F., *Formose*, Paris, 1959.

BENYOWSKY, COUNT, *Memoirs and Travels*, London, 1893.

BRIDGEMAN, E. C., *Rebellion of Choo Yihkwei in Formosa*, Canton, 1838.

CAMPBELL, W., *Past and Future of Formosa*, Hong Kong, 1889.

CORDIER, H., *Histoire Générale de la Chine*, Paris, 1920.

DAVIDSON, J. W., *The Island of Formosa*, London, 1903.

FISCHER, A., *Streifzüge durch Formosa*, Berlin, 1889.

TEN HOORN, JAN CLAEZ, *Formosa*, Amsterdam, 1675.

HOUSE, E. H., *Japanese Expedition to Formosa in 1874*, Tokyo, 1875.

IMBAULT-HUART, H., *L'île Formose*, Paris, 1893.

KLEINWACHTER, G., 'Formosa under the Chinese Government', *China Review*, 1884.

LEAVENWORTH, C. S., *The Loochoo Islands*, Shanghai, 1905.

MCGOVERN, B. J., *Headhunters in Formosa*, London 1903.

MACKAY, G. L., *From Far Formosa*, London, 1896.

PERRY, M. C., *American Expedition to the China Sea and Japan*, Washington, 1856.

PHILLIPS, G., 'Notes on the Dutch Occupation of Formosa', *China Review*, 1882.

——, *Dutch Trade in Formosa*, Shanghai, 1885.

——, 'The Life of Koxinga', *China Review*, 1885.

PICKERING, W. A., *Pioneering in Formosa*, London, 1826.

PLAUCHUT, E., *Formose*, Lyon, 1895.

RIESS, L., *Geschichte der Insel Formosa*, Tokyo, 1897.

SAVINA, F. N., *Histoire des Miao*, Hong Kong, 1924.

WIRTH, A., *Geschichte Formosas bis Anfang*, Bonn, 1896.

ZINKIN, M., *Asia and the West*, London, 1951.

Journals of the Academia Sinica

The biographies of Chiang Kai-shek by Mao Sse-chen, Chang Hsing-hai, Chen Tsung-hai, and Hollington Tong have been closely studied, as have the *T'aiwan Shih Hua* (Historical Records of Taiwan), published in Taipei in 1964.

Index

Aborigines, 3 ff.
Agriculture, *kaingin* method, 10; under Emperor Yu, 14–15; under Hoklos and Hakkas, 29–32; under Cheng Cheng-kung, 81–82. *See also* Land reform
America, *see* United States
Americanization, 209 ff.
Ami tribesmen, 107
Amoy, 30, 65, 74, 75–77, 87
Ampzingius, Jacobus, 60
Araki, General, 159
Arts, under the Chengs, 89; under the Ch'ings, 103, 106; during Japanese occupation, 165; under Chang Chi-yun, 198–200
Australia, possible influence in Formosa, 212
Australian trade union mission, 187
Awano, Dennojo, 14

'Black Flags', 153–5
'Blue Stars Society', 198
Bocarro, Antonio, 117
Bowman, Isaiah, 195
'Brotherhood of the Free', 165–6
Buck, Peter, 108
Bunum tribesmen, 147, 150
Burgevine, Henry, 118, 170

Cairo Declaration (1943), 166, 177
Camphor, 132
Candidius, Georgius, 58, 60
Captain China, *see* Li Han
Cassel, Commander, 151
Casteel Zeelandia, 52, 62, 69; besieged by Cheng Cheng-kung, 76–77; as Cheng Cheng-kung's capital, 78
Censorship, during Japanese war, 152
Chang Chi-yun, 16, 179, 185, 195–200, 208, 221
Chang Chih-tung, 148, 155
Chang Ing, Nancy, 33
Changhua, 68, 131, 151
Character, Formosan, xii

Chen Cheng, 179, 185–8, 200, 208, 221; introduces land reform, 188–94
Ch'en Ling, General, 19–20, 22, 36
Chen Tien, *see* Tainan
Chen Yi, 178
Cheng Cheng-kung (Koxinga), 67, 69, 70; early years, 72–75; besieges Casteel Zeelandia, 76–77; assumes control of Formosa, 78; his rule in Formosa, 78, 80–83; death, 84; influence of, 84–85; against Shih Lang, 92–93; introduction of examination system by, 97, 133; prayed to, during Japanese war, 149–50
Cheng Chih-lung, 63–71, 73, 92
Cheng Ching, 77, 83, 86–88, 93
Cheng Ho, Admiral, *see* Wan San-ho
Cheng K'o-tsang, 87, 91, 93–94
Cheng Shi-liang, 171–2
Cheng Shih-hsi, 87
Ch'eng Tang, 15
Ch'i Ju-shan, 198
Chia-luen Lo, 169
Chiang Kai-shek, achievements of, 179 ff., 200, 221; meaning of his name, 180; character, 180–2; spiritual beliefs of, 182; address to youth of Formosa, 183; believes Formosa is symbol of New China, 184; influence of, 185, 201; uniqueness of, 208
Chiang Kee, 104
Ch'ien Lung, 174–5
Chinese mainland, present relationship with, 213, 217
Ching Pao, 100–1
Chinlun, 1
Ch'iu Feng-chia, 90, 146, 148–9, 151, 176
Ch'iu Nien T'ai, 149
Choshiu-chi, 68
Christianity, 57–60, 127–8, 200
Chu Chi-hua, 178
Chu I-kwei, 169
Chu Yu-chien, *see* Lung Wu, Emperor
Chu Yu-lang, 73, 75
Ch'u Yuan, 17
Civil service, 97, 133, 216
Clarke, Samuel, 17

Clenk, Hermanus, 76
Climate, 96
Cocks, Richard, 41–42
Communications, 131
Communists, 178, 191, 212, 217
Confucianism, 97, 107, 128–9, 133–4, 137–9, 145–6, 200, 215–16
Coyett, Dutch Governor, 75–77
Crafts, aboriginal, 107
Creel, H. G., 112, 138
Customs, ancient, 11–12, 16–17, 33–34

David, Sir Percival, 198
Davidson, J. W., 78, 84, 144–5, 147
Democratic Socialist Party, 185
Dutch, arrival in Formosa (1623), 40; relations with Li Han, 42–43, 45–46; colonization of Formosa, 49 ff.; destined for disaster, 51 ff.; view Spaniards as a threat, 53; ineptness of, 54 ff.; clash with Japanese, 56; against Cheng Cheng-kung, 75–77; map of Formosa by, 81

East India Company, Dutch, 49 ff.; English, 41, 49, 87, 114
Economy, see Trade
Edgar, Henry, 151
Education, 87, 90, 133; under Japan, 162–163; present-day, 195 ff.
Electricity, first used in Taipei, 130
Epidemics, 100
Examination system, 97, 133, 216

Fa Hsien, 6
Family planning, 205–7
Feng Hsi-fan, 91, 94
Fengshan, 166
Festivals, 1–3, 34, 58
Food production, 194. See also Agriculture
Formosa, alternative names for, xvi–xvii
France, Formosan venture of, 129; offers to take over as caretaker Government, 143; present-day relations with Formosa, 213, 220
Franck, H. A., 163

Geology, x–xii
Giran, see Ilan
Government, first semblance of, 45; attempts at stable, 98–99; corruption in, 99. See also National Government, Republic

Goyer–Keyzer mission, 61
Great Britain, and trade with China, 102; and Opium War, 102, 113; trades with Formosa, 113; Government urged to occupy Formosa, 114; sets up consulate, 116–17; attitude to Japan over planned occupation of Formosa, 121; invited by China to take over Formosa, 143; present-day Formosa desires closer contact with, 210–12, 220
Grousset, René, 90

Hakkas, xiv, 24–29, 31–34, 80, 100, 147, 170
Hansen, Emanuel, 131
Harris, Townsend, 115
Herbs, medicinal, 35
Hideyoshi, 140, 142, 150
Hiranuma, Baron, 162
Ho Ping-sung, 219
Hoklos, 28–34, 51, 100, 147
Holland, see Dutch
Houses, earliest, 8; Hoklos', 30; Hakkas', 31
Houtman, Cornelius, 49
Hozan, see Fengshan
Hsia Chin, 198–9
Hsien Jung, 120
Hsinchu Temple, 134
Hsing Chung Hui, 156–7
Hsu Shen-mo, xvii, 79
Hsueh Fu-ch'eng, 128
Hsuing Wen-ts'an, 40, 50
Hu Shih, 220
'Huai Chun', 125
Hung Hsui-ch'uan, 118–19, 170, 175

Ilan, 95, 166
Industry, see Trade
Irrigation, 14, 96
Ito, Count, 141, 143
Iyeyasu, 150

Japanese, clash with Dutch, 56; a challenge to Formosa, 120–1; stays her hand, 121; spirit of aggression in, 140; war with China (1894), 141; invasion of Formosa by, 147–53; occupation, 158–67; migration to Formosa discouraged, 159; economic plans for Formosa, 160; corruption under, 161; basic purpose of occupation, 162; treatment of Formosans, 163–4; risings against, 164–5; occupation of Formosa ends, 166, 177

Jesuits, survey first carried out by, 95
Judo, General Saigo, 121
Junius, Robertus, 58–60

Kabayama, Count, 164
Kaiyuan Temple, assembly of literati at
  (1895), 150
K'ang Hsi, Emperor, 93
Keelung, first railway to, 132
Keng Ching-chung, 87
Kimberley, Lord, 143
Korea, 140–1, 147
Koxinga, see Cheng Cheng-kung
Kuang Hsu, Emperor, 143, 147, 156, 173
Kuomintang, 185, 209

Land reform, 188–94
Lanyu, 109
Le Gendre, General, 151
Li Han (Captain China), early life, 40–41 ;
  in Hirado, 41, 51 ; in Dutch employ,
  42–43, 51 ; as pirate, 43–46 ; disappear-
  ance of, 46–47 ; identification with Yen
  Ssu-ch'i, 47 ; place in history, 48 ; re-
  commends Cheng Chih-lung to Dutch
  as interpreter, 63
Li Hung-chang, 125–6, 128, 143
Li Kiang-jo, 171–2
Li Kuang-ti, 93
Li Shuai-t'ai, 86
Liang Ch'i-ch'ao, 219
Lien Heng, 89, 90, 165–6
Lin Ho-wan, 165
Lin Kuo-hua, 111–14, 116, 118
Lin Shao-hua, 165
Lin Shao-tsun, 165
Lin Shuang-wen, 169, 174
Lindley, A. F., 119
Literati, as dominant force, xiv, 110 ;
  doctrine becomes official Chinese policy,
  37–40 ; migrate to Formosa, 80, 175 ;
  visit Okinawa, 107 ; awakening of,
  109–10 ; meet in conference at Panch'-
  iao, 111 ff., 211 ; as custodians of
  Chinese culture, 112 ; establish Re-
  public of Formosa, 145 ; hold assembly
  in Kaiyuan Temple, 150 ; announce
  continuation of Republic in Japanese
  war, 151–2 ; underground activities
  during Japanese occupation, 165–7 ;
  under Chang Chi-yun, 195 ff.; fear of
  Americanization of Formosa, 213–15,
  220
Little, Mrs. Archibald, 142, 157

Liu Hou-tze, 17
Liu Ming-ch'uan, xiv ; first Governor of
  Formosa, 124 ; early career, 124-6 ; retirement and temporary recall, 126–7;
  appointed Governor of Fukien, 129 ;
  electrifies first Chinese city, 130 ; establishes first Chinese school for telegraph
  operators, 131 ; builds first Chinese
  railway, 132 ; develops industry, 132–
  133 ; education policies of, 133 ; taxation under, 135 ; dismissed, 136 ; death,
  136–7 ; evaluation of, 137–9 ; eagerness to retain Confucianism, 137–9 ;
  physical appearance, 139
Liu Wung-fu, 143, 145, 151, 153–6
Lung Wu, Emperor, 70–73
Lynch, E., 172

Ma Tso-po, goddess, 29, 72–73
Ma Tuan-lin, 20
MacArthur, Douglas, 48
McGovern, Janet, 164
Mackay, George Leslie, 3, 17
Mao Tse-tung, 175
Maps, 81, 95
Martinez, Bartolomé, 163
Matsu, goddess, 29
Mattau, seminary at, 60
Migrants, Chinese, xiii, 15, 24 ff., 68–69,
  80, 87, 95–97 ; earliest, 3 ff. ; Kwei-
  chow, 14–16 ; Japanese, 159–60
'Ming-tzu Chun', insurgents, 125
Missions, Chinese, 97 ; Christian, 57–60
Mola, Friar Francisco, 53
Morrison, Robert, 57
Mus, Petrus, 60
Mu-tan Shih She, 145–7, 211
Mutsu, Viscount, 143

National Government, Chinese, moves to
  Formosa, 178 ; parties in, 185–6 ;
  achievements of, 179 ff., 204 ; problems
  facing, 204 ff. ; future leadership of,
  208. See also Chiang Kai-shek
Nuyts, Pieter, 53–54, 66–67
Nye, Gideon, 115

Okinawa, 20–21, 107, 120
Opium War, Great Britain and China,
  102, 113

Paiwan wood-carvers, 107–9
Palafox, Bishop, 63–64
Panch'iao, 111 ff., 211

Perry, Commodore, 116, 140, 159
Pescadores, naval base at, 131
Pickering, W. A., 28, 137
Piracy, bases on Formosa, 43. *See also*
  Li Han
Pobete, see Story-tellers
Poetry clubs, 89–90, 107, 145–7, 198, 211
Population, xiii–xiv, 96–97, 204–8 ; of
  China, 101
Portilio, Gonsalo, 54
Postal system, first regular, 152
Pottinger, Sir Henry, 114–15
Priestesses, 2–3, 11–12
Proto-Malayans, 3–13, 19
Prussia, interest in Formosa shown by, 115
Putmans, Hans, 67

Railways, *see* Transport
Rebellions, against Government (1683–
  1843), 99 ; against Japanese, 164–5
Reijersen, Cornelius, 64–65
Religion, ancient, 11–13 ; Hoklos, 29 ;
  freedom of, 214. *See also* Christianity,
  Confucianism
Republic, Formosa an independent, 143–
  157 ; effect of, on China, 157
Ricci, Vittorio, in Amoy, 74; envoy to
  Manila, 82–83
Rice, 25, 30, 81, 96, 161
Riess, Ludwig, 13
Riru, 2–3

Sa Meng-wu, 219
Sakkam, feast at, 58
'San Ho Hui', secret society, 100–1, 150,
  169, 171–2
'San Min Chu I', of Sun Yat-sen, 173
Santissima Trinidad, 53–54
Schools, *see* Education
Seward, William, 116
Shao Yu-lien, 140
Shen Pao-chen, 121–3
Shen Ying, 16
Shigenabu, Okuma, 140
Shih Lang, 92–94, 123
Shih she, see Poetry clubs
Shih Shih-pang, 96
Shihmen reservoir, xii
Shimonoseki, Treaty of, 137, 141, 147, 148
Shiy De Jinn, 199
Shoin, Yoshida, 141
Shu Kuan, 19–21, 32, 36
Sino-American Mutual Defence Pact
  (1954), 204

Sino-Japanese Peace Treaty (1945), 166
Sonck, Martinus, 40, 42, 45–46, 50–51
Spain, establishes trading base, 53 ; Ricci
  as envoy to, 82–83
Story-tellers, on Lanyu, 109
Sugar, 25, 30, 81, 87, 96, 160, 161
Sun Moon Lake, power plant at, 160
Sun Yat-sen, demands revolution, 156–7,
  171–2 ; battle hymn of, 167 ; in
  Britain, 168 ; first visit to Formosa,
  168 ; vision of, 169, 170 ; plans to
  establish Republic on Chinese mainland,
  173 ; later visits to Formosa, 173 ; in-
  fluence of, on Formosa, 173–6 ; Chiang
  Kai-shek and, 182, 208 ; fears of over-
  population, 208 ; views on equality of
  men, 215–16
Survey (1714), 95. *See also* Maps

T'ai P'ings, rebels, 118–19, 125–7, 175
T'ai Tsung, Emperor, 23
Taihoku, *see* Taipei
Tainan, 82, 94, 123, 130, 135, 146, 149–
  150, 153, 155 ; Temple, 134
Taipei, 123, 129, 130–2, 135, 145–7, 209,
  210, 220, 221 ; Temple, 134 ; as
  Taihoku, Japanese capital, 168 ; uni-
  versity at, 162
Taiwan, xvi, xvii, 97, 123, 131. *See also*
  Tainan
'Taiwan Min-chu Kuo', *see* Republic,
  Formosa an independent
Taiyal tribesmen, 16, 17, 19, 147
Takekoshi, Yosaburo, 85, 144, 158, 160,
  162, 163
Takow, British vice-consulate at, 116
Tamsui, British and American consulates
  at, 116
T'ang Ching-sung, 140, 143, 146, 148,
  151, 156
T'ao, Captain, 136
Tao Kuang, Emperor, 100
Tavarong, 107
Taxation, under Dutch, 55, 61 ; under
  Cheng Cheng-kung, 80 ; under Cheng
  Ching, 87 ; under Liu Ming-ch'uan,
  135 ; under Japan, 161
Tea, 25, 132
Tientsin, Treaty of, 113, 127
Ting Jih-ch'ang, 131
Ting Tsu, 137
Tingchow, battle of, 71
Trade, 25, 30, 36, 44–45, 50 ff., 81, 87, 89,
  96, 113 ff., 132–3, 160–1, 187

Tradenius, Paulus, 54
Transport, 131–2
Ts'ai Shan-chi, 65–66
Tseng Kuo-fan, 119, 128
Tsung chu ch'uan, literati doctrine of, 38–39
Tuo Tuo, 26
Typhoons, xi–xii, 100

United States, starts trade with Formosa, 113; urged to occupy Formosa, 115; sets up consulate, 116–17; attitude to Japan over Formosan venture, 121; suspected of planning Japanese venture, 151; aid to Formosa from, 187. See also Americanization

Van de Laan, Admiral Jan, 76
Vonum tribesmen, 16, 17, 19

Wade, Sir Thomas, 121
Wan San-ho (Admiral Cheng Ho), 34, 35–36
Wang Hsien-chieh, 97

Wang Hsui-ch'u, 86
Wang T'ao, 128
Wang Yu-ch'eng, 23
Warren, Dr. Max, 139
Wasson, Lieutenant, 151
Wood-carving, 107–9
Wu Sha, 95
Wu Tzu-kuang, 90

Yahei, Yamada, 56
Yang Chien, 21
Yang Chih-shen, 96
Yang Ming Shan, Institute of Advanced Chinese Studies at, 198
Yang Ti, Emperor, 19, 21–23
Yang Tsiang, Admiral, 20
Yao Ying, 97–98, 211
Yen Ssu-ch'i, see Li Han
Yih Ching, ancient Chinese guide-book, 40
Young China Party, 186
Yu, Emperor, 14–15
Yuan-shan shell-mound, 14
Yueh, people, 15–16
Yung Cheng, Emperor, 100

PRINTED BY R. & R. CLARK, LTD., EDINBURGH

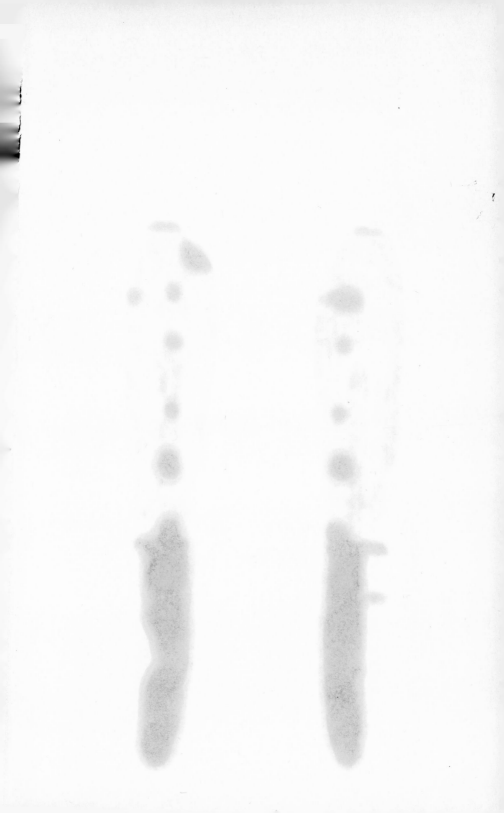